100

SOUTHERN On Occasion

SOUTHERN
On Occasion

A COMPANION TO INSPIRE GRACIOUS LIVING

THE JUNIOR LEAGUE OF COBB-MARIETTA, INC.

This cookbook is a collection of favorite recipes,
which are not necessarily original recipes.

SOUTHERN . . . ON OCCASION
A COMPANION TO INSPIRE GRACIOUS LIVING

Copyright© 1998 by
THE JUNIOR LEAGUE OF COBB-MARIETTA, INC.
P.O. Box 727, Marietta, Georgia 30060
770.422.5266

Library of Congress Catalog Number: 98-067390
ISBN: 0-9619983-1-8

Edited, Designed and Manufactured by
Favorite Recipes® Press
an imprint of

FRP

P.O. Box 305142, Nashville, Tennessee 37230
800.358.0560

Managing Editor: Mary Cummings
Art Director: Steve Newman
Book Project Managers: Jane Hinshaw, Debbie Van Mol
Cover and Book Design: Starletta Polster
Project Production: Sara Anglin

Manufactured in the United States of America
First Printing: 1998 15,000

ACKNOWLEDGEMENTS

CAMERON WOOD
Cameron Wood Photography – Atlanta

DONNA CREEL
Food Stylist – Atlanta

for opening your homes for our photography
MR. AND MRS. JAMES W. CORLEY, JR.
DR. AND MRS. WILLIAM W. HINKLE
M. L. JARVIS, INC.
MR. AND MRS. JEFFREY W. MARTIN
DR. AND MRS. BARRY MCKERRNAN
DR. AND MRS. HENRY RANDALL
MR. AND MRS. HANK RANDALL
THE WHITLOCK INN

Additional copies of SOUTHERN...ON OCCASION
may be obtained by writing or calling:
THE JUNIOR LEAGUE OF COBB-MARIETTA, INC.
P.O. Box 727, Marietta, Georgia 30060
770.422.5266
Fax 770.427.2253

TABLE OF *Contents*

COOKBOOK DEVELOPMENT COMMITTEE

Michi Rainey Newman
Chairman

Susan Morgan Martin
Assistant Chairman

Susann Meadows Braden
Recipe Development

Sue Boudreaux

Julia Harper Brown

Kim Connell Churchill

Virginia Webb Harrison

Jennifer Gardner Helms

Joanna Prater Martin

Diana Wiegand Mears

Lisa Forrest Mensch

Paige Hutto Monteith

Cherie Harlan Rudolph

Renee Porter Webster

Kris Anne Zenoni

We thank all who contributed to this extraordinary effort. Thank you for the constant encouragement and inspiration. Thank you for sharing your "southern-ness"—your traditions, recipes, ideas, and memories. Thank you to the families of each committee member, for all that you did and did without. Thank you to our spouses, children, parents and grandparents, friends, neighbors, employers, employees, and co-workers. And thank you to the many people we met along our creative journey, for your numerous talents and for allowing us to learn and discover. Thank you to our fellow members of the Junior League of Cobb-Marietta, Inc.—those current, past, and future. Thank you for believing in our concept and for your unwavering trust as we brought together the best efforts of so many. Thank you for your enthusiasm, always. And thank you for being, well... *Southern...On Occasion!*

THE JUNIOR LEAGUE OF COBB-MARIETTA, INC.

MISSION

THE JUNIOR LEAGUE OF COBB-MARIETTA, INC. IS AN ORGANIZATION OF WOMEN COMMITTED TO PROMOTING VOLUNTARISM, DEVELOPING THE POTENTIAL OF ITS MEMBERS AND IMPROVING THE COMMUNITY THROUGH THE EFFECTIVE ACTION AND LEADERSHIP OF TRAINED VOLUNTEERS. ITS PURPOSE IS EXCLUSIVELY EDUCATIONAL AND CHARITABLE.

VISION

THE JUNIOR LEAGUE OF COBB-MARIETTA, INC. IS A CATALYST FOR COMMUNITY CHANGE BY IMPROVING THE LIVES OF CHILDREN AND FAMILIES THROUGH THE ENCOURAGEMENT AND SUPPORT OF EFFECTIVE, QUALITY PARENTING.

ORGANIZED IN 1933 AS THE MARIETTA JUNIOR WELFARE LEAGUE, THE JUNIOR LEAGUE OF COBB-MARIETTA, INC. HAS DEDICATED MORE THAN 65 YEARS OF SERVICE TO ITS COMMUNITY. JLCM HAS WORKED TO POSITIVELY ADDRESS A MYRIAD OF COMMUNITY NEEDS THROUGH PROGRAMS INITIATED OR SUPPORTED BY ITS VOLUNTEERS AND MONETARY GRANTS. THE JUNIOR LEAGUE OF COBB-MARIETTA, INC. IS CURRENTLY FOCUSED ON THE DEVELOPMENT OF THE COBB PARENTING INITIATIVE—A PROGRAM WITH A MULTI-FACETED APPROACH TO PREPARING AND SUPPORTING PARENTS, WITH THE GOAL OF IMPROVING THE LIVES OF CHILDREN AND FAMILIES.

Introduction

We want to share just what it is

that makes us…well, southern.

Through six gentle seasons

we guide you through a year

in the South…

SOUTHERNERS…ARE VERY ENTERTAINING PEOPLE. FROM A SIMPLE BREAK-FAST ON THE PORCH TO A CORDIAL WELCOME FOR NEW NEIGHBORS, A SUMMER LEMONADE STAND OR A DAY SPENT RAKING FALL LEAVES…ALL ARE EVENTS WE BELIEVE AS IMPORTANT AS A HOLIDAY OPEN HOUSE FOR THE VERY BEST OF FRIENDS. THESE TREASURED TIMES AND SPECIAL TOUCHES ARE IN OUR NEWEST BOOK. WE WISH TO TELL THE WHY AND WHEN OF HOW WE ENTERTAIN. WE WANT TO SHARE JUST WHAT IT IS THAT MAKES US…WELL, SOUTHERN. THROUGH SIX GENTLE SEASONS, IF YOU WILL, WE GUIDE YOU THROUGH A YEAR IN THE SOUTH…AS GARDENS BEGIN TO SMILE WE CELEBRATE WITH OUTDOOR PARTIES AND SPRING LUNCHEONS. A TISKET, A TASKET AND OVERFLOWING PICNIC BASKETS… GRADUATION, WEDDING EVENTS, AND THE BEST OF SPRINGTIME…WHEN WE COME TOGETHER FOR A DAY OF PLAY AND NOTHIN' BUT BLUE SKIES. OH, MY STARS!!! WHAT A CLEAR EVENING SKY WHERE THE STARS SEEM TO DANCE…THESE SPLENDID SUMMER DAYS THAT ALLOW US TO BE A CHILD AGAIN…WITH ONLY THE SIMPLEST OF NEEDS FOR SIMPLE DAYS. A NIP IN THE AIR, THE FIRST TOUCHES OF AUTUMN REMIND US TO EMBRACE EACH DAY AS A GIFT FROM NATURE. TRADITIONS GATHERED FROM MANY HOMES, EACH CELEBRATING THE RITUALS THAT ENRICH OUR LIVES…QUIET OR ELABORATE…ALWAYS FAITHFUL. SILVERY SHADOWED DAYS FIND US NESTLED INSIDE BY A WARMING FIRE, PROTECTED FROM WINTER'S CHILL…BUT THESE ARE FLEETING MOMENTS! THERE ARE PARTIES TO ATTEND, MIDNIGHT SUPPERS, AND TRIUMPHANT JUBILEES…

YES, WE ARE *SOUTHERN...ON OCCASION.* ON OCCASION, WE TAKE OFF OUR SHOES AND WADE IN THE CREEK. A PACKED PICNIC AWAITS US ON THE BANK. PULL UP A BLANKET AND JOIN US. ON OCCASION, IT'S TIME FOR OUR HOLIDAY BEST. WE REJOICE WITH FRIENDS AND FAMILY, SHARING REGIONAL FAVORITES AND TIMELESS TRADITIONS. ON OCCASION, WE CELEBRATE A SPECIAL DAY, A FOND FAREWELL, A NEW ADDITION TO THE FAMILY. AND ON OCCASION, WE SIMPLY GATHER, FOR GOOD FOOD AND SPIRITED CONVERSATION. ALL OF OUR SELECTIONS ARE FRAMED IN A MENU FOR-MAT——MEANT TO INSPIRE, TO BE PREPARED IN-PART OR IN THEIR ENTIRETY. A THOROUGH INDEX WILL ALSO ALLOW YOU TO IDENTIFY THE PERFECT SIDE DISH OR DESSERT FOR OUR OCCASIONS, OR FOR ONE OF YOUR OWN DESIGN. WE HIGHLIGHT GIFTS TO GIVE, TEMPTING TREATS TO SHARE. FOOD AND WHINE SIGNALS ONE-DISH OR OTHER PORTABLES FOR A NEW MOTHER OR FOR A NEIGHBOR WHO'S UNDER THE WEATHER. WHILE SOME OF OUR ANCESTORS WERE BORN SIPPING TEA ON A WIDE ANTEBELLUM PORCH, OTHERS HAVE ARRIVED MORE RECENTLY. BUT NO ONE CAN SPEND TIME IN THE SOUTH WITHOUT BEARING THE IMPRINT OF OUR SLOWER-PACED "COME AND SIT A SPELL" VIEW OF THINGS. THIS PRIMER OF SORTS WAS COMPILED TO CAPTURE THE ESSENCE OF WHO WE ARE...HOW WE GREET OUR GUESTS...HOW WE HONOR A CHERISHED FRIEND...HOW WE PASS ON TRADITIONS. WE HAVE COLLECTED THE BEST OF SOUTHERN FAVORITES AND OCCASIONS. USE THIS BOOK AS A COMPANION, A FRIEND THAT IMPARTS HER OLD SECRETS AND "HOW TOS," AND AS A GUIDE FOR INSPIRATION ON DEFINING YOUR OWN SENSE OF STYLE.

Here we have it...a glimpse of how we cook, how we play...how we entertain, how we celebrate. Just how we are...Southern...On Occasion.

GARDENS IN ALL

THEIR GLORY...

BRIGHT WARM SUN

SPREADING ITS

ARMS WIDE...

THE GENTLE DAYS

OF SPRINGTIME...

MENUS

A PINCH OF SPRING

PEARLS AND PANSIES

THEY'RE HERE!!!

WICKER TO WICKETS

FIT FOR THE QUEEN

AS GARDENS BEGIN TO SMILE

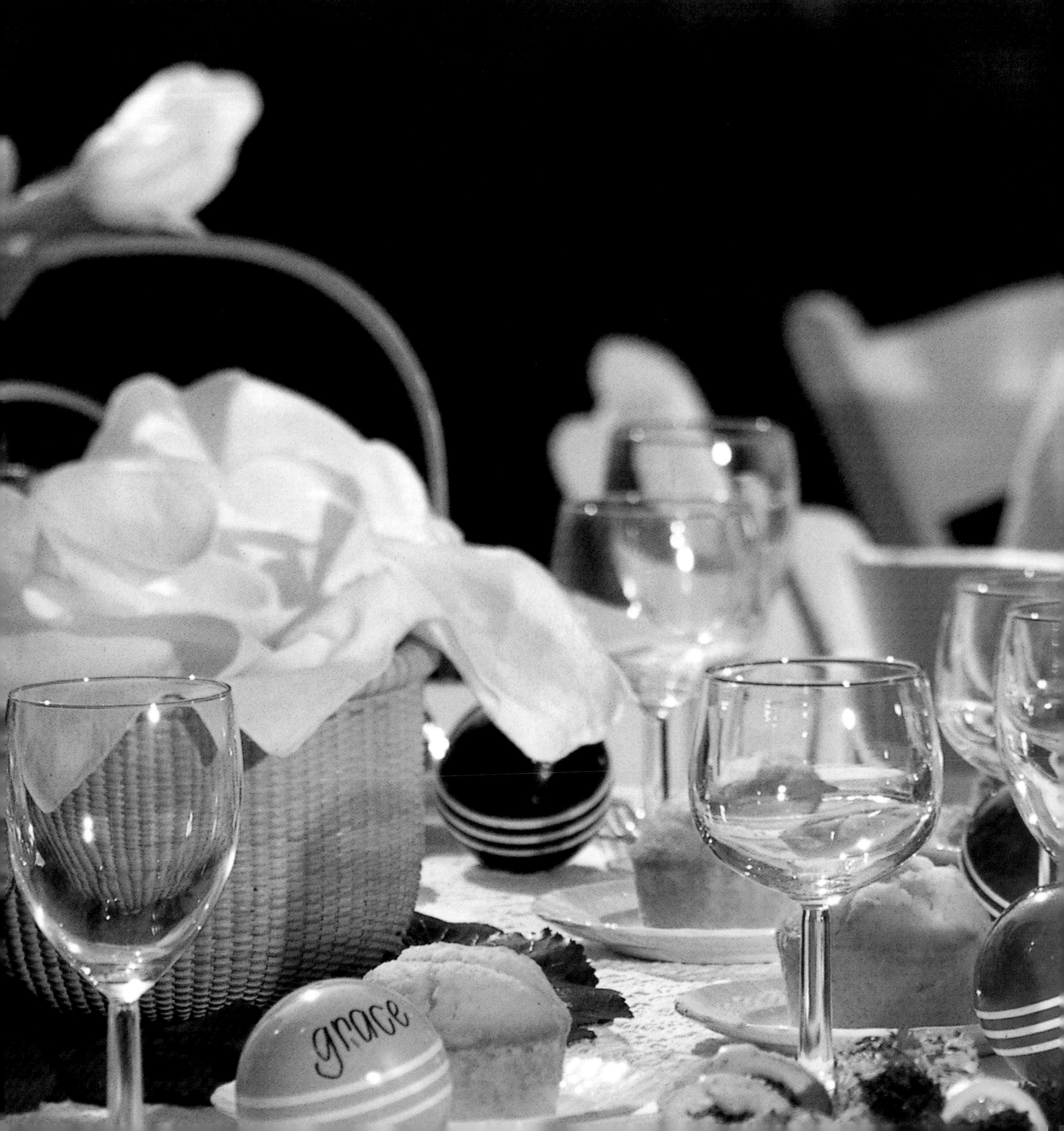

A PINCH OF SPRING

Menu

Pineapple Zucchini Bread

Jalapeño Fruit Salad

Crunchy Marinated Cucumbers

Baked Ham with Mustard and
Apricot Glaze

Fresh Spring Frittata

Traditional Dixie Biscuits with
Assorted Spreads

Fresh Fruit Tart

The Birthday Cake

Drizzled Dipped Fruit

On a certain day, year-in and year-out, each of us is allowed to feel "extra-special"—your birthday! A reason to celebrate..."jump for joy"...put some "spring in your step"...like finding a four-leaf-clover in a mass of green. But as the collection of clover keeps adding up, we observe them in a "big way" less often. Soon, only the digits followed by zeros are acknowledged, arriving much too quickly! If one of these "milestones" is fast approaching, consider rejoicing in a fresh way...Friends rise pre-dawn for an early morning surprise party. The bathrobed guests are quietly led inside. A brightly played bagpipe taps out a resounding announcement to a sleepy-eyed 40-year-old. A birthday breakfast is about to commence in his honor...Fifty finds "the girls" together for brunch, then appointments at the day spa and the required birthday shopping...A pre-tournament brunch for golfing buddies—will the 60-year-old last the entire eighteen holes?... For a birthday or simply to welcome a fine spring morning, enjoy this brunch...whatever your field of clover!

PINEAPPLE ZUCCHINI BREAD

3   CUPS FLOUR
2   CUPS SUGAR
1   TEASPOON SALT
1   TEASPOON BAKING SODA
1   TEASPOON CINNAMON
1   CUP CHOPPED PECANS OR WALNUTS
2   CUPS COARSELY SHREDDED UNPEELED ZUCCHINI
1   (20-OUNCE) CAN CRUSHED PINEAPPLE, DRAINED
1   CUP VEGETABLE OIL
3   EGGS, BEATEN
2   TEASPOONS VANILLA EXTRACT

Mix the flour, sugar, salt, baking soda and cinnamon in a bowl. Stir in the pecans. Combine the zucchini, pineapple, oil and eggs in a bowl and mix well. Stir in the vanilla. Add the zucchini mixture to the flour mixture, stirring just until moistened.

Spoon the batter into 5 greased and floured miniature loaf pans. Bake at 350 degrees for 45 to 50 minutes or until a wooden pick inserted in the center comes out clean. Cool in the pans for 10 minutes. Invert onto wire racks to cool completely.

May bake in 2 greased and floured loaf pans at 350 degrees for 70 minutes or until the loaves test done.

Makes five loaves

JALAPENO FRUIT SALAD

TANGY DRESSING
2   TABLESPOONS WHITE WINE VINEGAR
2   TABLESPOONS VEGETABLE OIL
1   TABLESPOON MINCED SEEDED JALAPEÑO
1   TABLESPOON SUGAR
½   TEASPOON PAPRIKA
⅛   TEASPOON PEPPER
SALAD
1   LARGE CANTALOUPE, CUT INTO BITE-SIZE PIECES
1   BUNCH ROMAINE, SEPARATED
1   CUP WHOLE STRAWBERRIES
½   CUP BLUEBERRIES
½   CUP SEEDLESS RED GRAPES
2   MEDIUM KIWIFRUIT, SLICED
    SPRIGS OF FRESH MINT

To prepare the dressing, combine the wine vinegar, oil, jalapeño, sugar, paprika and pepper in a jar with a tightfitting lid. Shake to mix.

To prepare the salad, mix the cantaloupe and dressing in a bowl, tossing to coat. Marinate in the refrigerator for 3 hours, stirring occasionally.

Spoon the cantaloupe onto a romaine-lined serving platter. Top with the strawberries, blueberries, grapes and kiwifruit. Garnish with mint.

To serve ten

For CRUNCHY MARINATED CUCUMBERS *score 5 large unpeeled cucumbers lengthwise with a fork to create a striped pattern. Cut the cucumbers into ¼-inch slices. Pour a mixture of ½ cup vegetable oil, ¼ cup rice wine vinegar and 2 teaspoons sugar over the cucumbers in a dish. Season with kosher salt and freshly ground pepper. Marinate, covered, in the refrigerator for 1 hour or longer. Toss gently before serving.*

Baked Ham with Mustard and Apricot Glaze

1   (10- to 12-pound) ham, trimmed
¼   cup (about) whole cloves
1   cup Dijon mustard
1   cup apricot jam
2   cups dry white wine, beer or ginger ale

Score the ham with a sharp knife to form a 1-inch diamond pattern. Insert a clove at each intersection of the lines.

Place the ham fat side up in a shallow baking pan. Spread the surface with the Dijon mustard. Spread the jam over the mustard. Pour the wine around the ham.

Bake at 300 degrees for 1 to 1½ hours or until a meat thermometer inserted in the center registers 140 degrees. Remove from oven.

Let stand for 10 minutes before slicing. Serve hot or at room temperature. Freeze the ham bone and fat for future use in soups and casseroles.

To serve fourteen to sixteen

Fresh Spring Frittata

1   small onion, chopped
2   tablespoons olive oil
6   eggs
1   teaspoon Tabasco sauce
    Salt and freshly ground pepper to taste
6   to 8 asparagus spears, steamed or blanched
1   medium red bell pepper, julienned
⅓   cup grated Parmesan cheese
1   tablespoon fresh snipped chives (optional)

Sauté the onion in the olive oil in a heavy skillet over medium heat for 3 to 5 minutes or until tender.

Beat the eggs, Tabasco sauce, salt and pepper in a bowl. Pour into a 9-inch round or heart-shape baking pan. Bake at 375 degrees for 3 minutes. Arrange the onion, asparagus and red pepper in a decorative pattern over the top.

Bake for 8 to 10 minutes longer or until set. Sprinkle with the cheese and chives. Broil for 2 to 3 minutes or until light brown. Cut into wedges. Serve warm or at room temperature.

To serve four to six

APRICOT JAM

8   OUNCES DRIED APRICOTS
¾   CUP SUGAR

Combine the apricots with enough water to cover in a saucepan. Bring to a boil over high heat; reduce heat to low. Simmer until the apricots are plump and tender, stirring occasionally. Add the sugar, stirring until dissolved. Cook for 10 minutes longer, stirring frequently. Process in a blender or food processor until of the desired consistency.

Makes one and one-half cups

CHUNKY HONEY BUTTER

½   CUP UNSALTED BUTTER, CHILLED
½   CUP ORANGE HONEY OR YOUR FAVORITE HONEY

Crumble the chilled butter in a bowl with a fork. Fold in the honey until combined. Chill, covered, in the refrigerator. Let stand at room temperature for 30 minutes before serving. Serve with hot biscuits.

Makes one cup

BERRY BUTTER

½   CUP BUTTER, SOFTENED
1   TABLESPOON FAVORITE BERRY JAM
1   TEASPOON GRATED ORANGE ZEST

Mix the butter, jam and orange zest in a bowl. Spoon into a mold. Chill, covered, until set. Serve with hot biscuits or spread over pancakes.

Makes one-half cup

TRADITIONAL DIXIE BISCUITS

Sift 4 cups flour, 2 teaspoons baking powder and 1 teaspoon salt into a bowl. Cut in 1 cup shortening until crumbly. Add 1½ cups milk, stirring just until moistened. Roll the dough ½ inch thick on a lightly floured surface; cut with a 2-inch biscuit cutter. Arrange the biscuits 2 inches apart on an ungreased baking sheet. Bake at 400 degrees for 15 minutes or until light brown. For Quickie Dixie Biscuits, drop the dough by tablespoonfuls directly onto the baking sheet and bake as above.

FRESH FRUIT TART

FRUIT TART PASTRY VARIATIONS

For a quicker version of the pecan crust for the FRESH FRUIT TART, *use a pie crust mix and add pecans. For a sweeter crust, substitute ready-to-use cookie dough and add the pecans before pressing the dough into the tart tin. For the easiest version of all, substitute all ready pie pastry and omit the pecans.*

PECAN CRUST
1¼	CUPS FLOUR
1	TEASPOON SUGAR
½	TEASPOON SALT
⅓	CUP FINELY CHOPPED PECANS
¼	CUP BUTTER, CUT INTO PIECES
3	TABLESPOONS SHORTENING, CHILLED
2	TO 3 TABLESPOONS WATER

CREAM CHEESE FILLING
3	OUNCES CREAM CHEESE, SOFTENED
½	CUP SUGAR
1	TEASPOON VANILLA EXTRACT
1	CUP WHIPPING CREAM
	FRESH RASPBERRIES, BLUEBERRIES, BLACKBERRIES, KIWIFRUIT OR APRICOTS

To prepare the crust, mix the flour, sugar, salt and pecans in a bowl. Cut in the butter and shortening with a pastry knife until crumbly. Add the water 1 tablespoon at a time, mixing until the dough forms a ball. Knead the dough lightly on a lightly floured surface with the heel of the hand. Shape into a ball. Chill, wrapped in waxed paper, for 30 to 60 minutes. Roll the dough into an 11-inch circle on a lightly floured surface. Fit into a 9-inch tart pan. Prick the bottom with a fork. Line with foil shiny side down. Fill with pie weights or dried beans. Bake at 350 degrees for 8 minutes. Remove the weights and foil. Bake for 10 to 13 minutes longer or until light brown. Let stand until cool.

To prepare the filling, beat the cream cheese, sugar and vanilla in a mixer bowl until blended, scraping the bowl occasionally. Beat the whipping cream in a chilled mixer bowl until stiff peaks form. Fold into the cream cheese mixture. Spoon into the prepared crust. Arrange the fruit in a decorative pattern, such as a star pattern, over the top. Chill until set. Serve slightly cooler than room temperature.

To serve six

THE BIRTHDAY CAKE

1   (2-LAYER) PACKAGE DEVIL'S FOOD CAKE MIX
2¼ CUPS SUGAR
¾   CUP WATER
3   EGG WHITES
1½ TABLESPOONS LIGHT CORN SYRUP
⅛   TEASPOON SALT
3   TO 4 DROPS OF OIL OF PEPPERMINT
3   TO 4 DROPS OF GREEN FOOD COLORING

Prepare and bake the cake using package directions for two 9-inch cake pans. Let stand until cool.

Combine the sugar, water, egg whites, corn syrup and salt in a double boiler and mix well. Cook over boiling water for 7 to 10 minutes or until stiff peaks form, beating constantly with an electric hand mixer. Remove from heat. Stir in the oil of peppermint and food coloring.

Spread the frosting between the layers and over the top and side of the cake.

One southern family ALWAYS had this wonderful cake for birthdays, and, in fact, the children in the family didn't recognize a traditional bakery cake at a birthday party. The original bottle of oil of peppermint that was always used still has the price tag of nineteen cents. Oil of peppermint can be found at pharmacies, but the current price is several dollars. Do not substitute peppermint extract for oil of peppermint in this recipe.

To serve twelve

ON OCCASION...

top it all off with DRIZZLED DIPPED FRUIT. *Pat pineapple spears, mandarin orange sections and cantaloupe cubes dry so the chocolate for dipping will adhere. Melt 1 cup of semisweet chocolate chips with 1 tablespoon shortening in a double boiler. Let stand until 110 degrees or until lukewarm. Dip each piece of fruit into the chocolate using wooden picks and place on a rack sprayed with nonstick cooking spray. Chill until set. Melt 1 cup of white chocolate chips with 1 tablespoon shortening in a double boiler. Cool as before. Drizzle over the chocolate coating. Chill until set and store in the refrigerator until serving time. Garnish with sprigs of fresh mint.*

PEARLS AND PANSIES

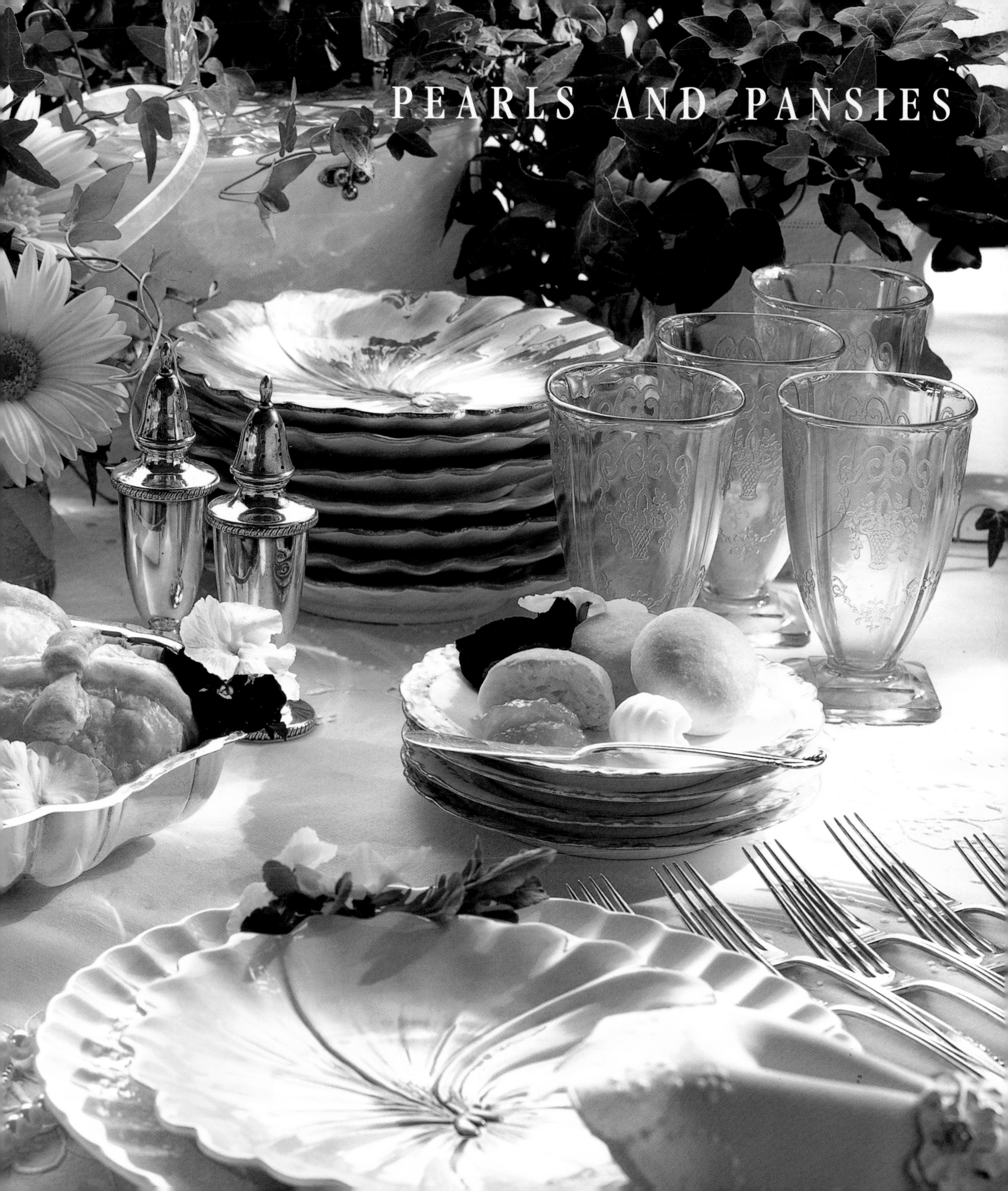

PEARLS AND PANSIES

Menu

Creamy Chutney Spread

Perfect Southern Mousse on
Perfect Toast Points

Rich Crab Cakes

Peach Bisque

Marinated Cherry Tomatoes

Chicken Presents

Spring Stuffing

Roasted Almond Asparagus

Angel Puffs

Raspberry Laces with
Caramel Sauce

Classic Layered Lemon Cake

Miss Priss's Punch

Pearls and pansies, white gloves and lace handkerchiefs...the ladies luncheon...so much a part of every Southern belle. This time-honored event has seen many faces——easy laughter, warm welcomes, heartfelt encouragement, shared joys. But the luncheon is more than well-wishes and light-hearted chatter——these gatherings are the ties that bind a community. Between soup and salad, ideas are coddled and nurtured. Strategies are soon developed and somewhere amidst dessert and coffee a commitment is made...a community embraced by determined backbone and focused energy. And all because an insightful woman knows that to garner support for a cause dear to her heart there is no better influence than a sampling of Southern fare. How could one say "no" while being wooed by raspberry and lemon? Imagination, dreams, a quiet goodness, positive challenges, best wishes...It is over lunch that foundations gain substance, a person's best is offered, and friendships come full circle...Pearls and pansies, white gloves and lace handkerchiefs...the ladies luncheon.

CREAMY CHUTNEY SPREAD

1   MEDIUM MANGO, PEELED, CHOPPED
¼   CUP APPLE JUICE
1   TABLESPOON SUGAR
½   TEASPOON SALT
8   OUNCES CREAM CHEESE, SOFTENED
¼   CUP FINELY CHOPPED FRESH CILANTRO
½   TEASPOON CURRY POWDER
    ASSORTED FRESH GREENS
    ASSORTED PARTY CRACKERS

Combine the mango, apple juice, sugar and salt in a double boiler. Cook for 20 to 30 minutes or until the mango is tender and the mixture is of a chutney consistency, stirring frequently. Let stand until cool.

Combine the mango chutney, cream cheese, cilantro and curry powder in a bowl and mix well. Spoon into a serving bowl.

Line a small serving platter with fresh greens. Place the serving bowl in the center of the platter. Serve at room temperature with assorted party crackers.

Save time by using a commercially prepared mango chutney.

Makes one and one-half cups

PERFECT SOUTHERN MOUSSE

2   ENVELOPES UNFLAVORED GELATIN
¼   CUP COLD WATER
2   CUPS CHOPPED COOKED SHRIMP
1½   CUPS MAYONNAISE-TYPE SALAD DRESSING
2   SMALL ONIONS, FINELY CHOPPED
2   HARD-COOKED EGGS, CHOPPED
     LETTUCE LEAVES

Combine the gelatin and cold water in a bowl and mix well. Let stand until the gelatin is softened. Combine the gelatin mixture, shrimp, salad dressing, onions and eggs in a bowl and mix well. Spoon into a mold.

Chill, covered, for 8 to 10 hours or until set. Invert onto a lettuce-lined serving platter. Serve with Perfect Toast Points.

To serve ten

∽

To prepare PERFECT TOAST POINTS *arrange 6 to 8 slices of white bread in a single layer on a baking sheet. Broil until light brown on 1 side. Trim the crusts with a serrated knife. Cut each slice into triangles. Arrange the triangles untoasted side up on a baking sheet. Broil until light brown. Store in an airtight container for up to 3 days.*

MARINATED CHERRY TOMATOES

24	FIRM RIPE CHERRY TOMATOES, CUT INTO QUARTERS
½	CUP CHOPPED FRESH BASIL
1	LEEK BULB, THINLY SLICED, CUT INTO QUARTERS
2	TABLESPOONS OLIVE OIL
2	TABLESPOONS BALSAMIC VINEGAR, OR TO TASTE
	SALT AND FRESHLY GROUND PEPPER TO TASTE
	RED LEAF LETTUCE

Combine the cherry tomatoes, basil, leek, olive oil, balsamic vinegar, salt and pepper in a bowl and toss to coat. Chill, covered, in the refrigerator. Toss and spoon onto a serving platter lined with red leaf lettuce.

To serve eight

PEACH BISQUE

5	CUPS SOUR CREAM
5	CUPS PLAIN YOGURT
3	CUPS APPLE JUICE
3	CUPS SUGAR
1	CUP PEACH SCHNAPPS
1	TEASPOON CINNAMON
1	TEASPOON NUTMEG
	WHIPPED CREAM
	NUTMEG TO TASTE

Combine the sour cream, yogurt, apple juice, sugar, peach schnapps, cinnamon and 1 teaspoon nutmeg in a bowl, stirring until blended. Chill, covered, in the refrigerator until serving time.

Ladle into soup bowls. Top each serving with a dollop of whipped cream and sprinkle with nutmeg to taste.

This may be prepared 1 day in advance and stored, covered, in the refrigerator. Stir before serving.

For a party, serve in a pretty soup tureen and arrange peaches, peach leaves and nasturtiums around the base. Dollop the whipped cream over the top and sprinkle with nutmeg.

To serve twelve

❧

Prepare RICH CRAB CAKES *by combining 1 pound backfin crab meat with 1 tablespoon flour in a bowl and stir gently to coat. Beat ¼ cup whipping cream, 1 egg, salt, black pepper and cayenne to taste in a bowl until blended. Add to the crab mixture and mix gently. Heat ¼ cup butter in a skillet until hot. Drop the crab mixture by heaping tablespoonfuls into the hot butter. Sauté until brown on both sides.*

CHICKEN PRESENTS

CHICKEN

  8   OUNCES GARLIC AND HERB CHEESE SPREAD

       FINELY CHOPPED ALMONDS TO TASTE

  6   BONELESS SKINLESS CHICKEN BREAST HALVES

       SALT AND PEPPER TO TASTE

  ¼   CUP BUTTER

  2   (17-OUNCE) PACKAGES PUFF PASTRY

  1   EGG WHITE, LIGHTLY BEATEN

CREAM SAUCE

  ½   CUP BUTTER

  2   TABLESPOONS FLOUR

  1   (16-OUNCE) CAN CHICKEN STOCK

  1   CUP WHIPPING CREAM

       GARLIC SALT TO TASTE

ON OCCASION...

dress up chicken bundles or customize other pastry dishes to the occasion. Cut leftover pastry into appropriate shapes such as flowers, flags, holly, bells, pumpkins, fruit, ribbons, hearts, etc. Moisten them with water and press lightly onto the pastry base. Brush with lightly beaten egg white before baking.

To prepare the chicken, combine the cheese spread and almonds in a bowl and mix well. Pound the chicken breasts between sheets of waxed paper with a meat mallet until flattened. Sprinkle the chicken with salt and pepper. Sauté in the butter in a skillet until light brown on both sides; drain.

Cut 3 sheets of the puff pastry vertically into halves on a lightly floured surface. Spread the cheese mixture evenly over 1 side of each pastry half. Place 1 chicken breast in the center of each half. Wrap the pastry around the chicken to enclose and seal the edges. Each bundle should resemble the shape of an egg. Smooth out any cracks that appear in the pastry with water. Arrange seam side down on a baking sheet. Cut the remaining sheet of puff pastry into twelve ¾-inch strips. Twist each strip. Arrange 1 strip horizontally around the center of each bundle. Arrange another strip vertically around the center to form a cross. Brush with the egg white. Chill for 1 hour. Bake at 350 degrees for 50 minutes.

To prepare the sauce, heat the butter in a saucepan until melted. Add the flour, stirring until blended. Cook until light brown, stirring constantly. Stir in the stock. Cook over low heat until reduced by ⅓, stirring constantly. Whisk in the whipping cream and garlic salt. Cook just until heated through; do not boil. Serve with the chicken.

To serve six

SPRING STUFFING

8 MEDIUM YELLOW SQUASH
1 CUP CHOPPED GREEN ONIONS
1 LARGE TOMATO, SEEDED, CHOPPED, DRAINED
1 CUP SHREDDED MONTEREY JACK CHEESE
4 SLICES CRISP-FRIED BACON, CRUMBLED
  SALT AND PEPPER TO TASTE
1 CUP BREAD CRUMBS
2 TO 3 TABLESPOONS MELTED BUTTER

Combine the squash with enough water to cover in a saucepan. Bring to a boil; reduce heat. Simmer for 10 minutes or until the squash are tender but firm; drain. Let stand until cool. Cut each squash horizontally into halves. Remove the pulp, leaving a thin shell. Arrange the squash shells on a nonstick baking sheet.

Combine the pulp, green onions, tomato, cheese, bacon, salt and pepper in a bowl and mix well. Spoon the squash mixture into the shells. Sprinkle with the bread crumbs; drizzle with the butter.

Bake at 400 degrees for 20 minutes or until brown and bubbly.

To serve eight

ROASTED ALMOND ASPARAGUS

½ CUP SLICED ALMONDS
2 TABLESPOONS BUTTER
1 POUND FRESH ASPARAGUS, TRIMMED
  SALT TO TASTE
  LEMON ZEST

Sauté the almonds in the butter in a skillet just until brown.

Blanch the asparagus in a small amount of boiling salted water in a saucepan for 4 to 6 minutes; drain. Toss the almonds with the asparagus in a serving bowl. Garnish with lemon zest. Occasionally . . . top roasted asparagus with HOLLANDAISE SAUCE.

To serve eight

❧

Don't ever allow the words "HOLLANDAISE SAUCE" to scare you again! Try this quick and easy version and wow your guests. Whisk ¼ cup melted butter, 1 tablespoon fresh lemon juice, 2 beaten egg yolks, 2 tablespoons half-and-half and ½ teaspoon dry mustard in a 2-cup microwave-safe dish. Season with salt and Tabasco sauce. Microwave for 1 minute, whisking every 15 seconds. You won't believe the results!

ANGEL PUFFS

2   ENVELOPES DRY YEAST
2   TABLESPOONS LUKEWARM WATER
5   CUPS FLOUR
5   TABLESPOONS SUGAR
1   TABLESPOON BAKING POWDER
1   TEASPOON SALT
1   TEASPOON BAKING SODA
1   CUP SHORTENING
2   CUPS BUTTERMILK
     MELTED BUTTER

Dissolve the yeast in the lukewarm water in a bowl and mix well. Sift the flour, sugar, baking powder, salt and baking soda into a bowl and mix well. Cut in the shortening until crumbly. Add the yeast mixture and buttermilk, stirring until mixed. Chill, covered, for 2 to 10 hours.

Roll the dough ½ inch thick on a lightly floured surface. Cut with a 2- or 3-inch biscuit cutter. Dip in butter. Arrange on a lightly greased baking sheet and fold over.

Let rise for 1 hour. Bake at 375 degrees for 20 minutes or until light brown. Serve with curls of butter. May store leftover dough, covered, in the refrigerator for up to 1 week.

Makes two and one-half dozen puffs

MISS PRISS'S PUNCH

2½   CUPS SUGAR
2½   CUPS WATER
1   (46-OUNCE) CAN PINEAPPLE JUICE
1   (46-OUNCE) CAN ORANGE JUICE
1½   CUPS FRESH LEMON JUICE
1   TEASPOON ALMOND EXTRACT
1   (2-LITER) BOTTLE GINGER ALE, CHILLED

Combine the sugar and water in a saucepan. Bring to a boil. Boil until the sugar dissolves, stirring constantly. Remove from heat. Stir in the pineapple juice, orange juice, lemon juice and flavoring. Pour into a freezer container. Freeze, covered, for 8 to 10 hours or until firm. Let stand at room temperature for several hours. Spoon into a punch bowl. Add the ginger ale and mix well. The mixture should have a slushy consistency. Ladle into punch cups. May substitute bottled lemon juice for the fresh lemon juice.

To serve twenty

For BLOOMIN' ICE, *place an edible flower blossom in each compartment of a plastic ice cube tray. Fill the trays halfway, or enough to cover the blossoms, with boiled water or ginger ale. Freeze until firm. Fill the rest of the way with water or ginger ale and freeze again. Serve in glasses, in a punch bowl, or in a large terra-cotta pot filled with bottled drinks.*

RASPBERRY LACES WITH CARAMEL SAUCE

FEAST OF FLOWERS

Brighten your tables and palate with a feast of edible flowers used as garnishes both on individual plates and serving plates. Edible flowers include pansies, Johnny-jump-ups, violets, roses, forget-me-nots, scented geranium leaves, nasturtiums, daisies, lavender, marigolds, and honeysuckle.

COOKIE CUPS

1	CUP FINELY GROUND BLANCHED ALMONDS
¾	CUP SUGAR
6	TABLESPOONS UNSALTED BUTTER, SOFTENED
4	TEASPOONS FLOUR
2	TABLESPOONS MILK

CARAMEL SAUCE

1	CUP PACKED LIGHT BROWN SUGAR
1	CUP WHIPPING CREAM
⅓	CUP SUGAR
¼	CUP MAPLE SYRUP
¼	CUP DARK CORN SYRUP

WHIPPED CREAM FILLING

½	CUP WHIPPING CREAM, CHILLED
¼	CUP SUGAR
⅛	TEASPOON UNFLAVORED GELATIN
2	PINTS FRESH RASPBERRIES

To prepare the cups, cut four 6-inch squares of parchment paper or waxed paper. Arrange the squares on a baking sheet. Beat the almonds, sugar, butter, flour and milk in a mixer bowl until blended. Spoon 1 tablespoon of the dough onto each square. Flatten the dough into 3-inch rounds with the back of a spoon dipped in cold water. Place the baking sheet on the middle oven rack. Bake at 350 degrees for 5 to 6 minutes or until golden brown. Remove from oven. Let stand for 45 seconds or just until the cookies are firm enough to hold their shape. Transfer the cookies on the parchment paper to inverted muffin tins or the bottom of inverted small glasses. Remove the paper. Mold the cookies to the tins to form cups. Let stand until cool. Repeat the process with the remaining dough.

To prepare the sauce, combine the brown sugar, whipping cream, sugar, maple syrup and corn syrup in a heavy saucepan. Cook over medium heat to 220 degrees on a candy thermometer; do not stir. Cool for 20 minutes. Store, covered, in the refrigerator for up to 1 week.

To prepare the filling, beat the whipping cream, sugar and gelatin in a chilled mixer bowl until soft peaks form, scraping the bowl occasionally.

To assemble, spoon approximately 3 tablespoons of the sauce onto each of 12 dessert plates. Spoon 2 heaping tablespoons of the filling into each cookie cup. Place the cookie cups on the dessert plates. Top with the raspberries.

To serve twelve

CLASSIC LAYERED LEMON CAKE

CAKE

1¾	CUPS SUGAR
¾	CUP BUTTER, SOFTENED
½	TEASPOON VANILLA EXTRACT
½	TEASPOON ALMOND EXTRACT
⅛	TEASPOON SALT
2	CUPS CAKE FLOUR
1	CUP ICE WATER
1	CUP CAKE FLOUR
1	TABLESPOON BAKING POWDER
6	EGG WHITES

LEMON FILLING

½	CUP BUTTER
1½	CUPS SUGAR
	GRATED PEEL AND JUICE OF
3	LEMONS
¼	TEASPOON SALT
12	EGG YOLKS, LIGHTLY BEATEN

DIVINE ICING

3	CUPS SUGAR
½	CUP WATER
¼	CUP LIGHT CORN SYRUP
⅛	TEASPOON SALT
3	EGGS WHITES
1	TEASPOON VANILLA EXTRACT

CANDIED FLOWERS

Candied edible flowers make a beautiful garnish for any plate. Begin with firm fresh flowers with stems cut close to the base of the blossom. Hold the blossoms with tweezers and dip completely into a wash of egg white diluted with water, coating completely. Sprinkle generously with superfine sugar and place gently on waxed paper. Let stand in a dry place for 2 to 4 days or until dry, rearranging gently each day to encourage even drying. Store for several months in a dry place.

To prepare the cake, grease and flour 2 round 9-inch cake pans. Line the bottom with waxed paper or parchment paper. Beat the sugar, butter, flavorings and salt in a mixer bowl until light and fluffy, scraping the bowl occasionally. Add 2 cups cake flour and ice water and mix well. Mix 1 cup cake flour and baking powder in a bowl. Add to the batter alternately with the egg whites 2 egg whites at a time, mixing after each addition. Do not overbeat. Spoon into the prepared pans. Bake at 350 degrees for 37 minutes. Cool in the pans for several minutes. Invert onto a wire rack to cool completely.

To prepare the filling, heat the butter in a double boiler over boiling water until melted. Stir in the sugar, lemon peel, lemon juice and salt. Add the egg yolks gradually, stirring constantly. Cook until thickened, stirring constantly. Let stand until cool.

To prepare the icing, combine the sugar, water, corn syrup and salt in a saucepan and mix well. Cook over medium heat to 240 degrees on a candy thermometer, stirring constantly. Beat the egg whites in a mixer bowl until stiff peaks form. Add the syrup mixture to the egg whites gradually, beating constantly. Add the vanilla. Beat until of a spreading consistency.

To assemble, split the cake layers horizontally into halves. Spread the filling between the layers. Spread the icing over the top and side of the cake.

To serve sixteen

THEY'RE HERE!!!

Menu

Goat Cheese Torta

Hearts of Palm Spread

Company Salad with
Pecan Croutons

Garden Lasagna

Pollo con Penne

French Loaf with Italian Oil

Roasted Garlic Spread

Orange Chess Pie

Raspberry Cheesecake Squares

Vanilla and Cherry Colas

A familiar sound is heard as the car pulls into the driveway. The doors fly open and suddenly everyone is hugging and telling tales. "They're here!"—for a weekend, a night, a visit of great proportion—with so much to do and much more to be said. How quickly the time will pass. And the weekend should not be spent only in the kitchen. For Saturday morning, make selections from our menus: A Pinch of Spring, Stay-at-Home Saturday, and Can't Wait 'til Morning. Keep lunch on-the-go with make-ahead items from A Tisket, A Tasket. For Saturday night serve from A Four-Star Day...or phone in a pizza order for the children and let the grown-ups go out for dinner. Plan ahead to take advantage of every second and make this a visit to remember!

GOAT CHEESE TORTA

6 OUNCES GOAT CHEESE

4 OUNCES CREAM CHEESE, SOFTENED

8 CLOVES OF GARLIC, CRUSHED OR FINELY CHOPPED

   SALT AND PEPPER TO TASTE

½ CUP PESTO

½ CUP FINELY CHOPPED OIL-PACK SUN-DRIED TOMATOES

   SPRIGS OF FRESH HERBS

1 LARGE BAGUETTE, CUT INTO ¼- TO ½-INCH SLICES

Line a 2- to 3-cup bowl with plastic wrap. Combine the goat cheese, cream cheese and garlic in a bowl and mix well. Season with salt and pepper.

Spoon ⅓ of the cheese mixture into the prepared bowl. Spread with the pesto. Spoon half the remaining cheese mixture over the pesto. Sprinkle with the sun-dried tomatoes. Top with the remaining cheese mixture. Chill, covered with plastic wrap, for 2 hours or up to 4 days.

Invert onto a serving platter. Garnish with fresh herbs. Serve with baguette slices. Store leftovers in the refrigerator for up to 1 week.

To serve twenty-four

ON OCCASION...

serve HEARTS OF PALM SPREAD. *Mix one 14-ounce can chopped drained hearts of palm, 1 cup shredded mozzarella cheese, ¾ cup mayonnaise, ½ cup grated Parmesan cheese and ¼ cup sour cream. Spoon into a lightly greased 9-inch quiche pan. Bake at 350 degrees for 20 minutes or until brown and bubbly. Serve with assorted party crackers.*

COMPANY SALAD WITH PECAN CROUTONS

FRENCH LOAF WITH ITALIAN OIL

Combine ½ cup extra-virgin olive oil, 1 large clove of minced garlic, 10 finely chopped basil leaves and freshly cracked pepper to taste in a bowl and mix well. Serve with a large loaf of French bread torn into bite-size pieces.

ROASTED GARLIC SPREAD

Cut the tops off 3 heads of garlic. Arrange in a baking pan. Drizzle with olive oil. Roast, loosely covered with foil, at 350 degrees for 45 to 60 minutes. Let stand until cool. Open any unopened cloves with a sharp knife. Squeeze the roasted garlic onto a cutting board and chop. (May be served at this point over melba rounds, allowing 1 head per guest.) Combine the garlic, 8 ounces softened cream cheese, 5 tablespoons mayonnaise and freshly cracked pepper in a bowl and mix well. Spread on toasted sliced French bread.

CANDIED PECAN CROUTONS
- ½ CUP SUGAR
- 2½ TABLESPOONS WATER
- ½ TEASPOON VANILLA EXTRACT
- 1 CUP PECAN HALVES OR ALMONDS

ORANGE VINAIGRETTE
- ⅓ CUP OLIVE OIL
- 2 TABLESPOONS RED WINE VINEGAR
- 1½ TEASPOONS FRESH ORANGE JUICE
- ½ TEASPOON GRATED ORANGE PEEL
- ¼ TEASPOON POPPY SEEDS
- ¼ TO ½ TEASPOON SALT
- ⅛ TEASPOON PEPPER

SALAD
- 8 CUPS MIXED SALAD GREENS
- 1 (11-OUNCE) CAN MANDARIN ORANGES, DRAINED
- 1 GREEN ONION, SLICED

To prepare the croutons, combine the sugar, water and vanilla in a saucepan and mix well. Bring to a boil; reduce heat. Cook over low heat for 5 minutes, stirring occasionally. Add the pecans, stirring until coated. Spread the pecans on a baking sheet. Let stand until cool. Break apart when cool.

To prepare the vinaigrette, combine the olive oil, wine vinegar, orange juice, orange peel, poppy seeds, salt and pepper in a jar with a tightfitting lid. Cover the jar and shake to mix.

To prepare the salad, mix the salad greens, mandarin oranges and green onion in a salad bowl. Drizzle with the vinaigrette and toss gently. Sprinkle with the croutons.

To serve eight

GARDEN LASAGNA

16 OUNCES LASAGNA NOODLES
1 LARGE SWEET ONION, CHOPPED
2 CLOVES OF GARLIC, MINCED
3 TABLESPOONS OLIVE OIL
2 LARGE CARROTS,
  COARSELY CHOPPED
1 RED BELL PEPPER,
  COARSELY CHOPPED
8 BUTTON MUSHROOMS,
  COARSELY CHOPPED
1 ZUCCHINI, COARSELY CHOPPED
1 YELLOW SQUASH,
  COARSELY CHOPPED
1 (14-OUNCE) CAN DICED
  TOMATOES
1 (10-OUNCE) CAN TOMATO
  PURÉE
1 TABLESPOON SUGAR
1½ TEASPOONS SALT, OR TO TASTE

1 TEASPOON PEPPER,
  OR TO TASTE
1 TABLESPOON CHOPPED FRESH
  BASIL
1 TABLESPOON CHOPPED FRESH
  OREGANO
1 TABLESPOON BALSAMIC
  VINEGAR
15 OUNCES RICOTTA CHEESE
1½ CUPS SHREDDED MOZZARELLA
  CHEESE
1 EGG, LIGHTLY BEATEN
1 TEASPOON GARLIC SALT
1 ZUCCHINI, SLICED
1 YELLOW SQUASH, SLICED
½ CUP SHREDDED MOZZARELLA
  CHEESE
¼ CUP GRATED PARMESAN
  CHEESE

Cook the noodles using package directions; drain. Sauté the onion and garlic in the olive oil in a large saucepan for 4 minutes or until the onion is tender. Stir in the carrots, red pepper, mushrooms, coarsely chopped zucchini and coarsely chopped yellow squash. Sauté for 4 minutes. Add the undrained tomatoes, tomato purée, sugar, salt and pepper and mix well. Simmer, covered, for 10 minutes, stirring occasionally. Stir in the basil, oregano and balsamic vinegar. Simmer for 5 minutes, stirring occasionally. Remove from heat.

Combine the ricotta cheese, 1½ cups mozzarella cheese, egg and garlic salt in a bowl and mix well. Layer ⅓ of the noodles in a greased baking dish. Top with half the vegetable sauce and half the remaining noodles. Layer with the cheese mixture, remaining noodles and remaining vegetable sauce. Arrange the sliced zucchini and sliced yellow squash over the top. Sprinkle with ½ cup mozzarella cheese and Parmesan cheese. Bake at 350 degrees for 35 to 40 minutes or until bubbly.

To serve six to eight

A ROOM AT THE INN

FOR UNEXPECTED GUESTS . . . *a glass and carafe for water; extra towels and toiletries; padded hangers; dryer sheet under chair cushions that can be flipped to freshen the room quickly; alarm clock; telephone book; notepad and pen; a pitcher of cut flowers and greenery from the yard; an assortment of small sweets*

FOR EXPECTED GUESTS . . . *basket of cookies, snacks, or fruit; fresh flowers; disposable camera; map of the city; wine with glasses; itinerary that includes some free time; books and magazines, particularly about the area; stationery, postcards, and stamps; extra top sheet over the blanket, two pillowcases per pillow, one slipped over the other in the opposite direction; full-length mirror; access to iron and ironing board; mint or chocolate on the pillow*

POLLO CON PENNE

CLASSIC COLAS

These lunch-counter classics are sure to awaken childhood memories!

For VANILLA COLAS, *pour 1 tablespoon vanilla syrup, from your local gourmet grocery, over crushed ice in a tall chilled glass. Fill the glass with cola and stir to mix well.*

For CHERRY COLAS, *pour 2 tablespoons maraschino cherry juice over ice cubes in a tall chilled glass. Fill the glass with cola and stir. Garnish with maraschino cherries on bamboo skewers.*

1	MEDIUM ONION, FINELY CHOPPED
2	TABLESPOONS OLIVE OIL
2	TABLESPOONS FINELY CHOPPED GARLIC
2	TEASPOONS BASIL
2	TEASPOONS OREGANO
4	(16-OUNCE) CANS DICED TOMATOES
2	CUPS WHIPPING CREAM
1½	TEASPOONS SALT
¾	TEASPOON FRESHLY GROUND BLACK PEPPER
¼	TEASPOON CAYENNE
6	BONELESS SKINLESS CHICKEN BREAST HALVES, GRILLED, CUT INTO BITE-SIZE PIECES
2	CUPS COARSELY CHOPPED FRESH BROCCOLI, STEAMED
8	OUNCES FRESH MUSHROOMS, SLICED
¾	CUP DRAINED CANNED CORN
1½	POUNDS PENNE, COOKED, DRAINED

Sauté the onion in the olive oil in a large saucepan for 5 to 7 minutes or until tender. Stir in the garlic, basil and oregano. Sauté for 1 minute. Add the undrained tomatoes, whipping cream, salt, black pepper and cayenne and mix well.

Bring to a boil. Boil for 5 minutes, stirring frequently. Stir in the chicken, broccoli, mushrooms, corn and pasta. Cook just until heated through, stirring frequently.

To serve eight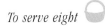

Orange Chess Pie

½ CUP BUTTER OR MARGARINE, SOFTENED
1 CUP SUGAR
3 EGGS
½ CUP ORANGE JUICE
3 TABLESPOONS CORNMEAL
1 TABLESPOON PLUS 1 TEASPOON GRATED ORANGE PEEL
1 TABLESPOON LEMON JUICE
1 UNBAKED (9-INCH) PIE SHELL
¼ CUP SHREDDED COCONUT
 FINELY CHOPPED MACADAMIA NUTS TO TASTE
 ORANGE SLICES (OPTIONAL)
 SPRIGS OF MINT (OPTIONAL)

Beat the butter in a mixer bowl until creamy. Add the sugar gradually, beating constantly at medium speed until light and fluffy. Add the eggs, beating until blended. Beat in the orange juice, cornmeal, orange peel and lemon juice.

Spoon into the pie shell. Sprinkle with the coconut and macadamia nuts. Bake at 350 degrees for 45 minutes or until a knife inserted in the center comes out clean. Garnish with orange slices and mint sprigs.

To serve six

Raspberry Cheesecake Squares

CHEESECAKE SQUARES
4 OUNCES BITTERSWEET CHOCOLATE, CHOPPED
2 OUNCES UNSWEETENED CHOCOLATE, CHOPPED
½ CUP UNSALTED BUTTER
1¼ CUPS SUGAR
3 EGGS
1½ TEASPOONS VANILLA
¾ TEASPOON SALT
¾ CUP FLOUR
TOPPING
8 OUNCES CREAM CHEESE, SOFTENED
⅔ CUP SUGAR
2 TEASPOONS LEMON JUICE
1 EGG
½ TEASPOON VANILLA EXTRACT
¼ TEASPOON SALT
2 TABLESPOONS FLOUR
1½ CUPS FRESH RASPBERRIES

To prepare the squares, heat the bittersweet chocolate, unsweetened chocolate and butter in a double boiler over hot water until blended, stirring frequently. Let stand until cool. Whisk the sugar into the chocolate mixture. Add the eggs 1 at a time, whisking well after each addition. Stir in the vanilla and salt. Add the flour, whisking just until blended. Spread in a buttered 9x13-inch baking pan.

To prepare the topping, beat the cream cheese and sugar in a mixer bowl until creamy. Add the lemon juice, egg, vanilla and salt and mix well. Beat in the flour. Spread over the prepared layer. Sprinkle with the raspberries.

Bake at 350 degrees for 35 to 40 minutes or until puffed and light golden brown. Chill, covered, for 6 hours or longer before cutting into squares.

Makes two dozen squares

WICKER TO WICKETS

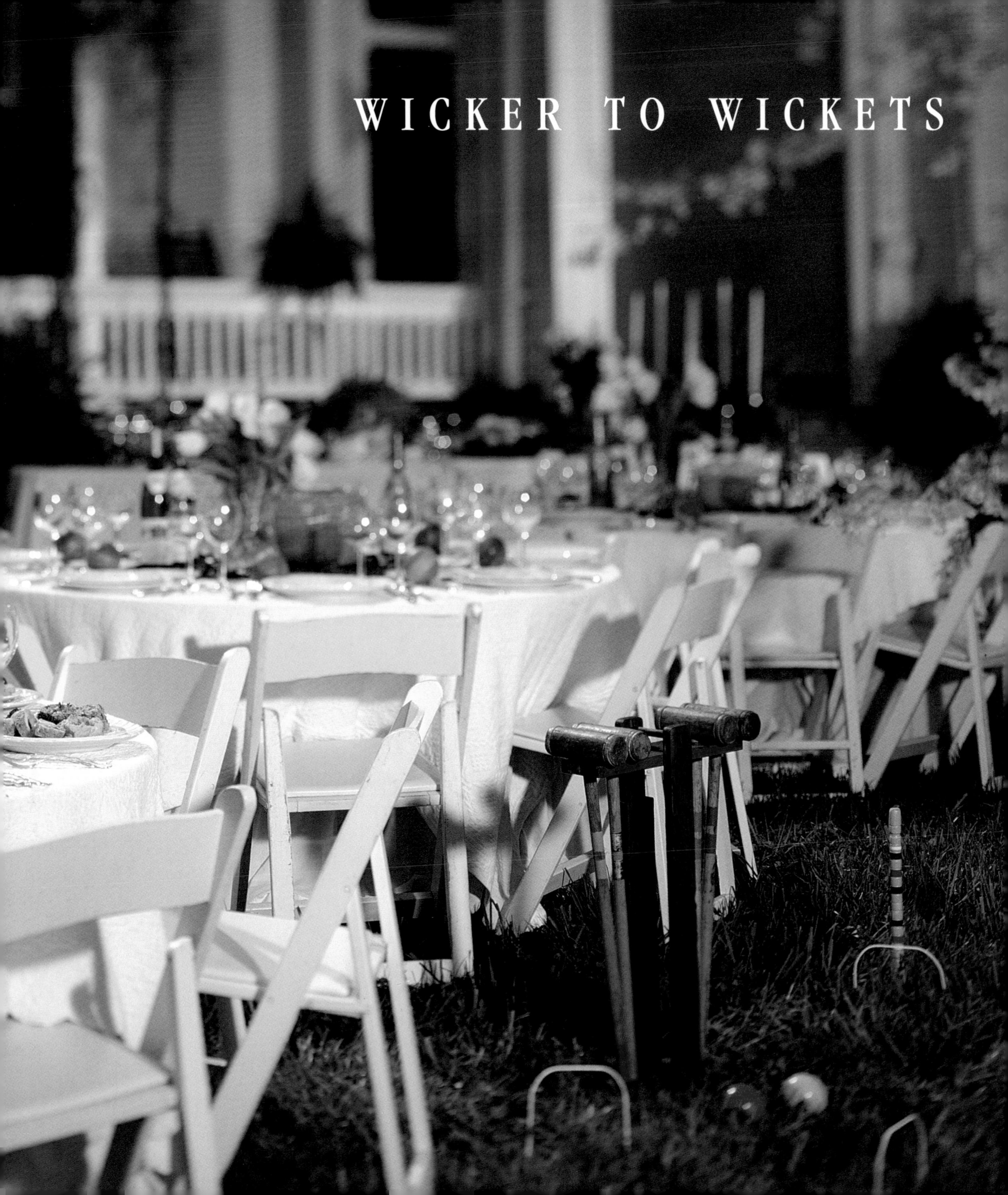

WICKER TO WICKETS

MENU

Smoked Salmon Breadsticks

All Wrapped Up

Kitty's Red Pear Salad

Mallet Chicken Medallions

Carrot Soufflés in Orange Cups

Lemoned Broccoli with Pecans

Sour Cream Muffins

Double Cookie Cheesecake

The Raspberry Meringue

Silver Pitcher Punch

White Wicker Punch

Gardens in all of their glory, bright warm sun spreading its arms wide. The gentle days of springtime when southern states put forth their best. Relaxing, taking it easy, 'tis a day for play—a classic lawn game perhaps. Mallets, wickets, and stakes...the blue ball strikes first, followed by red, black, and yellow. Take a fresh glance at the rule book, set up a course on a patch of grass, and sail through those wickets. A competitive spirit, teamwork, strategy, and concentration make for a lively afternoon. Then, conclude the match porchside. A row of wicker rockers, empty through the hilarity, now entice the competitors to rest easy. White linens and attire, ancient baskets, and ivory tulip blooms. Whether a wine-tasting, a dinner party, a couple's wedding shower, or a family day of outdoor games, welcome the promise of this season. We'll indulge in an early glimpse of spring by celebrating being southern...on occasion!

SMOKED SALMON BREADSTICKS

6	OUNCES CREAM CHEESE, SOFTENED		GROUND PEPPER TO TASTE
			CAPERS TO TASTE (OPTIONAL)
2	TABLESPOONS CHOPPED FRESH DILLWEED	48	ITALIAN GARLIC BREADSTICKS
1	TEASPOON LEMON JUICE	10	TO 11 OUNCES SLICED SMOKED SALMON, CUT INTO STRIPS
½	TEASPOON GRATED LEMON ZEST		LEMON SLICES
	SALT TO TASTE		SPRIGS OF DILLWEED

Beat the cream cheese, chopped dillweed, lemon juice, lemon zest, salt, pepper and capers in a mixer bowl until blended. Spread the cream cheese mixture on the breadsticks, leaving a small portion at the bottom to grasp. Wrap the salmon in a spiral fashion around the cream cheese mixture. Arrange the breadsticks on a serving platter. Garnish with lemon slices and sprigs of dillweed. These breadsticks must be prepared just before guests arrive or the breadsticks will become soggy.

Makes four dozen breadsticks

KITTY'S RED PEAR SALAD

¼	CUP RASPBERRY VINEGAR		MIXED SALAD GREENS
1	TEASPOON DIJON MUSTARD	3	RED PEARS, THINLY SLICED
¼	CUP HONEY	½	TO ¾ CUP CRUMBLED
¾	CUP EXTRA-VIRGIN OLIVE OIL		BLEU CHEESE
	SALT AND PEPPER TO TASTE	⅓	TO ½ CUP TOASTED WALNUTS

Mix the raspberry vinegar and Dijon mustard in a bowl. Stir in the honey. Whisk in the olive oil. Season with salt and pepper. Arrange the salad greens (red leaf lettuce, arugula, endive, etc.) on individual salad plates. Top with the pears and sprinkle with the bleu cheese and walnuts. Drizzle with the vinaigrette.

To serve eight

ALL WRAPPED UP

To set the tone, ol' Sport, revisit THE GREAT GATSBY *by F. Scott Fitzgerald. Daisy would have insisted on nothing but the finest silver, the sleekest bartender—perhaps a college student. Pass a silver tray filled with* ALL WRAPPED UP *hors d'oeuvre, which are simple, classic, and can be prepared ahead.*

For SCALLOPS WRAPPED WITH BACON, *wrap 1 pound sea scallops in ½-inch strips of bacon and secure with wooden picks. Bake at 400 degrees for 10 minutes or until bacon is crisp.*

For WATER CHESTNUTS WRAPPED WITH BACON, *wrap water chestnuts in bacon, drizzle with soy sauce, and bake in the same manner as above.*

For MELON WRAPPED WITH PROSCIUTTO, *wrap thin strips of thinly sliced prosciutto around wedges of melon.*

For DATES WRAPPED WITH BACON, *stuff blanched whole almonds into 1 pound of pitted dates. Wrap with thinly sliced bacon and secure with wooden picks. Bake at 400 degrees for 12 to 15 minutes or until the bacon is crisp. Drain. Serve warm.*

CARROT SOUFFLES IN ORANGE CUPS

6   ORANGES
1   POUND CARROTS, PEELED
1   CUP MILK, HEATED
½   CUP MELTED BUTTER
½   CUP SUGAR
3   EGGS
3   TABLESPOONS FLOUR
1   TEASPOON VANILLA EXTRACT

Rinse the oranges and cut off the top ⅓ of each orange. Scoop out the pulp and reserve for another use. Scallop the edges. Arrange the orange shells in a baking pan.

Steam the carrots in a steamer until tender. Drain and chop. Process the carrots, milk, butter, sugar, eggs, flour and vanilla in a food processor until smooth.

Spoon or pipe the carrot mixture into the orange shells, filling ⅔ full. Bake at 350 degrees for 1 hour.

If time is of the essence, prepare and bake only the carrot mixture in a greased baking dish for 1 hour.

To serve six

LEMONED BROCCOLI WITH PECANS

⅓   CUP CHOPPED PECANS
1   TABLESPOON BUTTER
1½   POUNDS FRESH BROCCOLI
¼   CUP LEMON JUICE
2   TEASPOONS CORNSTARCH
½   CUP DILUTED CANNED CHICKEN BROTH
1   TABLESPOON GRATED LEMON PEEL
1   TABLESPOON SUGAR
¼   TEASPOON PEPPER
     SALT TO TASTE

Sauté the pecans in the butter in a skillet until light brown. Set aside.

Separate the broccoli into spears. Steam in a steamer until tender-crisp; drain. Transfer to a serving bowl. Cover to keep warm.

Mix the lemon juice and cornstarch in a saucepan. Stir in the chicken broth, lemon peel, sugar, pepper and salt. Cook over medium heat until thickened, stirring constantly.

Pour the lemon sauce over the broccoli. Sprinkle with the pecans. Serve immediately.

To serve eight

❧

SOUR CREAM MUFFINS are quick and easy to prepare. Mix 1 cup softened butter, 2 cups self-rising flour and 1 cup sour cream with a fork. Spoon the batter into nonstick muffin tins. Bake at 350 degrees for 25 to 30 minutes or until light brown. For variety, add chopped fresh dillweed, basil, thyme or your favorite herb.

MALLET CHICKEN MEDALLIONS

2   (10-OUNCE) PACKAGES FROZEN CHOPPED SPINACH, THAWED
½   SWEET ONION, FINELY CHOPPED
2   CLOVES OF GARLIC, MINCED
2   TABLESPOONS OLIVE OIL
6   TO 8 BUTTON MUSHROOM CAPS, FINELY CHOPPED
1   EGG, BEATEN
¼   TEASPOON GROUND NUTMEG
    SALT AND PEPPER TO TASTE
8   BONELESS SKINLESS CHICKEN BREAST HALVES
¾   CUP SHREDDED SWISS CHEESE
½   CUP MELTED BUTTER
    SEASONED BREAD CRUMBS

Squeeze the moisture from the spinach.

Sauté the onion and garlic in the olive oil in a skillet until the onion is tender. Stir in the mushrooms. Sauté for 3 minutes. Add the spinach. Sauté for 3 minutes longer; drain. Let stand until room temperature. Stir in the egg, nutmeg, salt and pepper.

Place the chicken between sheets of waxed paper and pound ¼ inch thick with a meat mallet or other heavy object. Spread a thin layer of the spinach mixture onto the chicken and sprinkle with the cheese. Roll as for a jelly roll to enclose the filling.

Brush the chicken rolls generously with the butter and coat with the bread crumbs; secure with wooden picks. Place in a baking dish. Bake at 375 degrees for 45 minutes. Let stand for 10 minutes. Cut into ½-inch medallions. Serve warm from a chafing dish.

To serve eight

ON OCCASION...

enroll your guests in WINE TASTING 101, *or Pour, Smell, Swirl, Taste . . .*

Specify on the invitation that guests should bring two varieties of wine: a modestly priced one and something a bit more special. Instruct them to creatively cover the label (wrapping paper, a velveteen pouch, etc.). Allow no peeking during the tasting. Create a scorecard to rate wines, with a "10" meaning "Ooh, la, la, isn't that just the Eiffel Tower?" and "1" meaning "Stopped by the Quik Trip, did you?" The fun begins over dinner when guests reveal their mystery wines and comments. You may be pleasantly surprised!

DOUBLE COOKIE CHEESECAKE

A GRACIOUS TABLE

Galax leaves, which are available from the florist, make a luscious table cover. Starting at the center of a round table, arrange concentric circles of the leaves, layering them slightly and expanding to create a cover 36 inches or more in diameter. Secure the leaves to the table or tablecloth with double-face tape. Keep the greenery tablecloth cool until party time, then arrange votive candles and a bundle of fresh tulips at the table's center.

You can also decorate the votive candles with galax leaves, the tips of magnolia leaves, or rows of rose petals. Secure the leaves or petals with glue, trim the base of the leaves, and band with a ribbon or cording tied with a bow or knot. Exquisite!

CRUST

25 CHOCOLATE SANDWICH
   COOKIES
¼ CUP MELTED UNSALTED BUTTER

FILLING

32 OUNCES CREAM CHEESE,
   SOFTENED
1¼ CUPS SUGAR
2 TABLESPOONS FLOUR
4 EGGS, AT ROOM TEMPERATURE
3 EGG YOLKS, AT ROOM
   TEMPERATURE

⅓ CUP WHIPPING CREAM
1 TEASPOON VANILLA EXTRACT
1¾ CUPS COARSELY CHOPPED
   CHOCOLATE SANDWICH COOKIES
   (ABOUT 15)

TOPPING

2 CUPS SOUR CREAM
¼ CUP SUGAR
1 TEASPOON VANILLA EXTRACT

To prepare the crust, process the cookies in a food processor until of a crumb consistency. Add the butter. Process until mixed. Press the crumb mixture over the bottom and ¾ up the side of a greased 9-inch springform pan. Chill in the refrigerator.

To prepare the filling, beat the cream cheese in a mixer bowl until creamy, scraping the bowl occasionally. Add the sugar. Beat for 3 minutes or until light and fluffy, scraping the bowl occasionally. Beat in the flour. Add the eggs and egg yolks, beating constantly until smooth. Add the whipping cream and vanilla. Beat until blended. Spoon half the batter into the prepared pan. Sprinkle with the cookies. Spread with the remaining batter and smooth the top with a spatula. Place the pan on a baking sheet. Bake at 425 degrees for 15 minutes. Reduce the oven temperature to 225 degrees. Bake for 50 minutes longer or until set. Remove from oven. Reduce the oven temperature to 350 degrees.

To prepare the topping, mix the sour cream, sugar and vanilla in a bowl. Spread over the cheesecake. Bake for 7 minutes. Cool on a wire rack to room temperature. Chill, covered, for 2 to 10 hours before serving. May store, covered, in the refrigerator for up to 3 days.

To serve twelve

THE RASPBERRY MERINGUE

MERINGUE SHELL

½ CUP EGG WHITES (ABOUT 4)

½ TEASPOON CREAM OF TARTAR

1 CUP SUGAR

LEMON CUSTARD

4 EGG YOLKS, LIGHTLY BEATEN

½ CUP SUGAR

3 TABLESPOONS LEMON JUICE

1 TABLESPOON GRATED LEMON ZEST

¼ TEASPOON SALT

1 CUP WHIPPING CREAM, WHIPPED

RASPBERRY SAUCE

1 (12-OUNCE) PACKAGE FROZEN UNSWEETENED RASPBERRIES, THAWED

2 TABLESPOONS SUGAR

2 TABLESPOONS RASPBERRY LIQUEUR

1 TABLESPOON WATER

1 TEASPOON CORNSTARCH

1 CUP WHIPPING CREAM, WHIPPED

FRESH SEASONAL BERRIES

To prepare the shell, combine the egg whites and cream of tartar in a mixer bowl. Beat until foamy. Add the sugar gradually, beating constantly until stiff peaks form. Pipe the meringue in a 9-inch spiral with a 1½- to 2-inch side to form a shell on a parchment-lined baking sheet. Bake at 275 degrees for 1 hour or until light brown.

To prepare the custard, combine the egg yolks, sugar, lemon juice, lemon zest and salt in a double boiler. Cook over medium heat until thickened, stirring constantly. Remove from heat. Let stand until cool, stirring occasionally. Fold in the whipped cream. Spoon into the meringue shell. Chill for 6 hours or longer. May be prepared to this point up to 1 day in advance and stored, covered, in the refrigerator.

To prepare the sauce, combine the undrained raspberries, sugar and liqueur in a blender container; process until puréed. Strain into a saucepan, discarding the seeds. Stir in a mixture of the water and cornstarch. Bring to a boil over medium heat. Boil for 1 minute, stirring constantly. Let stand until cool. Drizzle over the lemon custard. Top with the whipped cream. Serve with sweetened seasonal berries.

To serve eight

FROM A SILVER PITCHER

Every beverage tastes better when served from a silver pitcher. Try SILVER PITCHER PUNCH, WHITE WICKER PUNCH, *sparkling white grape juice, or sparkling apple cider.*

For SILVER PITCHER PUNCH, *bring 1 gallon water to a boil. Add 3 family-size tea bags and steep for 3 minutes. Discard the tea bags. Add 2 cups sugar, stirring until dissolved. Stir in ¾ cup white grape juice and a 1.32-ounce packet of lemonade mix. Chill for 3 hours. Serve over ice with rock candy swizzle sticks and fresh mint.*

For WHITE WICKER PUNCH, *mix 2 quarts chilled white grape juice, 2 liters chilled ginger ale, and 750 milliliters chilled Champagne or dry white wine in a chilled punch bowl. Add ¾ cup grenadine if desired. Drape clusters of frozen grapes over the edge of the punch bowl to serve as a lovely garnish and to help keep the punch cool.*

FIT FOR THE QUEEN

Menu

Chicken Salad Drums

Cucumber Sandwiches

Whitlock Wedges

Tea Sandwich Spreads:
Creamy Mustard Spread
Strawberry Butter
Nutty Cream Cheese
Berry Cream Cheese

Chilled Olive Rolls

Cheese Buttons

Countryside Scones

Chocolate Chip Scones

Lemon Scones

Windsor Biscuits

Carriage Cookies

Colony Iced Tea
with Mint Syrup

It all began in that chilly harbor of our neighbors to the north. Tea was tossed and new traditions began for these rebellious colonies. As independence moved below the Mason-Dixon line, the brewed leaf eventually found its way inside tall glasses brimming with cubes of ice and a declaration of our own was created...THE DIXIE DECLARATION OF INDEPENDENCE...

"We, the people, in order to form a more perfect afternoon, establish teatime to insure domestic tranquility...provide for the common element—excellent company...promote the general well-being of all guests...secure the blessings of luxury for ourselves and our posterity...do ordain and establish this constitution for...Well,—for the pursuit of happiness!"

Whether a proper Brit or simply "Queen for the Day," delicately clasp your teacup—or tea glass—and make a gentle nod to the hostess as you judge the tea...fit for the queen!

CHICKEN SALAD DRUMS

12 THIN SLICES WHOLE WHEAT
    BREAD, CRUSTS TRIMMED
1 (6-OUNCE) BONELESS
    SKINLESS CHICKEN BREAST,
    POACHED, FINELY CHOPPED
1 RIB CELERY, FINELY CHOPPED
1 TABLESPOON MINCED GREEN
    ONION

1 TABLESPOON FRESH LEMON JUICE
¼ TEASPOON CURRY POWDER
3 TABLESPOONS MAYONNAISE
1 CUP SLICED ALMONDS,
    TOASTED, FINELY CHOPPED
    HOMEMADE MAYONNAISE
    TO TASTE

Cut the bread into 2-inch rounds with a biscuit cutter. Combine the chicken, celery, green onion, lemon juice and curry powder in a bowl and mix well. Stir in the mayonnaise. Spread half the bread rounds with the chicken mixture. Top with the remaining rounds. Spread additional mayonnaise around the side of each sandwich. Roll the sides in the almonds. Chill, covered, until serving time.

Makes two dozen sandwiches

CUCUMBER SANDWICHES

1 LOAF THIN-SLICED WHITE
    BREAD, CRUSTS TRIMMED
1 OR 2 ENGLISH CUCUMBERS
1 CUP BUTTER, SOFTENED
8 OUNCES CREAM CHEESE,
    SOFTENED
    JUICE OF 1 LEMON

1 TABLESPOON CHOPPED FRESH
    DILLWEED OR 1 TEASPOON DRIED
    SALT TO TASTE
    WHITE PEPPER TO TASTE
    RED CAVIAR
    SPRIGS OF FRESH DILLWEED

Cut 2 small rounds from each bread slice. Score the cucumber horizontally with the wide blade of a zester and cut into thin slices. Beat the next 6 ingredients in a mixer bowl until light and fluffy, scraping the bowl occasionally. Spread a thin layer of the butter mixture over 1 side of each round. Top with a cucumber slice. Garnish with red caviar and dillweed sprigs.

Makes one and one-half dozen sandwiches

COLONY ICED TEA WITH MINT SYRUP

Since Southerners always need iced tea at hand, it's a good idea to keep both the tea syrup and the mint syrup in the refrigerator. For COLONY ICED TEA, *bring 6 cups of water to a boil and remove from the heat. Add 4 ounces of tea, loose or in bags, to the water and steep for 15 minutes. Strain into a pitcher over 5 cups of sugar and stir to dissolve completely. To serve, pour the desired amount over ice in tall glasses and dilute with water to taste. This can be frozen or stored in the refrigerator for up to 2 weeks.*

For MINT SYRUP, *bring 2 cups of water and 2 cups of sugar to a boil. Add 1 bunch of fresh mint and simmer for 5 minutes. Let stand for 2 hours, strain, and store in the refrigerator.*

Now about that mint . . . every self-respecting southern garden has some! It is actually too easy to grow, because it spreads from the roots and may invade the garden. The answer is to plant it in an oversized container, either on the deck or sunk into the garden. You'll probably still have enough to share with friends.

WHITLOCK WEDGES

CRANBERRY MAYONNAISE
   1   CUP MAYONNAISE
   ¼   CUP WHOLE CRANBERRY SAUCE
WEDGES
   1   (16-OUNCE) LOAF PUMPERNICKEL BREAD,
        CRUSTS TRIMMED
   16   OUNCES SHAVED SMOKED TURKEY
         BEAN SPROUTS

For the cranberry mayonnaise, mix the mayonnaise and cranberry sauce in a bowl. Store, covered, in the refrigerator until serving time.

For the wedges, spread 1 side of each slice of bread with cranberry mayonnaise. Layer half the slices with turkey and bean sprouts. Top with the remaining bread slices. Cut each sandwich into wedges.

Makes twenty wedges

TEA SANDWICH SPREADS

CREAMY MUSTARD SPREAD

Mix 1 cup mayonnaise, 1 tablespoon freshly chopped chives, 2 teaspoons Dijon mustard and 2 teaspoons grated lemon peel or orange peel in a bowl. Store, covered, in the refrigerator until serving time. Makes 1 cup.

STRAWBERRY BUTTER

Mix ½ cup butter, 4 crushed strawberries and 2 tablespoons honey in a bowl. Store, covered, in the refrigerator. Makes ½ cup.

NUTTY CREAM CHEESE

Mix 8 ounces softened cream cheese and ¼ cup chopped walnuts, hazelnuts, almonds, pecans or raisins in a bowl. Store, covered, in the refrigerator. Makes 1 cup.

BERRY CREAM CHEESE

Mix 8 ounces softened cream cheese and ¼ cup raspberry preserves in a bowl. Store, covered, in the refrigerator. Makes 1¼ cups.

Don't forget some SPECIAL BITES FOR THE YOUNGER SET *at teatime. They might like miniature cinnamon-raisin bagels toasted with butter and cinnamon-sugar; peanut butter and purple jam diamonds; cheese crescent rolls; bear-shaped graham cookie sandwiches with sweetened cream cheese; miniature waffles with whipped cream and sprinkles; or shortbread cookies with strawberry cream cheese and a strawberry slice.*

CHILLED OLIVE ROLLS

8   OUNCES CREAM CHEESE, SOFTENED
½   CUP CHOPPED PIMENTO-STUFFED OLIVES
1   TABLESPOON SOUR CREAM
4   THIN SLICES WHEAT BREAD, CRUSTS TRIMMED
12   WHOLE PIMENTO-STUFFED OLIVES

Combine the cream cheese, chopped olives and sour cream in a bowl, stirring until mixed. Roll the bread slices on a hard surface until flattened. Spread each slice with some of the olive mixture. Line one edge of each slice with 3 olives end to end. Roll as for a jelly roll to enclose the filling. Chill, covered, in the refrigerator. Cut into ½-inch slices just before serving.

Makes two dozen

CHEESE BUTTONS

2   CUPS SHREDDED SHARP CHEDDAR CHEESE
1   CUP UNSALTED BUTTER, SOFTENED
2   CUPS FLOUR
2   CUPS CRISP RICE CEREAL
⅛   TEASPOON CAYENNE

Beat the cheese and butter in a mixer bowl until creamy, scraping the bowl occasionally. Add the flour and beat until blended. Stir in the cereal and cayenne. Chill, covered, for 30 minutes. Roll the dough into 1-inch balls. Arrange on a greased baking sheet; flatten. Bake at 350 degrees for 12 to 15 minutes or until light brown. Remove to a wire rack to cool.

Makes three dozen buttons

ON OCCASION...

treat the children to a memorable TEA PARTY. *It should be short, simple, and small. The child to be honored should be involved in the party planning and made to feel very special.*

To make everyone feel at home right away, start with a table covered in white paper. Place washable crayons and markers in an upturned hat (magic top hat, baseball helmet, straw boater...), a painted pail, or terra-cotta pots. Children can decorate the table cover while waiting for everyone to arrive.

For a special keepsake, substitute an inexpensive fabric cloth for the white paper and allow the wee folk to autograph or decorate it.

To answer "where do I sit?" try frosted cookies with names on them; a name painted on a bucket with a shovel; a personalized place setting drawn on a paper tablecloth; or a personalized tag on the tea bag dangling over the edge of a real teacup.

COUNTRYSIDE SCONES

¼ CUP DRIED PITTED TART RED CHERRIES
2½ CUPS FLOUR
1 TABLESPOON BAKING POWDER
½ TEASPOON SALT
½ CUP UNSALTED BUTTER, CHILLED
¼ CUP SUGAR
⅔ CUP MILK

Snip the cherries into halves. Combine with enough hot water to cover in a bowl. Let stand for 5 minutes; drain.

Combine the flour, baking powder and salt in a bowl and mix well. Cut in the butter with a pastry blender until crumbly. Stir in the sugar and cherries. Add the milk, stirring until a soft dough forms. Shape into a ball. Knead the dough 10 to 12 times on a lightly floured surface. Divide the dough into 2 portions. Knead each half lightly into a ball. Roll into a 6-inch circle.

Cut each circle into 6 to 8 wedges. Arrange the wedges slightly apart for crisp sides or touching for soft sides on an ungreased baking sheet.

Bake at 425 degrees for 12 minutes or until medium brown. Remove to a wire rack to cool.

Makes twelve to sixteen scones

CHOCOLATE CHIP SCONES

1 CUP UNSALTED BUTTER, SOFTENED
⅓ CUP SUGAR
3 EGGS
3 CUPS FLOUR
1 TABLESPOON BAKING POWDER
⅓ CUP BUTTERMILK OR PLAIN YOGURT
½ CUP SEMISWEET CHOCOLATE CHIPS

Beat the butter in a mixer bowl at high speed until creamy, scraping the bowl occasionally. Add the sugar. Beat for 3 to 5 minutes or until light and fluffy. Add the eggs 1 at a time, beating well after each addition. Scrape the side of the bowl.

Add a mixture of the flour and baking powder. Beat at low speed just until blended, scraping the bowl occasionally. Add the buttermilk and beat just until blended. Sprinkle the chocolate chips over the batter and fold in.

Drop ⅓ cupfuls of batter 2 inches apart onto an ungreased baking sheet. Chill, covered loosely with plastic wrap, for 45 minutes. Bake at 350 degrees for 15 minutes. Reduce oven temperature to 325 degrees.

Bake for 13 minutes longer or until light golden brown. Remove to a wire rack to cool.

Makes one dozen scones

Make LEMON SCONES *using the* COUNTRYSIDE SCONES *recipe by substituting 1 tablespoon freshly grated lemon peel for the cherries.*
Drizzle the wedges with a mixture of 2 teaspoons fresh lemon juice and 2 tablespoons confectioners' sugar after baking.

WINDSOR BISCUITS

2¼ CUPS FLOUR
¾ CUP FINELY GROUND ALMONDS
¼ TEASPOON SALT
1 CUP UNSALTED BUTTER, SOFTENED
¾ CUP CONFECTIONERS' SUGAR
2 TEASPOONS ALMOND EXTRACT
½ CUP MILK
½ CUP RASPBERRY JAM

Mix the flour, almonds and salt in a bowl. Beat the butter and ¾ cup confectioners' sugar in a mixer bowl until creamy. Add the flavoring and beat until blended. Add the milk and flour mixture alternately ⅓ at a time, beating well after each addition. Knead gently into a ball on a lightly floured surface. Chill, covered, for 3 hours or longer.

Divide the dough into 2 portions. Cover 1 portion and return to the refrigerator. Roll the remaining portion ⅛ inch thick on a surface dusted lightly with confectioners' sugar. Cut with a 1½-inch heart-shaped cookie cutter. Arrange on an ungreased baking sheet.

Bake at 350 degrees for 18 to 20 minutes or until the edges are golden brown. Remove to a wire rack. Repeat the process with the remaining dough, being sure to include any scraps of dough from the first portion.

Spread the bottom of half the hot cookies with the raspberry jam. Press the flat side of the remaining cookies over the jam to sandwich the filling. Cool on a wire rack. Dip the cookies in additional confectioners' sugar, shaking off the excess. Cool completely before storing.

Makes three dozen biscuits

CARRIAGE COOKIES

2 CUPS FLOUR
1 CUP MARGARINE, SOFTENED
⅓ CUP WHIPPING CREAM
  GRANULATED SUGAR TO TASTE
¾ CUP CONFECTIONERS' SUGAR
¼ CUP MARGARINE, SOFTENED
1 EGG YOLK
1 TEASPOON VANILLA EXTRACT
  FOOD COLORING

Beat the flour, 1 cup margarine and whipping cream in a mixer bowl until blended. Chill, covered, in the refrigerator.

Divide the dough into 3 portions. Roll each portion ⅛ inch thick on a lightly floured surface. Cut with a 1½-inch cookie cutter. Coat with granulated sugar. Arrange on an ungreased cookie sheet. Prick each cookie with a fork 4 times. Bake at 375 degrees for 10 to 15 minutes or until light brown. Cool on cookie sheet for 2 minutes. Remove to a wire rack to cool completely.

Beat the confectioners' sugar, ¼ cup margarine, egg yolk and vanilla in a mixer bowl until blended. Tint with food coloring as desired. Spread about 1 teaspoon of the filling on the bottom of half the cookies. Top with the remaining cookies.

To avoid raw eggs that may carry salmonella, we suggest using an equivalent amount of commercial egg substitute.

Makes two dozen cookies

A TISKET, A TASKET

AND OVERFLOWING

PICNIC BASKETS...

THE BEST OF TIMES

WHEN FRIENDS

COME TOGETHER FOR

A DAY OF PLAY...

MENUS

STAY-AT-HOME SATURDAY

FAREWELL FIESTA

A TISKET, A TASKET

I DO!!! I DO!!!

"FORE" THE NEIGHBORHOOD

FATHER'S DAY OUT

NOTHIN' BUT BLUE SKIES

STAY-AT-HOME SATURDAY

Menu

Broiled Grapefruit

Brown Sugar Bacon

Ruffled Canadian Bacon

Oatmeal Soufflé

Fluffy Crab Omelet

Baked Spinach

Stuffed French Toast

French Toast with Orange Zest

Streusel Crumb Muffins

Breakfast Bananas Foster

Strawberry Smoothies

Brunch Bellinis

Mimosas

Some days are meant to be taken ever so s-l-o-w-l-y. Sleep in this Saturday, rising only when the mood suits. Eventually...you'll saunter shiftlessly toward the kitchen. Flip the switch for a premade coffee brew and open your eyes enough to find the newspaper—just the comics, please. And, only when ready, commence with the day. To-Do List: Read the entire sports section, work a crossword puzzle, read one chapter out of the middle of a book, paint your toenails, take a long bubble bath, play the piano, watch a public television program, visit the backyard without pulling weeds, call a friend and talk for at least an hour, walk around the block. Then sit on the front porch, eat an extra piece of French toast...With a small friend, tie fishin' flies, get lost in a photo album, shell some peas. Pore over a magazine, watch an old movie, don't make your bed, and never look at a clock! For a morning of hiatus and hide-like-a-hermit, permit yourself these easygoing luxuries.

Oatmeal Souffle

SUGAR TO TASTE
1   CUP MILK
2   TABLESPOONS BUTTER
¾   CUP QUICK-COOKING OATS
⅓   CUP LOW-FAT CREAM CHEESE
½   CUP PACKED BROWN SUGAR
½   TEASPOON NUTMEG
½   TEASPOON CINNAMON
¼   TEASPOON SALT
3   EGG YOLKS, LIGHTLY BEATEN
½   CUP RAISINS
½   CUP CHOPPED WALNUTS
3   EGG WHITES

Coat the side and bottom of a 1½-quart soufflé dish or baking dish with butter. Sprinkle lightly with sugar.

Combine the milk and 2 tablespoons butter in a saucepan. Heat just until the mixture comes to a boil, stirring occasionally. Add the oats gradually, stirring constantly. Cook until thickened, stirring frequently. Remove from heat.

Add the cream cheese, brown sugar, nutmeg, cinnamon and salt to the oat mixture and mix until blended. Add the egg yolks gradually, beating constantly until mixed. Stir in the raisins and walnuts.

Beat the egg whites in a mixer bowl until stiff but moist peaks form. Fold into the oats mixture. Spoon into the prepared dish.

Bake at 325 degrees for 35 to 40 minutes or until the center is almost set. Serve immediately with cream or heated milk.

Do not discard the leftovers. This soufflé is just as tasty when cold and fallen.

To serve four

Brown Sugar Bacon

Fry 1 pound bacon in a cast-iron skillet over medium heat until the bacon is cooked through but slightly limp; drain. Arrange the bacon in a shallow baking pan or jelly roll pan. Sprinkle with ⅓ cup packed brown sugar. Broil for 2 to 5 minutes or until crisp.

Ruffled Canadian Bacon

Purchase Canadian bacon at your local deli and have the butcher cut the bacon into paper thin slices. Press 2 slices into standard muffin cups. Bake at 350 degrees for 10 minutes or until heated through. Serve ruffled cups alone or as a "bowl" for warmed syrup, cooked grits, jellies . . .

FLUFFY CRAB OMELET

1   SMALL ONION, MINCED
½   MEDIUM RED OR GREEN BELL PEPPER, MINCED
2   TABLESPOONS BUTTER
1   POUND LUMP BACKFIN CRAB MEAT, SHELLS REMOVED
4   EGG YOLKS
⅛   TEASPOON GINGER
     SALT AND PEPPER TO TASTE
4   EGG WHITES
2   TABLESPOONS BUTTER

Sauté the onion and red pepper in 2 tablespoons butter in a skillet over medium heat until tender-crisp; drain. Cool slightly. Combine the onion mixture with the crab meat in a bowl and mix gently.

Whisk the egg yolks in a bowl until blended. Stir in the ginger, salt and pepper. Add the crab meat mixture and mix gently.

Beat the egg whites in a mixer bowl until stiff but not dry peaks form. Fold ⅓ of the egg whites into the crab meat mixture. Stir in the remaining egg whites gently.

Heat 2 tablespoons butter in an ovenproof skillet over medium heat. Add the crab meat mixture, tilting the skillet to distribute evenly. Cook for 5 minutes or until set around the edge. Broil for 3 to 5 minutes or just until the omelet begins to brown. Let stand for 5 minutes. Cut into wedges.

To serve four

BAKED SPINACH

12   MEDIUM TOMATOES
1½   TEASPOONS EACH SALT AND SUGAR
1   MEDIUM ONION, CHOPPED
⅓   CUP BUTTER
3   TABLESPOONS FLOUR
1½   CUPS MILK
2   (10-OUNCE) PACKAGES FROZEN CHOPPED SPINACH, COOKED, DRAINED
¾   TEASPOON SALT
½   TEASPOON WHITE PEPPER
12   THIN SLICES BABY SWISS CHEESE

Slice the top quarter off each tomato and discard. Scoop out the pulp, leaving the shells intact. Sprinkle the inside of each tomato with ⅛ teaspoon salt and ⅛ teaspoon sugar. Invert onto paper towels to drain.

Sauté the onion in the butter in a saucepan until tender. Mix in the flour. Cook for 1 minute, stirring constantly. Add the milk gradually, stirring constantly. Cook over medium heat until thickened, stirring constantly. Add the spinach, ¾ teaspoon salt and white pepper and mix well. Arrange the tomato shells in a greased 9x13-inch baking dish. Spoon the spinach mixture into the shells. Top each tomato with a slice of cheese. Bake at 350 degrees for 20 minutes or until heated through.

May prepare 1 day in advance, store in the refrigerator and bake just before serving. Let stand at room temperature for 30 minutes before baking.

To serve twelve

For BROILED GRAPEFRUIT, *cut large grapefruit into halves crosswise; discard the seeds. Loosen the sections with a sharp knife. Spread 1 tablespoon of honey over the top of each half. Broil 4 inches from heat source for 3 minutes or until light brown and bubbly. For variety, drizzle 1 tablespoon light rum or amaretto over each half before broiling.*

STUFFED FRENCH TOAST

4   EGGS, LIGHTLY BEATEN
⅓   CUP SUGAR
1   CUP MILK
1   TEASPOON VANILLA OR ALMOND EXTRACT
⅛   TEASPOON SALT
8   OUNCES CREAM CHEESE, SOFTENED
½   CUP CONFECTIONERS' SUGAR, SIFTED
1   TEASPOON VANILLA OR ALMOND EXTRACT
¾   CUP CHOPPED PECANS, TOASTED
1   LOAF FRENCH BREAD, CUT INTO 2-INCH SLICES
    CREAM CHEESE, SOFTENED
    VEGETABLE OIL

TAKE A NOTE

Make notes in your cookbooks right next to the recipe you prepared. Jot down the occasion and guest list to remind you of when and to whom it was served—and how it was received. Note any changes to the basic recipe if you personalized it. If you have trouble finding a special recipe again in your cookbook library, use tape flags on recipe pages for quick reference.

Whisk the eggs and sugar in a bowl until mixed. Add the milk, 1 teaspoon vanilla and salt, whisking until blended. Set aside.

Beat 8 ounces cream cheese, confectioners' sugar and 1 teaspoon vanilla in a mixer bowl until creamy. Stir in the pecans.

Make a slit in each slice of bread, cutting to but not through the bottom edge to make a pocket. Spoon some of the cream cheese mixture into each pocket. Seal the edges with a thin layer of cream cheese.

Dip the slices in the egg mixture. Brown both sides of the bread on a hot griddle coated with vegetable oil, pressing down lightly when turning. Serve hot with your favorite syrup or dust with confectioners' sugar.

To serve six to eight

FRENCH TOAST WITH ORANGE ZEST

VEGETABLE OIL

1   CUP MILK

6   EGGS, LIGHTLY BEATEN

⅓   CUP GRAND MARNIER OR ORANGE LIQUEUR

JUICE OF 1 ORANGE

ZEST OF 2 ORANGES

2   TABLESPOONS (SCANT) SUGAR

¼   TEASPOON (SCANT) SALT

1   LOAF CHALLAH OR BRIOCHE, CUT INTO ¾-INCH SLICES

Heat a small amount of oil in a skillet over medium heat until hot.

Whisk the milk, eggs, Grand Marnier, orange juice, orange zest, sugar and salt in a bowl until mixed. Dip the bread slices in the egg mixture just until saturated.

Brown each slice on both sides in the hot skillet over medium heat, turning once; drain. Serve with maple syrup, confectioners' sugar, granulated sugar, fruit salad and/or orange marmalade.

Omit the Grand Marnier or orange liqueur if serving children.

To serve six

STREUSEL CRUMB MUFFINS

2   CUPS FLOUR

1½   CUPS PACKED BROWN SUGAR

¾   CUP BUTTER

1   CUP CHOPPED WALNUTS

1   CUP FLOUR

2   TEASPOONS BAKING POWDER

1   TEASPOON GROUND NUTMEG

1   TEASPOON GROUND GINGER

½   TEASPOON BAKING SODA

½   TEASPOON SALT

1   CUP BUTTERMILK

2   EGGS, BEATEN

Combine 2 cups flour and brown sugar in a bowl and mix well. Cut in the butter until crumbly. Mix ¾ cup of the crumb mixture and ¼ cup of the walnuts in a bowl. Set aside.

Combine the remaining crumb mixture, 1 cup flour, remaining ¾ cup walnuts, baking powder, nutmeg, ginger, baking soda and salt in a bowl and mix well. Add a mixture of the buttermilk and eggs, stirring just until moistened.

Fill greased muffin tins ⅔ full. Sprinkle with the reserved crumb mixture. Bake at 350 degrees for 20 to 25 minutes.

Makes eighteen muffins

BREAKFAST BANANAS FOSTER

⅓ CUP MELTED BUTTER

3 TABLESPOONS FRESH LEMON JUICE

6 FIRM RIPE BANANAS

⅓ CUP PACKED BROWN SUGAR

1 TEASPOON CINNAMON OR GROUND GINGER

Drizzle the bottom of a shallow 9x13-inch baking dish with a mixture of the butter and lemon juice. Arrange the bananas in a single layer in the dish, turning to coat. Sprinkle with a mixture of the brown sugar and cinnamon.

Bake at 375 degrees for 10 minutes; turn. Bake for 8 to 10 minutes longer or until the butter mixture bubbles. Serve warm with cream.

Bananas Foster is the traditional New Orleans dessert classic. Take this newfangled favorite and step back in time by adding Cognac, banana liqueur and/or rum. Flame as for Cherries Jubilee on page 231 and serve over vanilla ice cream. For breakfast? Mais oui!

To serve six

ON OCCASION...

make a special Saturday treat.

For BRUNCH BELLINIS, *combine 1 part chilled white peach juice with 3 parts chilled Champagne or sparkling wine in a Champagne flute.*

For MIMOSAS, *place 3 ounces of freshly squeezed orange juice in a Champagne flute. Fill the flute with chilled Champagne or sparkling wine. For variety, use the juice of blood oranges when they are in season.*

For the younger set, serve STRAWBERRY SMOOTHIES. *Blend fresh strawberries with orange juice and serve in glasses crowned with a whole strawberry on each rim.*

FAREWELL FIESTA

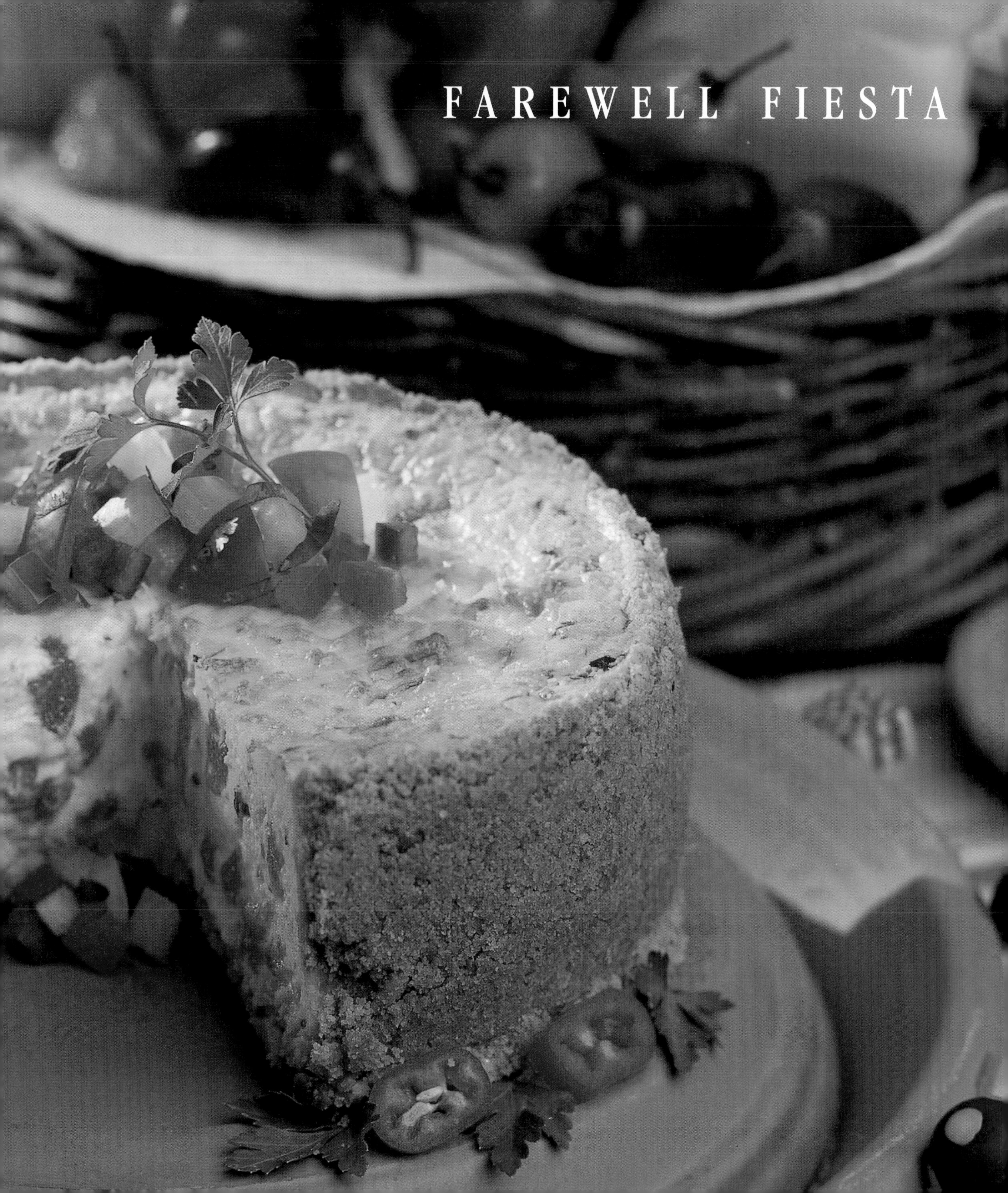

FAREWELL FIESTA

Menu

Roasted Red Pepper Cheesecake

Fresh Market Salsa

Black Bean and Corn Salsa

Cheese Tortilla Chips

Spiced Tortilla Soup

El Charro Raspberry Cilantro Vinaigrette with Mixed Greens

Tri-Pepper Steak over Border Rice

Chicken Artichoke Burritos

Skillet Paella

Black Beans

Farewell Cookies

Sunset Swirl Cookies

South of the Grande Ice Cream

Senior Sangría

Adiós! Adiós to all señors and señoritas! Farewell, graduating seniors! Forget finals—It's time for crepe-paper flowers, piñatas of penny candies, and big wide sombreros...Finally, time for a Fiesta!!! ∾ Get the graduating group poolside. Then throw in color and kitsch! Start with strands of lights, tin lanterns, or colored holiday bulbs strung from tree to tree. Bandannas of every shade can be tied to make lengths of bright pennants. Wrap serving tables with brown craft paper...add rough-hewn lumber for serving pedestals. Try brilliant copper, hammered pewter, and tin plates. Mix in palmetto branches, jute-bundled twigs, pots of vibrant red salvia, plus purple and yellow whatevers. Stack ten-inch terra-cotta saucers lined with flat tortillas for individual serving plates. Larger saucers edged with handmade clay beads are used for serving platters. Hollow out vegetables for serving dips and salsas, and then tie with raffia bands. ∾ What a send-off for the señors and señoritas!!!

ROASTED RED PEPPER CHEESECAKE

1 CUP CRUSHED SESAME BREADSTICKS
3 TABLESPOONS MELTED BUTTER
1 (7-OUNCE) JAR ROASTED RED PEPPERS, DRAINED
8 OUNCES GOAT CHEESE, CRUMBLED
1 CUP RICOTTA CHEESE
½ CUP WHIPPING CREAM
2 EGGS
2 TABLESPOONS FLOUR
1 CLOVE OF GARLIC, CHOPPED
2 TABLESPOONS CHOPPED FRESH CILANTRO
    SALSA
    ASSORTED PARTY CRACKERS

Mix the crushed breadsticks and butter in a bowl. Press over the bottom and 1 inch up the side of an 8-inch springform pan.

Chop ½ cup of the red peppers and set aside. Process the remaining red peppers, goat cheese and ricotta cheese in a food processor until smooth. Add the whipping cream, eggs, flour, garlic and cilantro. Process until smooth. Stir in the reserved red peppers. Spoon into the prepared pan. Place the pan on a baking sheet.

Bake at 350 degrees for 35 to 40 minutes or until the center is almost set. Cool pan on a wire rack for 15 minutes. Run a sharp knife around the edge of the pan to loosen the cheesecake. Cool for 30 minutes. Remove the side of the pan. Cool for 1 hour. Chill, covered, for 3 hours or longer.

Let stand for 30 minutes or until room temperature before serving. Serve with your favorite salsa and assorted party crackers.

To serve sixteen to eighteen

GIFTS FOR THE GRADUATE

Always money.

For survival . . . a laundry basket, detergent, roll of quarters, stain removal stick.

For keeping in touch . . . an address book with a note that the addresses be written in pencil, since they will change through the years; pre-paid telephone card; hometown telephone book; stationery; stamps.

For study . . . bookends, dictionary, book of quotes, thesaurus, electric pencil sharpener, personalized self-stick notes.

For the room . . . personalized bulletin board, linens and towels, iron or steamer, toaster oven, blender, popcorn popper, tool kit, alarm clock, microwave.

For fun . . . map of the college town and some gas money; ice chest with sunscreen, beach towel, beach music; stadium blanket and seat; sports tickets; backpack; football, frisbee, or baseball glove; restaurant gift certificates.

More personally . . . cosmetic bag, dopp kit, luggage, shoe shine kit, umbrella, monogrammed robe, camera, film.

Fresh Market Salsa

Cheese Tortilla Chips

Brush 1 side of 16 corn tortillas lightly with vegetable oil. Arrange the tortillas on 3 nonstick baking sheets.

Sprinkle with a mixture of 1 teaspoon salt, 1 teaspoon oregano and ¼ teaspoon cayenne. Sprinkle with 1½ cups shredded sharp Cheddar cheese.

Cut each tortilla into quarters with a sharp knife or pizza cutter. Bake at 400 degrees for 10 to 12 minutes or until golden and crisp.

Wine Vinaigrette
- ½ cup red wine vinegar
- ½ cup rice wine vinegar
- ½ cup olive oil
- ½ cup chopped fresh cilantro
- Juice of 2 limes
- ½ teaspoon salt
- ½ teaspoon pepper
- ½ teaspoon ground cumin

Salsa
- 1½ cups frozen corn
- 10 Roma tomatoes
- 2 (16-ounce) cans black beans, drained, rinsed
- 1 red bell pepper, chopped
- 1 yellow bell pepper, chopped
- 2 (or more) jalapeños, chopped
- 2 tomatillos, chopped
- 1 medium onion, chopped
- 2 cloves of garlic, minced

To prepare the vinaigrette, whisk the vinegars, olive oil, cilantro, lime juice, salt, pepper and cumin in a bowl.

To prepare the salsa, spread the corn in a shallow baking pan. Roast at 450 degrees for 10 minutes or until light brown, stirring every 2 minutes. Cut the tomatoes into quarters. Scoop out the seeds and membranes and discard. Chop the tomatoes.

Combine the corn, tomatoes, salsa, black beans, bell peppers, jalapeños, tomatillos, onion and garlic in a bowl and mix gently. Add the vinaigrette, tossing to coat. Serve with tortilla chips.

To serve twelve to fifteen

Spiced Tortilla Soup

2 MEDIUM ONIONS, CHOPPED
4 JALAPEÑOS, CHOPPED
3 CLOVES OF GARLIC, CHOPPED
2 (14-OUNCE) CANS DICED TOMATOES
2 (4-OUNCE) CANS DICED MILD GREEN CHILES
4 CUPS CHICKEN STOCK OR BROTH
12 CORN TORTILLAS, CUT INTO STRIPS
2 CUPS CHOPPED COOKED CHICKEN
   JUICE OF 1 LIME
   SALT AND CHILI POWDER TO TASTE
   TORTILLA CHIPS
   SHREDDED CHEDDAR CHEESE
   SOUR CREAM

Sauté the onions, jalapeños and garlic in a nonstick skillet sprayed with nonstick cooking spray until tender. Add the undrained tomatoes, chiles, chicken stock and tortillas. Bring to a boil; reduce heat.

Simmer until the tortillas are soft and moist, stirring occasionally. Stir in the chicken and lime juice. Season with salt and chili powder.

Ladle into soup bowls. Garnish with tortilla chips, cheese and/or sour cream.

To serve sixteen

El Charro Raspberry Cilantro Vinaigrette with Mixed Greens

1 BUNCH CILANTRO, FINELY CHOPPED
8 OUNCES FRESH RASPBERRIES, OR 12 OUNCES
   UNSWEETENED RASPBERRY PRESERVES
   JUICE OF 4 LIMES
1 CUP CANOLA OIL
½ CUP WHITE VINEGAR
   SALT AND PEPPER TO TASTE
   MIXED GREENS (ROMAINE, CHICORY, RED LEAF
   LETTUCE, RED CABBAGE), CHILLED

For the vinaigrette, process the cilantro, raspberries and lime juice in a blender until puréed.

Combine the canola oil and vinegar in a jar with a tightfitting lid. Shake to blend. Add the raspberry mixture and shake to mix. Season with salt and pepper. Chill until serving time.

For the salad, combine the mixed greens in a salad bowl. Drizzle with the desired amount of the chilled vinaigrette and toss to coat.

To serve eight to ten

For SENIOR SANGRÍA, mix 6 cups cranberry juice, 3 cups apple juice, 1½ cups orange juice and ¾ cup lemon juice. Chill in the refrigerator. Add two 28-ounce bottles chilled ginger ale or lemon-lime soda, 2 sliced oranges, 1 sliced lime and 1 sliced lemon just before serving. Add a citrus ice ring to your punch bowl if desired.

TRI-PEPPER STEAK

BORDER RICE

Bring 2 cups water to a boil. Stir in one 14-ounce can undrained black beans, 1 cup uncooked rice, ½ teaspoon salt and ½ teaspoon Tabasco sauce. Cook, covered, over low heat for 14 minutes; fluff with a fork.

2	POUNDS FLANK STEAK, COARSELY CHOPPED
1	LARGE ONION, CUT INTO QUARTERS
3	CUPS WATER
2	CLOVES OF GARLIC
2	ROASTED RED PEPPERS, SKINS REMOVED
½	YELLOW BELL PEPPER, CUT INTO STRIPS
½	RED BELL PEPPER, CUT INTO STRIPS
½	GREEN BELL PEPPER, CUT INTO STRIPS
2	LARGE ONIONS, CHOPPED
4	CLOVES OF GARLIC, MINCED
2	TABLESPOONS VEGETABLE OIL
1	(10-OUNCE) CAN TOMATO PURÉE
2	BAY LEAVES
½	CUP WHITE WINE
	BORDER RICE

Combine the steak, 1 onion, water and 2 cloves of garlic in a saucepan. Bring to a boil; reduce heat. Simmer for 1 hour. Drain, reserving 1½ cups liquid and discarding the onion and garlic. Shred the steak.

Process the roasted red peppers in a blender until puréed. Sauté the yellow pepper, red pepper, green pepper, 2 onions and 4 cloves of garlic in the oil in a saucepan. Stir in the puréed red peppers, tomato purée, bay leaves and white wine.

Cook for 3 minutes, stirring occasionally. Add the steak and the reserved liquid. Cook for 30 minutes longer, stirring occasionally. Discard the bay leaves. Serve over Border Rice.

To serve six

CHICKEN ARTICHOKE BURRITOS

2 ONIONS, THINLY SLICED
½ CUP BUTTER
1 ENVELOPE FAJITA SEASONING
4 BONELESS SKINLESS CHICKEN BREAST HALVES, POACHED, SHREDDED
1 (6-OUNCE) JAR MARINATED ARTICHOKES, DRAINED, CHOPPED
8 (8-INCH) FLOUR TORTILLAS
8 OUNCES CREAM CHEESE, SOFTENED
1 CUP SHREDDED MOZZARELLA CHEESE
3 TO 4 CUPS SHREDDED MEXICAN WHITE CHEESE
1½ CUPS CHOPPED ROMA TOMATOES

Sauté the onions in the butter in a skillet until tender. Stir in the fajita seasoning. Remove from heat. Add the chicken and artichokes and mix well.

Spread 1 side of each tortilla with the cream cheese. Spread the chicken mixture over the cream cheese. Sprinkle with the mozzarella cheese. Roll to enclose the filling.

Arrange seam side down side by side in a buttered baking dish. Sprinkle with the Mexican white cheese and tomatoes. Bake, covered with foil, at 350 degrees for 20 to 25 minutes or until heated through. Serve with sour cream and/or guacamole.

May be prepared 1 day in advance and stored, covered, in the refrigerator. Bake just before serving.

To serve eight

ON OCCASION...

surprise guests with FAREWELL FAVORS . . .

A group photograph taken at the party. It can be developed and a copy made for each guest at a one-hour photo shop during the party. Let each graduate sign the border of the picture frames in which the photograph will be presented.

Keepsakes, such as T-shirts, bandannas, or sombreros, to autograph or decorate with the class motto or year.

An address book and a pencil with the suggestion that the guests secure the addresses of their classmates as a mixer during the party.

A favorite class picture from a class trip, play, or party reproduced as a poster for each guest.

A monogrammed beach towel or bath sheet for each guest: They are less likely to disappear at college.

SKILLET PAELLA

BLACK BEAN MAGIC

To start from scratch for BLACK BEANS, *bring 8 cups cold water to a boil. Add 1 pound dried black beans. Boil for 2 minutes. Let stand, covered, for 1 hour and drain. Sauté 2 chopped Spanish onions, 1 chopped green bell pepper and 4 minced cloves of garlic in a nonstick saucepan until tender. Add the beans, 6 cups water, 1 smoked ham hock, 1 teaspoon ground cumin and salt and pepper to taste. Simmer for 1 hour, stirring occasionally. Stir in 2 sliced Spanish chorizos. Simmer for 1 hour longer or until the beans are tender, stirring occasionally.*

For BLACK BEAN AND CORN SALSA, *start with two 15-ounce cans of black beans that have been rinsed and drained. Add a 24-ounce jar of salsa, a drained 15-ounce can of diced tomatoes, a drained 11-ounce can of sweet corn, ½ to ¾ cup chopped onion and 1 tablespoon chopped cilantro. Chill until serving time and serve with tortilla chips.*

1	(2½- TO 3-POUND) CHICKEN, CUT UP
¼	CUP VIRGIN OLIVE OIL
2	MEDIUM ONIONS, CHOPPED
2	SMALL SPANISH CHORIZOS, SLICED, OR ANY SPICY SAUSAGE
1	RED BELL PEPPER, CHOPPED
1	GREEN BELL PEPPER, CHOPPED
4	OR 5 CLOVES OF GARLIC, MINCED
2	CUPS CHICKEN STOCK
1¾	CUPS STEWED TOMATOES
1½	CUPS RICE
⅛	TEASPOON SAFFRON
2	BAY LEAVES
	SALT AND PEPPER TO TASTE
2	ROASTED RED PEPPERS, SLICED, OR PIMENTO SLICES (OPTIONAL)

Brown 1 side of the chicken in the olive oil in a cast-iron skillet. Remove chicken with a slotted spoon to a platter, reserving the pan drippings.

Sauté the onions in the reserved pan drippings for 3 to 4 minutes. Stir in the chorizos, 1 chopped red pepper, green pepper and garlic. Sauté until the onions are tender, adding some of the chicken stock if the mixture becomes too dry. Add the stewed tomatoes and mix well.

Simmer for 3 to 4 minutes. Stir in the remaining chicken stock, rice, saffron, bay leaves, salt and pepper. Arrange the chicken brown side up over the rice mixture. Bake at 450 degrees for 45 minutes or until the chicken is cooked through and the rice is tender. Discard the bay leaves. Garnish with roasted red peppers or pimento slices.

To serve five to six

FAREWELL COOKIES

15   WHOLE GRAHAM CRACKERS
1   CUP UNSALTED BUTTER
1   CUP PACKED DARK BROWN SUGAR
1   TEASPOON VANILLA EXTRACT
1½   CUPS CHOPPED PECANS, TOASTED
1   CUP SEMISWEET CHOCOLATE CHIPS

Arrange the graham crackers in a single layer side by side on a buttered jelly roll pan.

Combine the butter and brown sugar in a saucepan. Cook over medium heat until the brown sugar dissolves, stirring constantly. Stir in the vanilla. Bring to a boil. Boil for 1 minute. Pour over the graham crackers. Sprinkle with the pecans.

Bake at 350 degrees for 10 minutes. Sprinkle with the chocolate chips. Let stand until cool. Cut along the edges of the graham crackers to separate.

Makes thirty cookies

SUNSET SWIRL COOKIES

1   CUP UNSALTED BUTTER, SOFTENED
1   CUP SUGAR
2   CUPS FLOUR
2   TEASPOONS GRATED ORANGE PEEL
1   TABLESPOON BAKING COCOA

Beat the butter and sugar in a mixer bowl until light and fluffy. Add the flour. Beat until of dough consistency, scraping the bowl occasionally.

Divide the dough into 2 portions. Knead the orange peel into 1 portion on a lightly floured surface. Knead the baking cocoa into the remaining portion on a lightly floured surface.

Roll each portion into a 7x12-inch rectangle on waxed paper. Stack the rectangles. Roll as for a jelly roll into a ¾-inch log. Chill, wrapped in waxed paper, for 45 minutes.

Cut the log into ¼-inch slices. Arrange on a lightly greased cookie sheet. Bake at 350 degrees for 10 to 15 minutes or until crisp around the edges. Cool on the cookie sheet for 2 minutes. Remove to a wire rack to cool completely.

Makes three to four dozen cookies

Serve SOUTH OF THE GRANDE ICE CREAM *with the cookies at any fiesta. Scoop vanilla bean ice cream into balls on a cookie sheet and freeze them until firm. Toast flaked coconut in a 350-degree oven for 10 to 15 minutes or until light brown. Roll the ice cream balls in the coconut and place on serving plates drizzled with fudge sauce. On occasion . . . try raspberry, lime, or orange sherbet for a different taste treat.*

A TISKET, A TASKET

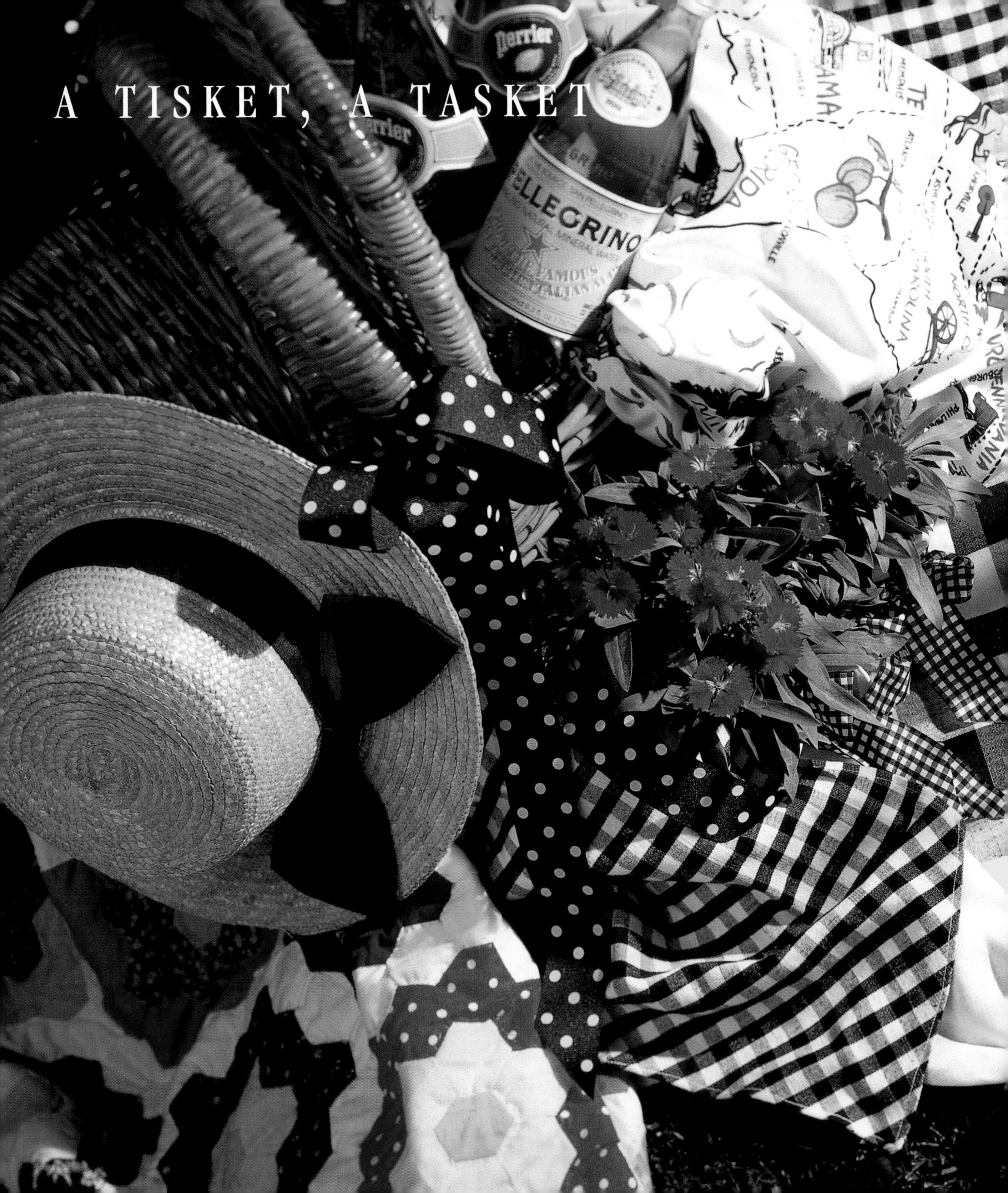

A TISKET, A TASKET

PICNIC (PIK' NIK), N. 1. A PLEASANT OR AMUSING EXCURSION, TYPICALLY ONE IN WHICH FOOD IS EATEN IN THE OPEN AIR. 2. (INFORMAL) AN ENJOYABLE EXPERIENCE, TIME, TASK, ETC., A TIME FREE OF ORDINARY CARES OR RESPONSIBILITIES... FINALLY! TIME FOR A PICNIC!!! AN OUTSIDE CONCERT, STARS AND GUITARS, FOLLY AND FRIENDSHIP...PACK A PORTABLE SOIRÉE (AND YOUR CAMERA) FOR A WONDERFUL TIME. PRISTINE OR GRANDIOSE, IN AN INSTANT OR WITH CAREFUL PLANNING ...THINK OF THE MEMORIES YOU WILL CREATE! TO START WITH: A CLASSIC ENGLISH PICNIC BASKET (SOMEDAY INVEST IN ONE...) OR A HANDSOME WICKER BASKET FILLED WITH PLATES, UTENSILS, AND MORE. "HAVE A GO" WITH BLACK AND WHITE TASSELED NAPKINS AND HAND-PAINTED STEMWARE FOR YOUR SOUTHERN SETTING...CANDELABRAS OF STERLING...OR MAYBE A PUNCHED TIN WITH A VOTIVE...FRESH FLOWERS...PICK SOME WILD ONES; THEY'LL LOOK GRAND TUCKED INSIDE A MASON JAR OR TRENDY WATER BOTTLE...A SIMPLE BALLAD FROM JAMES TAYLOR...AND ALWAYS—A HAT! SHOULDN'T EVERYONE HAVE A HAT?

LAWN PARTY SANDWICHES

1   CUP MARGARINE
1   MEDIUM ONION, MINCED
¼   CUP POPPY SEEDS
1   TABLESPOON PREPARED
    MUSTARD

3   (24-COUNT) PACKAGES PARTY
    ROLLS
1   POUND HAM, SHAVED
12 OUNCES SWISS CHEESE,
    THINLY SLICED

Heat the margarine in a microwave-safe dish for 1 to 2 minutes or until melted. Stir in the onion, poppy seeds and prepared mustard. Chill, covered, for 8 to 10 hours. Remove the poppy seed mixture from the refrigerator 1 hour before needed to prepare the recipe. Split each package of rolls horizontally with a serrated knife into 2 layers, leaving the bottom layer in the pan. Spread the cut sides of the rolls with the poppy seed mixture. Layer the ham and cheese on the bottom layer of rolls. Top with the remaining roll layer.

Bake at 350 degrees for 15 minutes. For variety, add chopped red bell pepper when assembling sandwiches. May be prepared in advance and frozen unbaked. Bake the frozen rolls at 350 degrees until heated through.

Makes six dozen sandwiches

MARMALADE TARTS

1   CUP SHREDDED CHEDDAR
    CHEESE
½   CUP BUTTER, SOFTENED

1   CUP SIFTED FLOUR
    ORANGE MARMALADE, APRICOT
    PRESERVES OR PEPPER JELLY

Beat the cheese and butter in a mixer bowl until creamy. Add the flour, beating until blended. Shape into a ball. Chill, wrapped in waxed paper, for 8 to 10 hours.

Roll the dough thin on a lightly floured surface. Cut with a 3- or 4-inch round cutter. Spoon ½ teaspoon of the marmalade on each round. Fold over to enclose the filling. Press the edges with a fork to seal. Arrange on a baking sheet. Bake at 400 degrees for 12 to 15 minutes or until light brown.

Makes one dozen tarts

THE BASKET NECESSITIES

Begin to gather these favorites for your next jaunt . . .

A Swiss army knife
An ice chest with wheels
*Lantern, candles—and remember
    the matches*
Folding trays and chairs
*Plastic wine glasses—even small hands
    can hold these well*
Plastic storage bowls with tightfitting lids
Serrated knife
Paper towels and wet wipes
*Trash bags, sealable plastic bags,
    including some large enough to hold the
    used dishes and utensils*
Salt and pepper
Sunblock and insect repellent
*Ponchos and a clear drop cloth for a
    summer concert shower*
Binoculars and a bird book
*A gallon jug of water, always needed for
    something*
*A deck of cards, an easy board game,
    summer reading, or nothing at all!*

HOPPIN' JOHN SALAD

3 CUPS COOKED LONG GRAIN RICE
2 CUPS DRAINED COOKED BLACK-EYED PEAS
½ CUP CHOPPED PURPLE ONION
¼ CUP CHOPPED CELERY
1 JALAPEÑO PEPPER, SEEDED, MINCED
¼ CUP CHOPPED FRESH PARSLEY
¼ CUP LOOSELY PACKED CHOPPED FRESH MINT (OPTIONAL)
1 CLOVE OF GARLIC, MINCED
¼ CUP OLIVE OIL
½ TEASPOON SALT
3 TABLESPOONS FRESH LEMON JUICE
   CRACKED PEPPER TO TASTE

Mix the rice, black-eyed peas, onion, celery and jalapeño in a bowl. Stir in the parsley, mint and garlic.

Whisk the olive oil, salt, lemon juice and pepper in a bowl until mixed. Add to the rice mixture and toss gently to coat.

To serve eight

BASKET CHICKEN SALAD

1 CUP MAYONNAISE
¼ CUP (OR MORE) MAJOR GREY'S CHUTNEY
2 TEASPOONS GRATED LIME PEEL
1 TEASPOON CURRY POWDER
½ TEASPOON SALT
¼ TEASPOON LIME JUICE
4 CUPS CHOPPED COOKED CHICKEN
2 (13-OUNCE) CANS PINEAPPLE CHUNKS, DRAINED
2 CUPS DIAGONALLY SLICED CELERY
1 CUP SLICED GREEN ONIONS
½ CUP SLIVERED ALMONDS
   PITA BREAD, CUT INTO HALVES

Combine the mayonnaise, chutney, lime peel, curry powder, salt and lime juice in a bowl and mix well. Stir in the chicken, pineapple, celery, green onions and almonds.

Spoon into pita bread. Store leftover chicken salad in the refrigerator.

To serve ten to twelve

Take a long lazy afternoon drive or just a short hop. Visit a neighboring county, state, or national park—often the trip we never get around to taking. Make a stop at a roadside stand, a hokey tourist trap, an unusual antique store, a flea market, or a dollar store. Take along a camera. Look for still life compositions, perhaps a horse in a pasture or the edge of a riverbank and see things in a new light.

BROCCOLI TOSS

	FLORETS OF 2 BUNCHES BROCCOLI
1	RED ONION, THINLY SLICED OR CHOPPED
1	CUP RAISINS
1	CUP PECANS
1	POUND BACON, CRISP-FRIED, CRUMBLED
1	CUP MAYONNAISE OR YOGURT
½	CUP SUGAR
2	TABLESPOONS CIDER VINEGAR

Toss the broccoli, onion, raisins, pecans and bacon in a salad bowl. Stir in a mixture of the mayonnaise, sugar and vinegar up to 1 hour prior to serving. Store, covered, in the refrigerator until serving time.

May use low-fat or nonfat mayonnaise. Cut the bacon into small pieces with kitchen shears prior to cooking if desired.

To serve eight to ten

GARLIC AND HERB POTATO SALAD

3	POUNDS NEW POTATOES, CUT INTO WEDGES
1	TEASPOON SALT
½	CUP SALAD OIL
½	CUP CHOPPED FRESH PARSLEY
⅓	CUP FINELY CHOPPED GREEN ONIONS
¼	CUP RED WINE VINEGAR
3	LARGE CLOVES OF GARLIC, CRUSHED
1	TABLESPOON CHOPPED FRESH CHIVES
1½	TEASPOONS CHOPPED FRESH OREGANO
1	TEASPOON CHOPPED FRESH THYME
½	TEASPOON SALT
¼	TEASPOON WHITE PEPPER

Place the potatoes in enough cold water to cover in a saucepan. Let stand until crisp. Stir in 1 teaspoon salt. Bring to a boil. Boil for 10 minutes or until tender-crisp; drain. Do not overcook.

Combine the salad oil, parsley, green onions, wine vinegar, garlic, chives, oregano, thyme, ½ teaspoon salt and white pepper in a jar with a tightfitting lid. Shake to mix. Pour over the hot potatoes in a bowl and toss gently to coat. Serve hot or cold.

To serve eight

Serve THE RECIPE *at your next gathering and your guests will want "the recipe." Squeeze the juice of 3 lemons and 2 oranges into a bowl and chill, reserving the peel. Place 9 family-size tea bags, 1 cup chopped fresh mint and the reserved lemon and orange peel in 2 quarts boiling water. Steep for 30 minutes; strain. Add 2½ cups sugar, stirring until dissolved. Chill for up to 24 hours. Stir in the lemon juice mixture, ¼ cup maraschino cherry juice and 1½ quarts cold water. Freeze in a 1-gallon container until of a slushy consistency. Garnish each serving with a mint sprig and maraschino cherry. Psst . . . secret ingredient—top with a splash of bourbon.*

BUTTERMILK FRIED CHICKEN

1 (2½- to 3-pound) chicken, cut up
1 quart buttermilk
1 teaspoon salt
1 teaspoon black pepper
2 cups flour
   Salt and black pepper to taste
½ teaspoon cayenne, or to taste
   Vegetable shortening, melted, or peanut oil
   for frying
3 tablespoons bacon drippings

Soak the chicken in the buttermilk in a bowl in the refrigerator for 8 to 10 hours. Drain and pat dry. Sprinkle with 1 teaspoon salt and 1 teaspoon black pepper.

Combine the flour, salt and black pepper to taste and cayenne in a sealable plastic bag. Add the chicken 2 to 3 pieces at a time, shaking to coat.

Pour a mixture of shortening and bacon drippings to measure 1 inch in a cast-iron skillet. Heat until hot. Fry the chicken in the hot oil mixture for 15 minutes per side or until golden brown; drain. Place in a nonrecycled brown paper bag in a warm oven until serving time.

To serve four to six

RHUBARB CUSTARD PIE

1 recipe (2-crust) pie pastry (page 35)
2 cups sugar
¼ cup flour
¾ teaspoon nutmeg
3 eggs, lightly beaten
2⅔ tablespoons milk
4 cups chopped fresh rhubarb
1 (8-ounce) can crushed pineapple
1 tablespoon margarine

Prepare the pastry, reserving 1 portion for another use. Line a 10-inch deep-dish pie plate with half the remaining pastry.

Combine the sugar, flour and nutmeg in a bowl and mix well. Stir in the eggs and milk. Add the rhubarb and undrained pineapple and mix gently.

Pour into the prepared pie plate. Top with the remaining pastry, fluting the edge and cutting vents. Dot with the margarine.

Bake at 400 degrees for 50 to 60 minutes or until light brown.

To serve eight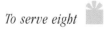

For PERFECT PIE CRUSTS *that never fail, cut 1¾ cups shortening into 4 cups flour and a pinch of salt in a bowl. Add 1 egg, 1 tablespoon white vinegar and ½ cup ice water. Mix to form a dough. Divide into 3 equal portions to use right away or wrap for storage in the freezer for up to 3 months.*

OATMEAL CRANBERRY WHITE CHOCOLATE COOKIES

2   CUPS QUICK-COOKING OATS

2   CUPS FLOUR

1   TEASPOON BAKING SODA

½   TEASPOON SALT

1   CUP BUTTER OR MARGARINE, SOFTENED

1   CUP PACKED BROWN SUGAR

2   EGGS

1½   CUPS SWEETENED DRIED CRANBERRIES

1   CUP WHITE CHOCOLATE CHIPS

Mix the oats, flour, baking soda and salt in a bowl.

Beat the butter and brown sugar in a mixer bowl until light and fluffy, scraping the bowl occasionally. Beat in the eggs. Add the oats mixture gradually, mixing well after each addition. Stir in the cranberries and white chocolate chips.

Drop by rounded teaspoonfuls onto an ungreased cookie sheet. Bake at 375 degrees for 10 to 12 minutes or until golden brown. Cool on cookie sheet for 2 minutes. Remove to a wire rack to cool completely.

Makes two and one-half dozen cookies

ON OCCASION . . .

the children will need fun too . . .

Take along a jar of solution for bubbles that are guaranteed to hang in the air. Just shake together 1 cup of dishwashing detergent with 3 cups of water and 6 tablespoons of white corn syrup. Let the mixture settle for four hours and use a large bubble wand to create giant floating bubbles.

Make a floating armada at the pond. Cut white 3x5-inch index cards into halves and fold up 2 edges to form a U. Anchor birthday candles with drops of melted wax and set them afloat. They will be easier to retrieve if you tie them together in a row.

Make a daisy chain or clover chain. Use that Swiss army knife from the basket necessities to cut small slits in the stems below the base of 20 or 30 flowers. Thread a second flower through and repeat the process.

Lie on your back and search the blue for cloud dragons, grizzly bears, and angels—or whatever you fancy. And later . . . twinkling or falling stars.

I DO!!! I DO!!!

Menu

Pecan Cheese Taddies

Chilled Strawberry Soup

Frozen Fruit Salad

Waldorf Salad

Chesapeake Bay Chicken

Spinach Elegante

Sautéed Cherry Tomatoes

Hazelnut Pear Tea Bread

Lemon Straws

Little Lime Tarts

Champagne 'n Strawberries

The Flower Girls' Baskets

It's almost her big day...the flowers ordered, engraved invitations sent, brother's morning coat fits just dandy...Nothing left to do but wipe away the tears as she floats down the aisle...except the bridesmaids' luncheon. Hosted by a cherished friend, this gathering allows dear friends to reflect fondly on fleeting girlhood days. Consider a Tiffany-inspired table...Powder blue boxes banded in white ribbon invite a giggling girl to be seated. Slip satin ribbons around anything sitting still—wine goblets, tulle-covered chairs, the chandelier—and make a ribboned wreath for the puppy's dressy collar. Clusters of ivory peonies grace the lace-veiled table, with vintage white plates for each guest. Delight in one of life's sparkling moments ...a passage, a ritual, a promise...a marriage. Enjoy this luncheon menu also, to honor mothers and daughters, to say hello or farewell, or to herald a friend's special day! Uh-oh!...Time to put on that dress...and those shoes!!

PECAN CHEESE TADDIES

1 CUP FINELY SHREDDED SHARP CHEDDAR CHEESE
½ CUP BUTTER
1 TEASPOON SALT
½ TEASPOON CAYENNE
1 CUP FLOUR
24 PECAN HALVES

Beat the cheese, butter, salt and cayenne in a mixer bowl until creamy, scraping the bowl occasionally. Add the flour, beating until blended. Knead into a ball.

Shape the dough into 1-inch balls. Arrange on an ungreased baking sheet. Press 1 pecan half in the center of each ball to flatten.

Bake at 350 degrees for 15 minutes. Cool on baking sheet for 2 minutes. Remove to a wire rack to cool completely.

May be prepared in advance and stored, wrapped in foil, in the freezer. Bake the day of serving.

Makes two dozen taddies

CHILLED STRAWBERRY SOUP

6 CUPS FRESH STRAWBERRIES
2 CUPS ORANGE JUICE
1 CUP SOUR CREAM
¼ CUP GRAND MARNIER

Reserve 12 large strawberries. Process the remaining strawberries in a blender until puréed. Pour the purée into a pitcher.

Whisk in the orange juice, sour cream and Grand Marnier. Chill, covered, for 6 to 10 hours.

Pour the chilled soup into soup bowls. Cut the reserved strawberries lengthwise into ¼-inch slices. Arrange 3 to 4 slices in a star pattern on top of each serving.

May be prepared 1 day in advance and stored, covered, in the refrigerator.

To serve eight

To create a YOGURT FLOWER GARNISH for soup, drizzle a narrow stream of yogurt onto the top of the soup serving, beginning at the center and expanding to form a circle 3 inches in diameter. Then spoon a dollop of yogurt into the center. Using a wooden pick, pull lines from the outer edge of the circle into the center and back again to form a flower.

CHESAPEAKE BAY CHICKEN

A BRIDE'S PRAYER

*. . . to be presented to her on the eve
of her wedding, so that it can be
in her thoughts as she wakes on a day
with new beginnings.*

*Oh, Father, my heart is filled with
happiness so wonderful that I am almost
afraid. This is my wedding day, and I
pray Thee that the beautiful joy of this
morning may never grow dim.
Rather, may its memories become
more sweet and tender with each
passing anniversary.*

*Thou hast sent to me one who seems all
worthy of my deepest regard. May I
indeed prove steadfast, a helpmate,
sweetheart, and friend. Grant to me the
skill to make our home the best-loved
place of all. Help me to make its
light shine farther than any glow that
could dim its radiance.*

*Walk Thou with us even to the end of
our journey, hand in hand, lightening
each day with the sunshine of good
and happy lives.*

Amen.

8	BONELESS SKINLESS CHICKEN BREAST HALVES
	SALT AND PEPPER TO TASTE
½	CUP CHOPPED ONION
½	CUP CHOPPED CELERY
3	TABLESPOONS BUTTER
8	OUNCES FRESH OR CANNED CRAB MEAT
3	TABLESPOONS WHITE WINE
½	CUP SEASONED STUFFING MIX CUBES
2	TABLESPOONS FLOUR
½	TEASPOON PAPRIKA
2	TABLESPOONS MELTED BUTTER
	HOLLANDAISE SAUCE (PAGE 26)
1	CUP SHREDDED SWISS CHEESE
¼	CUP WHITE WINE

Place the chicken in a sealable plastic bag. Pound with a wooden meat mallet until flattened. Season with salt and pepper.

Sauté the onion and celery in 3 tablespoons butter in a skillet until tender. Remove from heat. Stir in the crab meat, 3 tablespoons white wine and stuffing.

Spoon some of the stuffing mixture in the center of each chicken breast. Roll to enclose the filling; secure with wooden picks. Coat the rolls with a mixture of the flour and paprika. Arrange seam side down in a baking dish. Drizzle with 2 tablespoons butter. Bake at 375 degrees for 1 hour.

Mix the Hollandaise Sauce, cheese and ¼ cup white wine in a bowl. Drizzle over the chicken. Bake for 25 to 30 minutes longer or until the chicken is cooked through. Need a shortcut? Try Knorr's Hollandaise Sauce mix.

To serve eight

SPINACH ELEGANTE

VEGETABLE OIL
BREAD CRUMBS
¼ CUP GRATED PARMESAN
  CHEESE
1 POUND MUSHROOM CAPS,
  FINELY CHOPPED
2 SHALLOTS, FINELY CHOPPED
2 TABLESPOONS OLIVE OIL
1 CLOVE OF GARLIC, MINCED

SALT AND PEPPER TO TASTE
4 (10-OUNCE) PACKAGES
  FROZEN CHOPPED SPINACH,
  COOKED, DRAINED
6 TABLESPOONS MELTED BUTTER
1 TEASPOON SALT
4 EGG YOLKS, LIGHTLY BEATEN
4 EGG WHITES, STIFFLY BEATEN

Coat a baking sheet with sides with vegetable oil and line with heavy-duty foil. Spray the foil with nonstick cooking spray. Sprinkle with bread crumbs and cheese. Sauté the mushrooms and shallots in the olive oil in a skillet until the liquid is absorbed. Stir in the garlic, salt and pepper. Remove from heat. Squeeze the moisture from the spinach. Combine the spinach, butter, salt and egg yolks in a bowl and mix well. Fold in the egg whites. Spread the spinach mixture over the bread crumbs and cheese. Bake at 350 degrees for 12 to 15 minutes. Cut into halves. Spread the mushroom mixture over 1 half. Top with the remaining half crumb side up. Cut into squares.

To serve eight

SAUTEED CHERRY TOMATOES

2 POUNDS CHERRY TOMATOES
¼ CUP OLIVE OIL
2 TEASPOONS SUGAR
  SALT AND FRESHLY GROUND
  PEPPER TO TASTE

½ CUP FINELY CHOPPED BASIL
¼ CUP FINELY CHOPPED PARSLEY
2 CLOVES OF GARLIC, MINCED

Rinse the tomatoes and pat dry. Heat the olive oil in a skillet over high heat until hot. Add the tomatoes, stirring to coat. Sprinkle with the sugar, salt and pepper. Add the basil, parsley and garlic and toss to mix. Serve immediately.

To serve eight

A STITCH IN TIME

For a really special wedding gift, pass along a basket or box with sewing essentials; attach a ribbon inside to hold loose needles and pins. Include a good pair of scissors and a sterling silver thimble; assorted needles and threads; shirt buttons, snaps, hooks and eyes, and safety pins; seam binding, elastic, and iron-on tape; straight pins and a plump pin cushion; seam ripper, tape measure, and a needle threader.

To wrap it all up, use several layers of organdy, lace, or tulle around the box and cinch it at the top. Tie it with wide double-face satin ribbon. Be generous with the fabric and trimming. Finish the fabric edges, and the bride has a new dresser scarf, napkin, or table topper. This wrap will be a welcome change from white paper. Use for other than wedding gifts as well.

FROZEN FRUIT SALAD

1½   CUPS SOUR CREAM
¾   CUP CONFECTIONERS' SUGAR
2   TABLESPOONS LEMON JUICE
⅛   TEASPOON SALT
1   (20-OUNCE) CAN CRUSHED PINEAPPLE, DRAINED
¾   CUP SEEDLESS GRAPE HALVES
1   BANANA, CHOPPED (OPTIONAL)
½   CUP SLICED OR CHOPPED MARASCHINO CHERRIES
½   CUP CHOPPED PECANS
½   CUP SOUR CREAM
½   CUP PACKED LIGHT BROWN SUGAR

Combine 1½ cups sour cream and confectioners' sugar in a bowl and mix well. Stir in the lemon juice and salt. Add the pineapple, grapes, banana, cherries and pecans and mix gently. Spoon into paper-lined muffin cups or a 9x11-inch dish. Freeze, covered, until firm.

Mix ½ cup sour cream and brown sugar in a bowl. Top each serving with a dollop of the sour cream mixture.

To serve fifteen

WALDORF SALAD

2   RED DELICIOUS APPLES, CHOPPED
2   GOLDEN DELICIOUS APPLES, CHOPPED
     JUICE OF ½ LEMON
1   CUP RAISINS (OPTIONAL)
1   CUP BROKEN PECAN HALVES, TOASTED
1   CUP RED GRAPE HALVES
1   CUP CHOPPED CELERY
½   CUP SOUR CREAM
½   CUP MAYONNAISE
2   TEASPOONS SUGAR
⅛   TEASPOON SALT

Toss the apples with the lemon juice in a bowl. Stir in the raisins, pecans, grapes and celery.

Mix the sour cream, mayonnaise, sugar and salt in a bowl. Add to the apple mixture and toss gently to mix. Chill, covered, until serving time.

To serve sixteen

For something old, fill a recipe file with a number of your favorite recipes as a gift for the bride. These recipes for good old-fashioned FROZEN FRUIT SALAD *and* WALDORF SALAD *would be perfect to include. For something new, present a cookbook with some of the latest trends in cooking, making sure to include your notes about specific recipes in the book.*

Hazelnut Pear Tea Bread

⅓	CUP HAZELNUTS
1½	CUPS ALL-PURPOSE FLOUR
½	CUP WHOLE WHEAT FLOUR
1¼	TEASPOONS BAKING POWDER
¾	TEASPOON GROUND CINNAMON
½	TEASPOON SALT
½	TEASPOON BAKING SODA
1	CUP COARSELY SHREDDED PEELED PEAR
¾	CUP SUGAR
3	TABLESPOONS VEGETABLE OIL
½	TEASPOON GRATED LEMON PEEL
½	TEASPOON VANILLA EXTRACT
1	EGG, LIGHTLY BEATEN
1	EGG WHITE, LIGHTLY BEATEN

Spread the hazelnuts in a single layer on a baking sheet. Toast at 350 degrees for 15 minutes, stirring occasionally. Invert the hazelnuts onto a tea towel. Roll up the towel and rub off the skins. Chop the hazelnuts. Mix the hazelnuts, all-purpose flour, whole wheat flour, baking powder, cinnamon, salt and baking soda in a bowl.

Combine the pear, sugar, oil, lemon peel, vanilla, egg and egg white in a bowl and mix well. Add the hazelnut mixture, stirring just until moistened. Spoon into a 5x9-inch loaf pan sprayed with nonstick cooking spray.

Bake at 350 degrees for 65 minutes or until the loaf tests done. Cool in the pan on a wire rack for 10 minutes. Remove to a wire rack to cool completely.

To serve twelve

Lemon Straws

Beat 2 cups butter and 2 cups confectioners' sugar until light and fluffy. Mix in ¼ cup reconstituted lemon juice. Add 4½ cups flour gradually, beating just until blended. Add 1 teaspoon citric acid and mix well. Chill for 10 minutes. Spoon the dough into a cookie press fitted with a bar cookie or star plate. Pipe the dough in rows ½ inch apart on an ungreased baking sheet. Bake at 350 degrees for 15 minutes or until light brown on the edges. Cut the rows into 2-inch strips, dust liberally with confectioners' sugar and cool on a wire rack.

LITTLE LIME TARTS

CHAMPAGNE 'N STRAWBERRIES

For a beverage that will make everyone say, "I do! I do!" mix 3 thawed 6-ounce cans of frozen lemonade concentrate with 5 cups water and 1 pint of sliced fresh strawberries. Chill the mixture for 4 hours. Stir in 1 quart of chilled ginger ale and two 750-milliliter bottles of chilled dry Champagne just before serving.

TART SHELLS
- 1   CUP FLAKED COCONUT
- ½   CUP GINGERSNAP CRUMBS
- ½   CUP GRAHAM CRACKER CRUMBS
- ¼   CUP MELTED BUTTER
- 2   TABLESPOONS FLOUR

KEY LIME FILLING
- 1   (14-OUNCE) CAN SWEETENED CONDENSED MILK
- 8   OUNCES CREAM CHEESE, SOFTENED
- ½   CUP KEY LIME JUICE
- 1   CUP SOUR CREAM

TOPPING
- ½   CUP WHIPPING CREAM
- 2   TABLESPOONS CONFECTIONERS' SUGAR
-      GRATED LIME PEEL

To prepare the shells, mix the coconut, gingersnap crumbs, graham cracker crumbs, butter and flour in a bowl. Press over the bottoms and ¾ inch up the sides of 8 small tart pans. Place on a baking sheet. Bake at 350 degrees for 5 minutes. Chill for 3 to 4 hours.

To prepare the filling, beat the condensed milk and cream cheese in a mixer bowl until light and fluffy. Add the Key lime juice and mix well. Stir in the sour cream. Spoon into the prepared tart shells. Chill, covered, for 2 hours or longer.

To prepare the topping, beat the whipping cream in a mixer bowl until soft peaks form. Add the confectioners' sugar. Beat until stiff peaks form. Spread over the tarts. Sprinkle with lime peel. Serve immediately.

To serve eight

THE FLOWER GIRLS' BASKETS

2   CUPS SEMISWEET CHOCOLATE CHIPS
6   OUNCES CHOCOLATE CANDY COATING
½   CUP BLACKBERRY PRESERVES
2   TABLESPOONS BLACKBERRY LIQUEUR
2   CUPS SWEETENED WHIPPED CREAM

Heat the chocolate chips and candy coating in a double boiler over hot water until blended, stirring frequently. Remove from heat. Let stand until the chocolate mixture is cool enough to handle but still pliable.

Invert 2 miniature muffin tins. Spray backs lightly with nonstick cooking spray. Cut squares of plastic wrap large enough to press over each muffin cup; edges can overlap.

Spoon the melted chocolate mixture into a pastry bag fitted with a small round tip, or use a sealable plastic bag snipping a tiny hole in 1 corner. Drizzle the chocolate gradually over each muffin cup using a figure-8 pattern draped from edge to edge of the cup in order to form the side of the basket as well as the base. Make sure the baskets do not touch each other or they will break apart when you try to remove them from the muffin cups. If the chocolate drizzles too fast, let it cool longer. If it becomes too hard, reheat slightly. Chill baskets for 10 minutes.

Pipe a second layer of chocolate over each basket, filling in the sides and any other sparse areas. Chill for 1 to 10 hours. Remove the baskets by lifting 1 corner of the plastic wrap very carefully; baskets and plastic wrap should easily pull away from the cups. Peel the plastic from the inside of the baskets. Place in an airtight container, separating the layers with loose balls of plastic wrap. Store in the refrigerator.

Fold the preserves and liqueur into the whipped cream. Spoon into the baskets. Garnish with fresh berries and fresh mint.

Makes thirty baskets

ON OCCASION...

chill the punch or wine with RINGS AND ROSES.

Arrange edible rose blossoms in a ring mold and fill it half full with boiled water, ginger ale, or fruit juice. Freeze until firm. Fill the mold completely with the liquid chosen and freeze again until firm. Let stand at room temperature for 5 to 10 minutes, then unmold the ring into the punch bowl just as the first guests arrive.

If serving wine, place a wine bottle of equal size filled with dried beans in the center of a narrow plastic container. Arrange flower blossoms, greenery, beads, or other decorative items in the bowl. Fill it half full with boiled water and freeze until firm. Fill the bowl completely with water and freeze several days or until firm. Let stand for 5 to 10 minutes and remove from the plastic bowl to a decorative container. Remove the bean-filled bottle and slip the bottle of wine to be served into the center.

Ray Young ©

3

"FORE" THE NEIGHBORHOOD

MENU

Double Bogey Dip

Gingered Chicken Wings

Birdie Food

Herb Cheese
Sandwiches with Salsa

Country Club Salad

Sugar Snap Pea Salad

Vidalia Onion Slaw

Grilled Shrimp with
Hot Lime Butter or
Garlic Ginger Butter Sauce

Kielbasa Kabobs

Even Par Cake

Bloody Mary Bar

Rally young and old, swingers and hackers for a hilarious round to remember! Neighbors each design a golf hole in their yard...A bucket on a raft floating in the Miller's pool (a water hazard coming and going), Rover's dog bowl resting on the crest of his humble dwelling...Get the idea? Think clever yet attainable. Collect a tournament fee——for the rented margarita machine and the prizes for longest ball, lowest score, cutest dog, most outrageous golfin' get-up... At a two o'clock shotgun start at the "clubhouse," have the "Marshal" review the rules—— creative and shrewd. Pass out scorecards (no pencils, no erasin') and Bloody Marys. Hit a few...then catch up to the "Kooler Kart" driven by enterprising youngsters. Spend the afternoon hacking Wiffle balls (have more than you can count) and replacing divots up and down the block. Finish with a lazy evening of grilling...then...begin scheming for next year!

DOUBLE BOGEY DIP

1   (16-OUNCE) CAN SAUERKRAUT
1½ POUNDS SLICED CORNED BEEF,
    FINELY CHOPPED
2   CUPS SHREDDED SWISS CHEESE
½   CUP MAYONNAISE
1   TABLESPOON (ABOUT)
    COCKTAIL SAUCE, OR TO TASTE

2   TABLESPOONS PICKLE RELISH,
    DRAINED
¼   CUP WATER
    RYE SQUARES
    TOASTED PARTY RYE

Place the sauerkraut in a colander. Drain for 15 minutes. Layer the corned beef, sauerkraut and cheese in a 9x13-inch baking dish sprayed with nonstick cooking spray or coated with olive oil. Mix the mayonnaise, cocktail sauce and pickle relish in a bowl. Stir in the water. Spoon over the prepared layers. Bake at 325 degrees for 20 minutes or until bubbly. Serve with rye squares and/or toasted party rye.

To serve eight

GINGERED CHICKEN WINGS

1½ CUPS SOY SAUCE
¾   CUP SHERRY
½   CUP CHOPPED GINGERROOT
6   TABLESPOONS SUGAR

6   TABLESPOONS PEANUT OIL
8   CLOVES OF GARLIC, CRUSHED
6   POUNDS CHICKEN WINGS

Combine the soy sauce, sherry, gingerroot, sugar, peanut oil and garlic in a bowl and mix well. Pour over the chicken in a large plastic bowl or sealable plastic bag, turning to coat. Marinate in the refrigerator for 6 to 12 hours, stirring occasionally. Drain the chicken, discarding the marinade. Arrange the chicken in a single layer on a baking sheet lined with foil. Bake at 400 degrees for 20 to 30 minutes or until the chicken is cooked through. Serve at room temperature.

Substitute 6 boneless, skinless chicken breast halves for the wings and turn this appetizer into an entrée. Grill the chicken over medium-hot coals until cooked through, turning and basting with the marinade several times.

To serve six

TEE UP A BLOODY MARY BAR

You can't leave the clubhouse without the breakfast of champions. Leaded or unleaded, it's the perfect start to a winner-of-a-day. Just arrange all or some of the following ingredients on a bar, buffet, or an outdoor table. For an extra touch, rim French jelly glasses with the lemon or lime and dip in the coarse salt or Old Bay Seasoning. Add a celery stick, carrot stick or shrimp on a skewer.

THE BASICS
vodka
tomato juice and V-8 juice
prepared horseradish
Tabasco and Worcestershire sauces
salt and pepper

THE NOT-SO-BASICS
lemon and lime wedges
whole steamed shrimp, peeled with
    the tail intact
whole blanched green beans
    and asparagus
crisp celery and carrot sticks
coarse salt
Old Bay Seasoning

GRILLED SHRIMP WITH HOT LIME BUTTER

BAMBOO SKEWERS

2 POUNDS LARGE PEELED DEVEINED SHRIMP WITH TAILS

2 CUPS MELTED BUTTER

JUICE OF 2 LIMES

1½ TEASPOONS CAYENNE

Soak the skewers in water to cover in a bowl for 30 minutes; drain. Thread the shrimp on the skewers.

Combine the butter, lime juice and cayenne in a bowl and mix well. Reserve 1½ cups for dipping. Baste the shrimp with some of the remaining butter sauce.

Grill over medium-hot coals for 2 to 3 minutes per side or until the shrimp are pink, basting with the butter sauce occasionally. Serve with the reserved butter sauce.

To serve four

HERB CHEESE SANDWICHES WITH SALSA

SALSA

3 ROMA TOMATOES, SEEDED, FINELY CHOPPED

1 (14-OUNCE) CAN ARTICHOKES, DRAINED, FINELY CHOPPED

2 CLOVES OF GARLIC, MINCED

1 TABLESPOON OLIVE OIL

HERB CHEESE SANDWICHES

6 OUNCES GOAT CHEESE, CRUMBLED

½ CUP CHOPPED FRESH BASIL

3 GREEN ONIONS, FINELY CHOPPED

½ TEASPOON FRESHLY CRACKED PEPPER

1 LOAF PARTY RYE OR PUMPERNICKEL

To prepare the salsa, combine the tomatoes, artichokes and garlic in a bowl and mix gently. Stir in the olive oil. Store, covered, in the refrigerator until serving time.

To prepare the sandwiches, mix the goat cheese, basil, green onions and pepper in a bowl. Spread the bread slices with the goat cheese mixture. Top with the salsa.

Makes one dozen sandwiches

❧

Prepare GARLIC GINGER BUTTER SAUCE *by combining 2 cups butter, 6 tablespoons brown sugar, 1 tablespoon ground ginger, 1½ teaspoons grated orange peel and 6 cloves of minced garlic in a saucepan. Cook over medium heat until the brown sugar dissolves, stirring constantly. Serve with grilled shrimp.*

COUNTRY CLUB SALAD

BALSAMIC VINAIGRETTE

- 3 TABLESPOONS BALSAMIC VINEGAR
- 1 TABLESPOON DIJON MUSTARD
- 1 CLOVE OF GARLIC, MINCED
- ½ CUP OLIVE OIL
  SALT AND FRESHLY GROUND PEPPER TO TASTE

SALAD

- 1½ POUNDS FARFALLE, COOKED AL DENTE, DRAINED
- 6 ROMA TOMATOES, SEEDED, CHOPPED
- ½ CUP KALAMATA OLIVE HALVES
- 3 OUNCES FETA CHEESE, CRUMBLED
- ⅓ CUP CHOPPED RED ONION
- 4 TEASPOONS DRAINED CAPERS
- 10 BASIL LEAVES, JULIENNED

To prepare the vinaigrette, whisk the balsamic vinegar, Dijon mustard and garlic in a bowl until mixed. Add the olive oil gradually, whisking constantly until mixed. Season with salt and pepper.

To prepare the salad, mix the pasta, tomatoes, olives, feta cheese, red onion, capers and basil in a salad bowl. Add the vinaigrette and toss gently.

To serve eight

SUGAR SNAP PEA SALAD

- 1 POUND FRESH SUGAR SNAP PEAS
- ½ CUP GARLIC VINEGAR
- ½ CUP EXTRA-VIRGIN OLIVE OIL
- ½ CUP CHOPPED FRESH BASIL
- 1 SHALLOT, MINCED
  SALT AND PEPPER TO TASTE

Blanch the peas in boiling water in a saucepan for 2 minutes. Drain and rinse with cold water.

Whisk the balsamic vinegar, olive oil, basil, shallot, salt and pepper in a bowl until mixed. Pour over the peas in a bowl, tossing to coat.

To serve eight

Prepare BIRDIE FOOD *by mixing 6 cups popped popcorn, 2 cups corn twists and 2 cups pretzel twists in a roasting pan. Pour a mixture of ⅓ cup melted butter or margarine, 1 teaspoon lemon pepper, ½ teaspoon chili powder, ½ teaspoon oregano, ¼ teaspoon onion powder and ¼ teaspoon garlic powder over the popcorn mixture and stir to coat. Bake at 325 degrees for 30 minutes, stirring twice. Cool before storing in an airtight container.*

Kielbasa Kabobs

Vidalia Onion Slaw

Slice 6 large Vidalia onions and separate into rings. Arrange in a shallow dish. Mix 2 cups boiling water, 1 cup sugar and ½ cup cider vinegar in a saucepan until the sugar dissolves. Pour over the onions. Marinate, covered, in the refrigerator for 8 to 10 hours; drain. Combine the onions with 1 cup mayonnaise and 2 teaspoons celery seeds. Chill in the refrigerator. Serve with saltines. Great on hot dogs, hamburgers, everything!

Honey Mustard Sauce
| 1 | cup Dijon or Grey Poupon mustard |
| ½ | cup honey |

Kabobs
10	new potatoes
2	quarts water
2	onions, cut into halves
1	pound kielbasa sausage, cut into 1-inch slices
	Red and green bell peppers, cut into 1-inch chunks

To prepare the sauce, mix the mustard and honey in a bowl. Prepare 3 to 4 hours before serving.

To prepare the kabobs, combine the new potatoes and water in a saucepan. Bring to a boil. Boil for 10 minutes or until tender; drain. Let stand until cool. Cut the potatoes into halves.

Cut the onion halves into quarters. Thread the kielbasa, onions, bell peppers and potatoes on skewers. Grill for 4 minutes per side or until the sausage and vegetables begin to brown. Serve with the sauce.

To serve eight

EVEN PAR CAKE

CAKE

1 TEASPOON BAKING SODA

½ CUP BUTTERMILK

½ CUP BUTTER

1 CUP WATER

½ CUP VEGETABLE OIL

2 CUPS FLOUR

2 CUPS SUGAR

2 TABLESPOONS BAKING COCOA

2 EGGS, BEATEN

1 TEASPOON VANILLA EXTRACT

½ TEASPOON SALT

CHOCOLATE FROSTING

½ CUP BUTTER, SOFTENED

6 TABLESPOONS BUTTERMILK

¼ CUP BAKING COCOA

1 (1-POUND) PACKAGE CONFECTIONERS' SUGAR

1 TEASPOON VANILLA EXTRACT

1 CUP FINELY CHOPPED PECANS

To prepare the cake, dissolve the baking soda in the buttermilk in a small bowl and mix well. Heat the butter in a saucepan until melted. Remove from heat. Stir in the water and oil. Fold in the flour and sugar. Stir in the baking cocoa. Fold in the eggs. Add the buttermilk mixture, vanilla and salt and mix well. Spoon into a greased 9x13-inch cake pan. Bake at 375 degrees for 20 minutes.

To prepare the frosting, beat the butter, buttermilk and baking cocoa in a mixer bowl until smooth. Add the confectioners' sugar, beating until blended. Stir in the vanilla and pecans. Spread over the hot cake. Cool before serving.

The flavor is enhanced if prepared 1 day in advance.

To serve fifteen

ON OCCASION...

enterprising youngsters can accompany the golfers with a Kids' Kooler Kart—an upgraded little red wagon lined with lawn bags. Place a small cooler in the front of the wagon for the "dry" items and fill the back with ice. Add such summer necessities as frozen ice cream bars, Yoo-Hoos, juice boxes, sodas, candies, and boiled peanuts in brown lunch bags.

Convert the "Fore" the Neighborhood party to a party for the kids. The invitations might read "A Party 'Fore' Molly" or "Michael Is 'Fore.'" Kiddie golf sets, sandbox sand traps, and visors painted with MCC for Molly's Country Club round out the backyard fun.

For Kids' Kabobs at the nineteenth hole, grill hot dog bites and fresh pineapple chunks threaded on bamboo skewers that have been soaked in water.

FATHER'S DAY OUT

Menu

Deviled Eggs

Zucchini Fries

Caesar Salad with
Rich Dressing

Pan-Seared Garlic Pork Roast

"The Grove" Steaks and Salmon

Vidalia Onion and Rice Bake

Green Beans with
Horseradish Sauce

Papa's Mashed Potatoes

Sourdough Bread

Peachy Polka-Dot Crumb Pie

Blackberry Shortcake

Sparkling Gin Cooler

King for a Day, Top of the Heap, Big Man on Campus, He's the Man! In keeping with this fine June tradition, we celebrate once again with Dad's favorites—his pipe and slippers and that age-old rectangular box with the proverbial tie or socks. Ward Cleaver never spent a day this relaxing! But does it have to be this way every year? Last time, for some Junior League "widowers" we know, it was slightly different. With wives hard at work contributing countless volunteer hours away from the home fires, innumerable dads were driving carpool and making the dental appointments. The twist? A surprise golf outing for the guys—but on Mother's Day! Planned all along, the girls kept mum. When he woke her with a bouquet and mushy card, she one-upped him with a new sleeve of balls and an eleven o'clock tee-time. As he set off to make his foursome, she spent all day making...reservations for dinner! Enjoy a day for honoring dads—and moms—with a menu of family favorites.

DEVILED EGGS

6   HARD-COOKED EGGS, CUT HORIZONTALLY INTO HALVES
3   SLICES COOKED LEAN HAM
3   TABLESPOONS MAYONNAISE
1   TABLESPOON SOUR CREAM
1   TABLESPOON DIJON MUSTARD
1   TABLESPOON CHOPPED SCALLIONS
    SALT AND PEPPER TO TASTE
2   TABLESPOONS CHOPPED FRESH THYME

Place the egg yolks in a bowl and arrange the whites on a serving platter. Mince 2 slices of the ham. Julienne the remaining slice.

Mash the egg yolks with a fork or process in a food processor. Stir in the minced ham, mayonnaise, sour cream, Dijon mustard and half the scallions. Season with salt and pepper. Spoon or pipe into the egg whites. Garnish each half with the remaining scallions, thyme and julienned ham. Chill, covered with plastic wrap, until serving time.

To serve twelve

ZUCCHINI FRIES

2   MEDIUM ZUCCHINI
1   EGG
2   TEASPOONS MILK
⅓   CUP SEASONED BREAD CRUMBS

Cut the zucchini crosswise into halves. Cut the halves into ½-inch strips. Whisk the egg and milk in a bowl until blended. Sprinkle the bread crumbs on a sheet of waxed paper. Dip each strip into the egg mixture and coat with the bread crumbs. Arrange the strips in a single layer on a baking sheet sprayed with nonstick cooking spray. Bake at 400 degrees for 8 minutes; turn. Bake for 7 minutes longer. Serve immediately.

To serve six

ON OCCASION...

give something special to dear old Dad!

Metal ruler, flashlight, any cordless tool, rechargable batteries.

Tire gauge and car wash kit, car emergency kit, jumper cables in a case, small air compressor, journal to log car services and mileage, car wash gift certificates.

Inexpensive watch for yard work, pruners, gardening tools, work gloves, gardening books.

Croquet set, volleyball set, golf balls, tennis balls, magazine subscriptions, puzzles, monogrammed sports towels, fact books, how-to books, cookbook with chef tools.

Shoe shine kit, wooden hangers, brass collar stays, leather belt, calculator with paper tape.

Honey-Do Buckets—Line 5-gallon plastic buckets with canvas liners and fill them with the tools necessary for a particular type of chore.

CAESAR SALAD WITH RICH DRESSING

2   CLOVES OF GARLIC
1   (2-OUNCE) CAN ANCHOVIES, DRAINED
6   OUNCES PARMESAN CHEESE, GRATED
    JUICE OF 2 LEMONS
½   CUP OLIVE OIL
1   TEASPOON CRACKED PEPPER
⅛   TEASPOON WORCESTERSHIRE SAUCE
    MIXED GREENS (ROMAINE AND ENDIVE)
    CROUTONS

Process the garlic in a food processor fitted with a chopping blade. Add the anchovies. Pulse until chopped. Add the cheese and lemon juice. Process until smooth. Add the olive oil in a thin stream, processing constantly until blended. Add the pepper and Worcestershire sauce. Process until blended. Store, covered, in the refrigerator.

Serve over mixed greens. Top with croutons made of pumpernickel, wheat or rye bread, seasoned with Greek seasoning and toasted in butter or olive oil.

To serve six to eight

PAN-SEARED GARLIC PORK ROAST

6   CLOVES OF GARLIC, MINCED
1   TEASPOON OREGANO
1   TEASPOON PAPRIKA
    SALT AND PEPPER TO TASTE
1   (3- TO 4-POUND) PORK LOIN ROAST
    VEGETABLE OIL
2   BAY LEAVES
    JUICE OF ½ LEMON
¼   CUP BUTTER
    JUICE OF ½ LEMON
2   LARGE ONIONS, THINLY SLICED
2   CLOVES OF GARLIC, MINCED

Mix 6 cloves of garlic, oregano, paprika, salt and pepper in a bowl. Coat the roast with oil. Press the garlic mixture into the roast. Brown the roast on all sides in a skillet. Remove the roast to a roasting pan, reserving the pan drippings. Press the bay leaves on top of the roast. Drizzle with the juice of ½ lemon. Bake at 350 degrees for 1 to 1½ hours or until a meat thermometer registers 160 degrees. Discard the bay leaves.

Heat the butter and juice of ½ lemon with the reserved pan drippings. Add the onions and 2 cloves of garlic and mix well. Sauté until the onions are tender. Spoon over the roast on a serving platter. Slice and serve.

To serve eight

Prepare THE GROVE MARINADE *by mixing ¾ cup packed brown sugar, ½ cup white wine, ¼ cup honey, 3 or 4 finely chopped scallions and 3 tablespoons teriyaki sauce. Pour over beef or salmon steaks. Marinate in refrigerator for 8 to 10 hours. Let stand at room temperature for 15 minutes before grilling. For a special treat, accompany the salmon or steak with* GRILLED VIDALIA ONIONS. *Peel large Vidalia onions and remove a small cavity from the top of each with a melon baller. Fill the cavity with softened butter, seasonings or bread crumbs. Place on the grill before the steaks so they will have time to grill for 30 to 45 minutes or until tender.*

VIDALIA ONION AND RICE BAKE

5   CUPS BOILING WATER
1   CUP RICE
8   CUPS CHOPPED VIDALIA ONIONS
¼   CUP BUTTER OR MARGARINE
1   CUP SHREDDED SWISS CHEESE
⅔   CUP HALF-AND-HALF
¼   TO ½ TEASPOON TABASCO SAUCE, OR TO TASTE
    GARLIC POWDER TO TASTE

Combine the boiling water and rice in a saucepan and mix well. Cook for 5 to 7 minutes; drain.

Sauté the onions in the butter in a skillet until tender. Remove from heat. Stir in the rice, cheese, half-and-half, Tabasco sauce and garlic powder. Spoon into a 2-quart greased baking dish. Bake at 350 degrees for 1 hour.

To serve eight

GREEN BEANS WITH HORSERADISH SAUCE

HORSERADISH SAUCE
1   CUP MAYONNAISE
3   HARD-COOKED EGGS, CHOPPED
1   TABLESPOON (HEAPING) PREPARED HORSERADISH
1   TABLESPOON CHOPPED FRESH PARSLEY
    JUICE OF 1 LEMON
1   TEASPOON WORCESTERSHIRE SAUCE
    SALT, PEPPER, GARLIC POWDER, CELERY SALT AND ONION SALT TO TASTE
GREEN BEANS
2   (16-OUNCE) CANS GREEN BEANS
1   ONION, SLICED
    CHOPPED BACON TO TASTE (OPTIONAL)

To prepare the sauce, combine the mayonnaise, eggs, horseradish, parsley, lemon juice, Worcestershire sauce, salt, pepper, garlic powder, celery salt and onion salt in a bowl and mix well. Let stand at room temperature for 10 to 15 minutes for flavors to marry.

To prepare the beans, combine the undrained green beans, onion and bacon in a saucepan. Cook over medium heat for 30 minutes, stirring occasionally; drain. Spoon into a serving bowl. Spoon the sauce over the top.

To serve eight

To make PAPA'S MASHED POTATOES, *peel and coarsely chop 5 pounds russet potatoes. Boil until tender but still firm; drain. Beat with 6 tablespoons butter or 3 tablespoons olive oil, 1 to 1½ cups milk, salt and pepper until smooth. For add-ins, try 1 cup crumbled feta cheese; 1 cup shredded Cheddar, Swiss or smoked provolone cheese; ½ cup crumbled bleu cheese; ⅓ cup chopped black or green olives; ⅓ cup drained prepared horseradish; ¼ cup barbecue sauce; ⅓ cup pesto and/or 6 cloves of crushed* ROASTED GARLIC, *page 32.*

SOURDOUGH BREAD

A SOURDOUGH TIMETABLE

Friday morning: remove the entire jar of starter from the refrigerator and let stand on the kitchen counter.

Friday evening: stir the starter well with a wooden spoon. Remove 1 cup of the starter. Either make bread with it, discard it, or give it to a friend. Feed the starter. If you make bread, let the dough rise overnight.

Saturday morning: place the risen dough in baking pans. Return the starter to the refrigerator.

Saturday evening: bake the bread and leave it on our back porch!

SOURDOUGH STARTER
2 CUPS WARM WATER
1 CUP SUGAR
6 TABLESPOONS INSTANT POTATO FLAKES
2 ENVELOPES DRY YEAST

SOURDOUGH BREAD
6 TO 7 CUPS BREAD FLOUR
¼ CUP SUGAR
2 TEASPOONS SALT
1½ CUPS WARM WATER
1 CUP STARTER
½ CUP CORN OIL
MELTED BUTTER

To prepare the starter, combine the warm water, sugar and potato flakes in a large glass jar. Let stand, covered with foil, at room temperature for 4 days, stirring once or twice with a wooden spoon. Always use a wooden spoon.

Stir in the yeast. Let stand at room temperature for 24 hours. Remove 1 cup of the starter before feeding to make bread, give to a friend or discard. Let the starter stand at room temperature for 8 to 12 hours before using. Store the remaining starter in the refrigerator and feed it every 3 to 5 days with ½ cup sugar, 3 tablespoons instant potato flakes and 1 cup warm water.

To prepare the bread, combine the bread flour, sugar and salt in a bowl sprayed with nonstick cooking spray and mix well. Stir in the warm water, starter and corn oil. Let stand, covered with plastic wrap, at room temperature for 8 hours or longer. Punch the dough down.

Divide the dough into 3 equal portions. Shape each portion into a loaf in a loaf pan sprayed with nonstick cooking spray. Brush the tops with melted butter. Let rise, covered with a tea towel, in a warm place for 8 to 12 hours or until doubled in bulk. Bake at 325 degrees for 25 to 30 minutes or until the loaves test done. Invert onto a wire rack to cool.

Makes three loaves

PEACHY POLKA-DOT CRUMB PIE

1   UNBAKED (10-INCH) DEEP-DISH PIE SHELL
2½ CUPS SLICED FRESH PEACHES
½   CUP BLUEBERRIES
1   CUP SUGAR
⅓   CUP FLOUR
⅛   TEASPOON SALT
½   CUP SOUR CREAM
2   EGGS, BEATEN
1   CUP FLOUR
1   CUP SUGAR
½   CUP BUTTER
    SLICED PEACHES
    FRESH BLUEBERRIES

Line the bottom of the pie shell with a mixture of 2½ cups peaches and
½ cup blueberries. Combine 1 cup sugar, ⅓ cup flour and salt in a bowl and
mix well. Stir in the sour cream and eggs. Spoon over the peaches.

Mix 1 cup flour and 1 cup sugar in a bowl. Cut in the butter until crumbly.
Sprinkle over the top. Bake at 350 degrees for 55 to 60 minutes
or until brown. Garnish with sliced peaches and blueberries.

To serve eight

BLACKBERRY SHORTCAKE

1   QUART FRESH BLACKBERRIES
2   TEASPOONS SUGAR
2   CUPS FLOUR
2   TABLESPOONS SUGAR
1   TABLESPOON BAKING POWDER
½   TEASPOON SALT
¼   CUP BUTTER, CHILLED
½   CUP FINELY CHOPPED PECANS
1   CUP WHIPPING CREAM
    SUGAR TO TASTE
1   CUP WHIPPING CREAM, WHIPPED
    SPRIGS OF MINT
    BLACKBERRIES

Toss 1 quart blackberries and 2 teaspoons sugar in a bowl. Chill in the
refrigerator. Mix the flour, 2 tablespoons sugar, baking powder and salt in a
bowl and mix well. Cut in the butter until crumbly. Stir in the pecans. Add
1 cup whipping cream and mix well.

Roll the dough thin on a lightly floured surface. Cut into 3-inch rounds.
Coat each round with sugar to taste. Arrange on a baking sheet lined with
parchment paper. Bake at 400 degrees for 10 to 13 minutes or until brown
and puffed. Remove to a wire rack to cool completely.

For each serving, layer 1 shortcake round, chilled blackberries and
whipped cream on a dessert plate. Repeat the process. Top with a pastry
round. Garnish with blackberries and sprigs of mint.

To serve six to eight

Treat Dad to a SPARKLING GIN COOLER. *Combine 3 cups chilled orange juice and ¾ cup gin. Stir in 1 cup chilled
ginger ale. Pour over ice cubes in a glass. Garnish each serving with a lime slice and maraschino cherry.*

A LATE AFTERNOON

TURNS INTO A

LUMINOUS EVENING...

A CLEAR SKY

WHERE THE STARS

SEEM TO DANCE...

SPLENDID SUMMER

DAYS THAT

ALLOW US TO BE

A CHILD AGAIN...

MENUS

WASHED ASHORE

SILVER AND SADDLES

GOOD HEAVENS!!!

★★★★ A FOUR-STAR DAY ★★★★

OH, MY STARS!!!

WASHED ASHORE

Menu

Summer Scallops

Avocado and Feta Salsa

Chopped Salad with
Pepper Dressing

Shrimp Salad

Horseradish-Crusted Grouper

Briny Boiled Shrimp

Frogmore Stew

Caribbean Rice

Garlic Green Beans

Margarita Pie

Lemon Ice Cream with Cookies

Chocolate Éclair Cake

Sun Fizz

"On the Rocks"

Chi Chis

The best-laid plans for a summer trek to the beach is...to have no plans a'tall!!! Keep a vacation journal for great fun and lots of laughs... Or mail home postcards. With or without written messages, begin a collection of postmarks and destinations, to revisit down the road. Take along The Beach Boys and Jimmy Buffett... Indulge in the luxury of two cameras...a Brownie special, waterproof disposable, or your finest Nikon. Load one with black-and-white film for instant nostalgia. Teach everyone to dance the Carolina Shag to old favorites from The Embers, The Drifters, The Tams... Observe the universe. Learn the constellations. The North Star is where? Rediscover shell shops, battleships, museums...those places you meant to visit on a day filled with raindrops. Pack your summer book, plenty of playing cards, Scrabble, and a dictionary. And obey the eleventh commandment...thou shalt take at least one long nap a day while...washed ashore.

SUMMER SCALLOPS

2 SLICES BACON	¼ CUP FINELY CHOPPED ONION
½ CUP PEELED SEEDED CHOPPED TOMATO	1 POUND SMALL BAY SCALLOPS
	SALT AND WHITE PEPPER
¼ CUP FINELY CHOPPED GREEN BELL PEPPER	TO TASTE
	FRESHLY GRATED PARMESAN
¼ CUP FINELY CHOPPED YELLOW BELL PEPPER	CHEESE (OPTIONAL)

Fry the bacon in a skillet until cooked through but not crisp. Drain, reserving 1 to 2 teaspoons pan drippings. Chop the bacon. Sauté the tomato, green pepper, yellow pepper and onion in the reserved pan drippings for 2 to 3 minutes or until tender-crisp. Remove to a bowl with a slotted spoon. Sauté the scallops in the pan drippings for 2 to 3 minutes or just until brown.

Combine the scallops, vegetables, bacon, salt and white pepper in a bowl and mix gently. Spoon the scallop mixture into individual baking shells. (May use cleaned oyster or clam shells.) Arrange on a baking sheet. Broil for 2 minutes. Garnish with Parmesan cheese.

To serve four

AVOCADO AND FETA SALSA

1 LARGE AVOCADO	1 TABLESPOON BALSAMIC VINEGAR
2 PLUM TOMATOES	
¼ CUP CHOPPED PURPLE ONION	1½ TEASPOONS RED WINE VINEGAR
1 CLOVE OF GARLIC, MINCED	½ TEASPOON CHOPPED FRESH OREGANO
1 TABLESPOON CHOPPED PARSLEY	
1 TABLESPOON OLIVE OIL	2 OUNCES FETA CHEESE, CRUMBLED

Chop the avocado and plum tomatoes coarsely and mix in a bowl. Add the onion, garlic, parsley, olive oil, balsamic vinegar, wine vinegar and oregano and mix gently. Fold in the cheese. Serve immediately with corn chips.

Makes two cups

ON OCCASION...

dream up a new wrinkle for that most challenging entertainment situation of them all: How to keep children occupied on the road. To get you started, try some of the following ideas:

THE ALPHABET GAME: *Find letters on road signs and billboards. The first one to "Zephyrhills" wins!*

AUTO TAG BINGO: *Create a bingo board of squares with five across and five deep. Dad fills them with assorted states and places. The first one with five in a row is the champ.*

SURPRISE STASH: *Dole out surprise treats at each 100-mile interval of road. The kids will look forward to discovering what fruit roll, comic book, or travel game will appear next.*

SWEET 'N' SOUR: *As you travel, wave to the people you pass. If they wave back, they're sweet; if they don't . . .*

LICENSE PLATE PLUS: *Give a new spin to the old favorite by also tallying the state's capital, largest body of water, state motto, its most unique tourist attractions, etc. Carry a pocket atlas or an almanac to verify answers.*

CHOPPED SALAD WITH PEPPER DRESSING

PEPPER DRESSING
- 1   CUP MAYONNAISE
- 1   TABLESPOON DRAINED RINSED CAPERS
- 1   TABLESPOON FRESHLY CRACKED PEPPER
- 1   TEASPOON LEMON JUICE

SALAD
- 1   HEAD ICEBERG LETTUCE, COARSELY CHOPPED
- 2   TOMATOES, SEEDED, CHOPPED

To prepare the dressing, whisk the mayonnaise, capers, pepper and lemon juice in a bowl until mixed.

To prepare the salad, mix the lettuce and tomatoes in a salad bowl. Add the dressing and toss to coat. Serve immediately.

When cutting iceberg lettuce with a knife, serve immediately as the edges will turn brown.

To serve eight

HORSERADISH-CRUSTED GROUPER

- 2   POUNDS GROUPER OR WHITE FISH FILLETS
-    JUICE OF 1 LEMON
-    SALT AND PEPPER TO TASTE
- ½   CUP PREPARED HORSERADISH
- 3   TABLESPOONS BREAD CRUMBS
- 1   TABLESPOON OLIVE OIL

Arrange the grouper on a baking sheet sprayed with nonstick cooking spray. Drizzle with the lemon juice and sprinkle with salt and pepper.

Mix the horseradish, bread crumbs and olive oil in a bowl. Spread over both sides of the fish.

Bake at 400 degrees for 10 minutes or until the fish flakes easily. Broil for 1 minute or until light brown.

To serve four

~

FROGMORE STEW, a recipe from the JLCM classic GEORGIA ON MY MENU, is a snap to make for a crowd of up to 12 people. Just combine 2 gallons water, 3 pounds Polish sausage pieces, 2 large chopped onions, 2 sliced lemons, 2 tablespoons seafood seasoning, salt and pepper in a large stockpot. Bring to a boil, then simmer for 45 minutes. Stir in ½ cup butter and add 15 ears of corn. Cook for 10 minutes, stirring occasionally. Add 4 pounds unpeeled shrimp. Cook for 5 minutes or until the shrimp turn pink; drain. Remove to a large serving platter.

BRINY BOILED SHRIMP

 5   QUARTS WATER
     COARSE SALT
 1   LEMON, THINLY SLICED
 1   TEASPOON CAYENNE
 5   POUNDS LARGE SHRIMP, WITH OR WITHOUT HEADS

Combine the water with coarse salt until the water appears briny. Mix in the lemon slices and cayenne. Bring to a boil. Add the shrimp. Cook for 5 minutes or until the shrimp turn pink; drain. Serve in a large bowl over cracked ice.

Shrimp with heads are less expensive and more messy to fool with, but therein lies the Gulf Coast charm. OK, OK, you may also use large shrimp with heads removed.

To serve ten

SHRIMP SALAD

 1   POUND SHRIMP, COOKED, PEELED
 1   CUP FINELY CHOPPED CELERY
 2   HARD-COOKED EGGS, CHOPPED
 2   TABLESPOONS CHOPPED FRESH PARSLEY
 2   GREEN ONIONS, THINLY SLICED
     JUICE OF ½ LEMON
     GARLIC SALT TO TASTE
     FRESHLY GROUND PEPPER TO TASTE
 ¾   CUP MAYONNAISE

Chop, cut into halves or leave the shrimp whole. Combine the shrimp, celery, eggs, parsley, green onions, lemon juice, garlic salt and pepper in a bowl and mix gently. Stir in the mayonnaise. Chill, covered, until serving time. Serve with croissants. May substitute lump crab meat for shrimp.

To serve four

TO COOL YOURSELF . . .

Serve summer coolers over crushed ice in tall glasses for a special treat.

For a SUN FIZZ, *combine ginger ale with orange juice or pineapple juice.*

*For "*ON THE ROCKS,*" combine pineapple juice with a splash of Malibu rum.*

For CHI CHIS, *combine 1 part CoCo Lopez coconut milk with 2 parts vodka and 4 parts pineapple juice in a freezer container and freeze. Let stand at room temperature for 5 minutes and shake well. Fill glasses ¾ full and top off with ginger ale. Garnish with fresh pineapple wedges.*

CARIBBEAN RICE

1½   CUPS ORANGE JUICE
1½   CUPS WATER
1   TEASPOON SALT
1   TEASPOON CUMIN
½   TEASPOON PEPPER
1½   CUPS LONG GRAIN RICE
½   CUP CURRANTS OR GOLDEN RAISINS
4   GREEN ONIONS, SLICED

Bring the orange juice, water, salt, cumin and pepper to a boil in a saucepan. Stir in the rice, currants and green onions.

Cook, covered, over low heat for 12 to 15 minutes or until the rice is tender and the liquid has been absorbed.

May substitute 3 cups orange juice for 1½ cups orange juice and 1½ cups water.

To serve six to eight

GARLIC GREEN BEANS

2   POUNDS FRESH GREEN BEANS, TRIMMED
2   CLOVES OF GARLIC, THINLY SLICED
2   TABLESPOONS BUTTER
   SALT AND PEPPER TO TASTE

Blanch the green beans in boiling water in a saucepan for 4 minutes; drain. Rinse with cold water.

Sauté the garlic in the butter in a skillet for 1 minute; do not brown. Add the green beans and mix well. Season with salt and pepper.

To serve six

NAPKINS can be . . . bandannas, dish towels, gingham, plaid, starched white, bright cotton, paper, elegant ecru . . . folded, knotted, wrapped, tucked, tied, monogrammed, numbered, personalized, stitched, painted, edged, bordered, tasseled, hem-stitched, corded, pinked, sheared . . . from the fabric store, flea market, dime store, grandma's trunk, kitchen store, attic, basement, estate sale, any sale table, china shop

MARGARITA PIE

1¼ CUPS FINELY CRUSHED PRETZELS
½ CUP MELTED MARGARINE
¼ CUP SUGAR
1 (14-OUNCE) CAN SWEETENED CONDENSED MILK
⅓ CUP FROZEN LIME JUICE CONCENTRATE
3 TABLESPOONS TEQUILA
3 TABLESPOONS COINTREAU OR TRIPLE SEC
1 CUP WHIPPING CREAM, WHIPPED
  LIME CURLS

Combine the pretzels, margarine and sugar in a bowl and mix well. Press the crumb mixture over the bottom and up the side of a lightly buttered 9-inch pie plate.

Combine the condensed milk, lime juice concentrate, tequila and Cointreau in a bowl and mix well. Fold in the whipped cream. Spoon into the prepared pie shell. Freeze until firm. Garnish with lime curls.

For variety, omit the condensed milk and whipped cream. Whip the ingredients with 1½ quarts softened vanilla ice cream. Freeze until firm.

To serve six to eight

CHOCOLATE ECLAIR CAKE

2 (4-OUNCE) PACKAGES FRENCH VANILLA INSTANT
  PUDDING MIX
3 CUPS COLD MILK
12 OUNCES WHIPPED TOPPING, THAWED
1 (16-OUNCE) PACKAGE GRAHAM CRACKERS, SEPARATED
  INTO 3x3-INCH SECTIONS
1 (15-OUNCE) CAN MILK CHOCOLATE FROSTING

Whisk the pudding mix and milk in a bowl until thickened. Fold in the whipped topping.

Cover bottom of a 9x13-inch dish with ⅓ of the graham crackers. Spread ½ of the pudding mixture over the graham crackers. Layer with ½ of the remaining graham crackers and the remaining pudding mixture. Top with the remaining graham crackers.

Remove the plastic lid and paper liner from the frosting can. Lay the plastic lid loosely over the opening. Microwave for 30 seconds or until the frosting is of pouring consistency. Pour over the prepared layers. Chill for 12 hours before serving.

To serve twelve

The best LEMON ICE CREAM *is simply made by mixing 1 quart of softened vanilla ice cream with one 6-ounce can of frozen lemonade or limeade concentrate. Freeze it in a plastic container, and serve it over shortbread cookies. For a party, freeze it in lemon or orange shells, garnish with a sprig of mint, and serve with fancy cookies.*

SILVER AND SADDLES

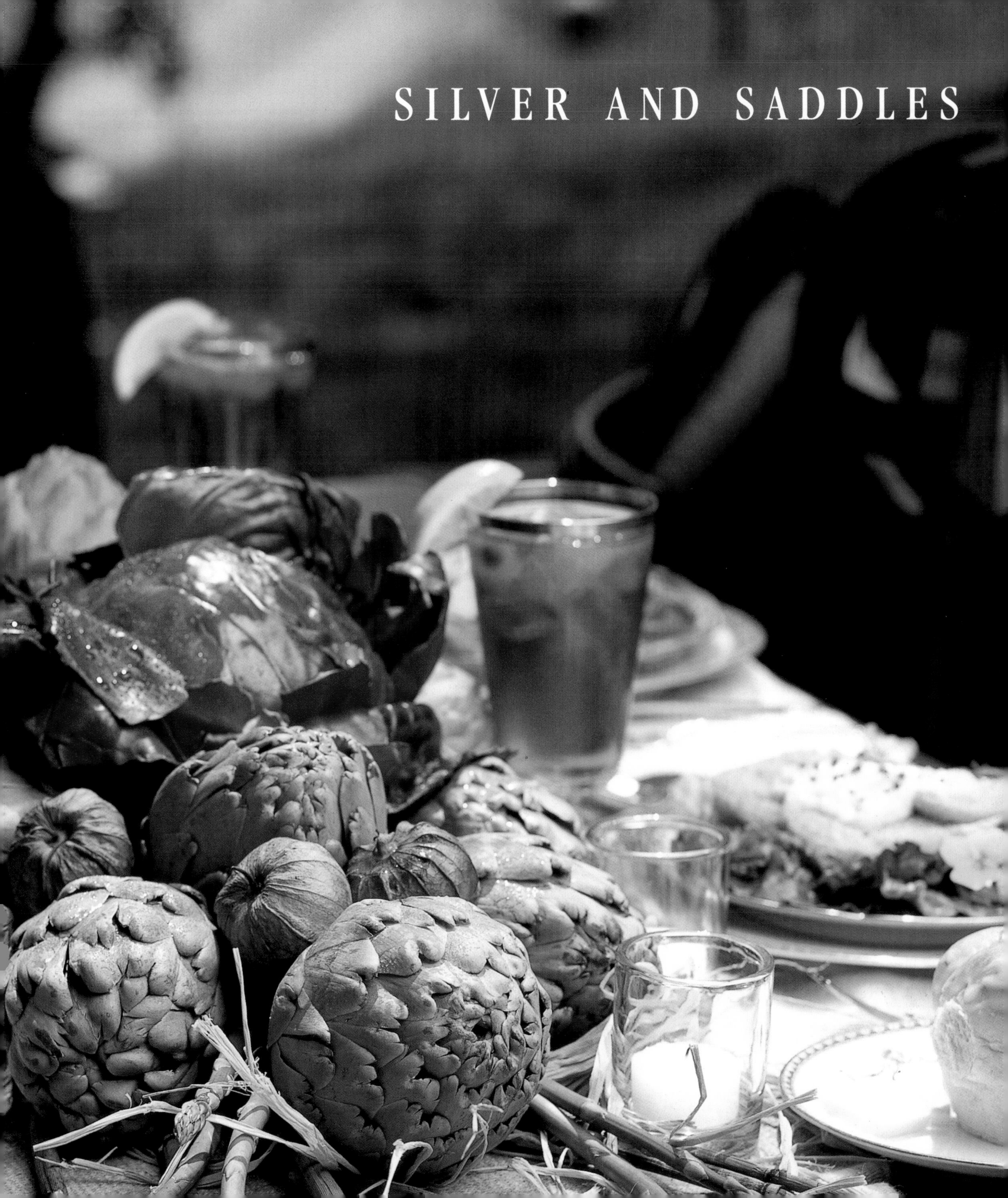

SILVER AND SADDLES

MENU

Clam Puffs on
Artichoke Blossoms

Bruschetta

Broiled Artichokes with
Bagna Cauda

Fried Green Tomato Salad with
Cayenne Mayonnaise

Beef au Poivre

Chilean Sea Bass

Green Bean Bundles

Bow Tie Pasta with Walnuts

Orange Knots

Fallen-for-Chocolate Torte

Amaretto Nectarines

Enjoy a flavorful feast at a table bedecked with finery as you rear back in complete comfort. Bring out the Wedgwood, along with your oldest denim…and ensure your guests do the same! Tonight, the touch of silver may be one of simple elegance or a flourish of fancy. Either way, it will be just right with saddle leather, riding crop, and worn blue jeans…maybe a little dust still on your boots. Grab the table and move it outside…to the "back forty," out on the porch, or to the prime place on your spread—smack in the middle of the backyard. Amass fresh fruits and vegetables, nature's summer yield, and provide an early glimpse of the meal to come. Mix all your china and glassware, then set atop tag-sale linens. This is the time to use the family heirlooms and uncover those flea market finds for a summertime supper. Raise the Waterford…Revel in bending some of the rules…Take pleasure in the home you've created…Embrace your own sense of style!

CLAM PUFFS ON ARTICHOKE BLOSSOMS

3   (14-OUNCE) CANS ARTICHOKE BOTTOMS, DRAINED, TRIMMED
2   (7-OUNCE) CANS MINCED CLAMS, DRAINED
6   OUNCES CREAM CHEESE, SOFTENED
¼   CUP WHIPPING CREAM
3   GREEN ONIONS, FINELY CHOPPED
1   TEASPOON WORCESTERSHIRE SAUCE
½   TEASPOON DRY MUSTARD
½   TEASPOON SALT

Snip the edges of the artichoke bottoms with kitchen shears to resemble flower petals or create your own design. Arrange in a single layer on a nonstick baking sheet.

Mix the clams, cream cheese, whipping cream, green onions, Worcestershire sauce, dry mustard and salt in a bowl. Mound some of the clam mixture on each artichoke bottom. Broil until puffy. Serve immediately. Substitute melba rounds for the artichoke bottoms for a more economical appetizer.

To serve six to eight

BRUSCHETTA

1   FRENCH BAGUETTE, THINLY SLICED
    OLIVE OIL
1   (15-OUNCE) CAN CHOPPED TOMATOES WITH GARLIC
    SALT AND FRESHLY GROUND PEPPER TO TASTE
    FRESH BASIL LEAVES
    FINELY GRATED PARMESAN CHEESE

Brush each baguette slice lightly with olive oil. Arrange in a single layer on a baking sheet sprayed with nonstick cooking spray. Broil for 2 to 3 minutes or until light brown. Spread each slice with 1 teaspoon of the tomatoes and sprinkle with salt and pepper. Arrange 1 leaf of basil on top of each serving; sprinkle with cheese. Serve immediately.

To serve twelve

GRACIOUS LIVING...

begins with approaching everyday tasks from a fresh viewpoint. Find ways to add order, simplicity, and grace to each day.

Daily . . .
allow 15 minutes for yourself; make ample notes in a journal; exercise, take a vitamin; make a list of things to do

Weekly . . .
clean out your car, backpack, purse, or briefcase; make Sunday night supper a family time to plan and reflect; mail a quick postcard to a friend; wrap presents for the week ahead

Monthly . . .
send birthday cards; clean off your desk; fertilize plants; turn the mattress; clean the telephone; ask someone over for coffee and a chocolate; lunch with a friend

Twice a year . . .
rearrange the indoor plants; move a piece of furniture; make a trip to the frame shop or upholstery shop; set a special day for a massage

And once a year . . .
click a family photograph; start a collection or add to one; plan a weekend retreat

FRIED GREEN TOMATO SALAD WITH CAYENNE MAYONNAISE

BAGNA CAUDA

Serve BAGNA CAUDA as a dipping sauce for artichokes which have been steamed, then cut into halves, brushed with olive oil and grilled. For the sauce, heat ½ cup olive oil and ½ cup butter in a double boiler over hot water. Sauté 3 to 5 finely chopped garlic cloves in 1 tablespoon olive oil until tender. Add 6 chopped and mashed anchovy fillets, chopped green onions and salt and pepper to taste. Cook for 5 minutes or until of a pasty consistency. Stir into the olive oil mixture. Serve in a crock with the grilled artichokes. Guests pull the leaves from the artichoke, dip them into the sauce, and gently pull them between the teeth to extract the delicious pulp.

CAYENNE MAYONNAISE

4	EGG YOLKS
¼	CUP FRESH LEMON JUICE
½	TEASPOON SALT
½	TEASPOON FRESHLY GROUND BLACK PEPPER
9	CLOVES OF GARLIC
½	TEASPOON DRY MUSTARD
¼	TEASPOON CAYENNE
¼	TEASPOON PAPRIKA
1½	CUPS OLIVE OIL
	SALT AND FRESHLY GROUND BLACK PEPPER TO TASTE

SALAD

6	LARGE GREEN TOMATOES
1½	CUPS CORNMEAL
½	CUP FLOUR
	SALT AND FRESHLY GROUND BLACK PEPPER TO TASTE
¼	TEASPOON CAYENNE, OR TO TASTE
3	EGGS, BEATEN
	VEGETABLE OIL FOR FRYING
1½	CUPS BOSTON OR BIBB LETTUCE, SHREDDED
2½	CUPS SHREDDED ROMAINE ARUGULA

To prepare the mayonnaise, process the egg yolks, lemon juice, ½ teaspoon salt and ½ teaspoon black pepper in a food processor or blender until blended. Add the garlic, dry mustard, cayenne and paprika. Process until smooth. Add the olive oil in a steady stream, processing constantly until the mixture thickens. Season with salt and black pepper to taste.

To avoid raw eggs that may carry salmonella, we suggest using an equivalent amount of commercial egg substitute.

To prepare the salad, cut the tomatoes into twenty-four ¼-inch slices. Mix the cornmeal, flour, salt, black pepper and cayenne in a bowl. Dip the tomatoes in the eggs; coat with the cornmeal mixture.

Heat the oil in a cast-iron skillet over medium heat to 375 degrees. Add the tomatoes a few at a time. Fry for 2 to 3 minutes per side or until golden brown; drain.

Toss the Boston lettuce, romaine and arugula in a bowl. Divide the lettuce mixture among 8 salad plates. Top each serving with 3 fried tomato slices. Drizzle with the mayonnaise.

To serve eight

BEEF AU POIVRE

12 TO 16 OUNCES BEEF TENDERLOIN, CUT INTO
   1½-INCH MEDALLIONS
   COARSELY GROUND PEPPER
1 TO 2 TABLESPOONS COGNAC
¾ CUP (ABOUT) WHIPPING CREAM

Coat the edges of the medallions with pepper. Heat a nonstick skillet over medium-high heat until hot. Brown the medallions in the hot skillet on all sides, including the pepper-coated edges. Remove the beef to a platter and cover to keep warm.

Stir the Cognac into the pan drippings. Ignite the Cognac; let the flames subside. Add just enough whipping cream to cover the bottom. Bring to a boil, stirring constantly. Cook until of a sauce consistency. Return the medallions to the skillet, stirring to coat. Serve immediately.

To serve two

GREEN BEAN BUNDLES

2 POUNDS FRESH GREEN BEANS, TRIMMED
1 POUND BACON, CUT INTO HALVES
1 CUP PACKED LIGHT BROWN SUGAR
2 TABLESPOONS LIGHT SOY SAUCE
½ TEASPOON GARLIC POWDER
½ CUP BUTTER

Blanch the green beans in boiling water in a saucepan for 5 minutes. Wrap 8 to 10 green beans with 1 bacon strip, twisting the ends of the bacon; secure with a wooden pick. Place in a dish. Repeat the process with the remaining green beans and bacon. Microwave the brown sugar, soy sauce, garlic powder and butter in a microwave-safe dish until blended, stirring twice. Pour over the green beans. Marinate in the refrigerator for 24 hours.

Arrange the bundles in a single layer in a baking dish. Reheat any marinade that has hardened in the dish and pour over the bundles. Bake at 350 degrees for 30 minutes. Broil for 5 minutes.

May substitute four 16-ounce cans drained and rinsed European-cut green beans for the fresh green beans. Or, instead of wrapping as bundles, arrange the green beans on a baking sheet with sides. Sprinkle with crumbled crisp-fried bacon. Pour the marinade over the beans. Marinate, covered, for 24 hours. Bake, uncovered, for 30 minutes. Spoon the beans and any remaining marinade into a serving bowl.

To serve eight

To prepare CHILEAN SEA BASS, *allow 8 ounces sea bass per guest. Arrange the sea bass on a baking sheet. Drizzle generously with lemon juice and sprinkle with oregano and Creole seasoning. Broil for 5 to 8 minutes and turn. Drizzle the other side generously with lemon juice and sprinkle with oregano and Creole seasoning. Broil for 5 to 8 minutes or until the fish flakes easily. Garnish with orange twists. For a more casual dinner, try salsa as a topping.*

BOW TIE PASTA WITH WALNUTS

1   CUP COARSELY CHOPPED WALNUTS
3   TABLESPOONS BUTTER
¼   CUP FLOUR
2   CUPS MILK
    SALT AND PEPPER TO TASTE
1   TABLESPOON CHOPPED FRESH BASIL AND OREGANO
1   (16-OUNCE) PACKAGE BOW TIE PASTA, COOKED
    AL DENTE, DRAINED
½   CUP FRESHLY GRATED PARMESAN CHEESE
½   CUP FRESHLY GRATED ROMANO CHEESE

Spread the walnuts on a baking sheet. Toast at 350 degrees for 10 minutes, stirring occasionally.

Melt the butter in a large saucepan over medium heat. Add the flour, stirring until blended. Add the milk gradually, whisking constantly. Cook until thickened, whisking constantly. Season with salt and pepper. Stir in the herbs. Remove from heat. Add the pasta and toss to coat. Add the Parmesan cheese and Romano cheese and toss. Spoon into a serving bowl. Top with the walnuts. Toss before serving.

To serve eight to twelve

ORANGE KNOTS

BREAD
1   ENVELOPE DRY
    YEAST
¼   CUP WARM WATER
1   CUP MILK,
    SCALDED
½   CUP SHORTENING
⅓   CUP SUGAR
1   TEASPOON SALT
5   TO 5½ CUPS
    SIFTED FLOUR

2   EGGS, BEATEN
2   TABLESPOONS
    GRATED ORANGE PEEL
¼   CUP ORANGE JUICE
ORANGE ICING
1   CUP SIFTED
    CONFECTIONERS' SUGAR
2   TABLESPOONS
    ORANGE JUICE
1   TEASPOON
    GRATED ORANGE PEEL

To prepare the bread, soften the yeast in the warm water and mix well. Combine the milk, shortening, sugar and salt in a bowl and mix well. Let stand until lukewarm. Stir in 2 cups of the flour. Add the eggs and mix well. Stir in the yeast mixture. Mix in the orange peel, orange juice and just enough of the remaining flour to make a soft dough. Let rest, covered, for 10 minutes. Knead the dough on a lightly floured surface for 8 to 10 minutes or until smooth and elastic. Place in a greased bowl, turning to coat the surface. Let rise, covered, in a warm place for 2 hours or until doubled in bulk. Punch the dough down. Let rest, covered, for 10 minutes.

Roll the dough into a ½-inch-thick 10x18-inch rectangle on a lightly floured surface. Cut into 10-inch strips ¾ inch wide. Tie each strip loosely into a knot. Arrange on a greased baking sheet and tuck the ends under. Let rise, covered, in a warm place for 45 minutes or until almost double in size. Bake at 400 degrees for 12 minutes or until light brown. Cool on a wire rack.

To prepare the icing, mix the confectioners' sugar, orange juice and orange peel in a bowl until of spreading consistency. Brush over the knots.

Makes two dozen

FALLEN-FOR-CHOCOLATE TORTE

CHOCOLATE TORTE

4	OUNCES SEMISWEET CHOCOLATE
1¾	CUPS PECANS OR WALNUTS
2	TABLESPOONS SUGAR
½	CUP UNSALTED BUTTER, SOFTENED
½	CUP SUGAR
3	EGGS, AT ROOM TEMPERATURE
1	TABLESPOON GRAND MARNIER OR RUM

CHOCOLATE GLAZE AND GARNISH

6	OUNCES SEMISWEET CHOCOLATE, CHOPPED
6	TABLESPOONS UNSALTED BUTTER
20	TO 24 PECAN OR WALNUT HALVES, TOASTED

To prepare the torte, grease a round 8-inch baking pan. Line the bottom with parchment paper or waxed paper. Grease the paper. Heat the chocolate in a double boiler over hot water until melted. Cool slightly. Process the pecans and 2 tablespoons sugar in a food processor until ground. Pour into a bowl. Process the butter and ½ cup sugar in a food processor until smooth. Add the eggs and Grand Marnier. Process until blended. Add the pecan mixture. Pulse once or twice until mixed. Pour the batter into the prepared pan. Bake at 375 degrees for 25 minutes. Cool in the pan on a wire rack for 20 minutes. Invert onto the wire rack to cool completely. May be prepared up to 2 days in advance and stored at room temperature or frozen, tightly wrapped, for future use.

To prepare the glaze and garnish, heat the chocolate and butter in a double boiler over hot water until blended, stirring occasionally. Dip half of each pecan into the glaze. Arrange on a baking sheet lined with waxed paper. Chill until set. Let the glaze stand until slightly thickened or of a consistency that will coat the torte.

To assemble, place the torte on a rack over a baking sheet. Pour the glaze onto the middle of the torte, tilting so the glaze flows down the side. Smooth the side with a knife dipped in hot water. Do not touch the top once the glaze is poured over or it will not be smooth. Arrange the chocolate-dipped pecans around the outer edge of the torte. May prepare 1 day in advance and store, uncovered, at room temperature.

To serve eight

ON OCCASION...

treat yourself or guests to AMARETTO NECTARINES—*served in silver bowls, of course. Cut 4 nectarines into halves and remove the pits. Arrange them on a baking sheet with sides. Sprinkle with a mixture of 10 crumbled vanilla wafers or shortbread cookies, ½ cup packed light brown sugar and 1 cup miniature chocolate chips. Dot with ½ cup butter. Drizzle with ¼ cup amaretto. Bake at 350 degrees for 10 to 15 minutes. Beat 1 cup whipping cream and ⅛ teaspoon unflavored gelatin in a mixer bowl until stiff peaks form. Serve with the warm nectarines.*

To keep your silver shining longer, use tarnish-resistant felt bags. The bags are not inexpensive, but you don't have to buy enough for all your silver at once. To start with, because it is exposure to air that tarnishes silver, keep flatware and small serving trays in sealable plastic bags. Wrap other items in large plastic bags and secure them with a twist tie. Then, treat yourself to one or two felt bags a year—or stitch your own. It's a great idea for a gift!

GOOD HEAVENS!!!

MENU

LAYERED MUSHROOM PASTRY

SALMON PÂTÉ

SPINACH AND CHEESE SQUARES

STUFFED NEW POTATOES

TWENTY-FOUR-HOUR FRUIT SALAD

MARINATED BLUE CRAB CLAWS

CHICKEN AND PECAN PASTRY PIE

HEAVENLY CHEESE GRITS

BANANA BLUEBERRY BREAD

CELEBRATION FRUIT DIPS

LEMON CLOUD DESSERT

SUNDAE ICE CREAM TORTE

PINEAPPLE AND MINT LEMONADE

TOMATO SPRITZER

Sleep, baby sleep.
Our cottage vale is deep:
The little lamb is on the green,
with woolly fleece so soft and clean.
Sleep, baby, sleep.

"LET'S SEE...THE DINING ROOM IS ALMOST READY. THE PINK TOILE COVERING THE TABLE...LATER I'LL SEW PILLOWS AND SHAMS FOR HER ROOM—MAYBE BEFORE SHE'S SIX. AND THE OLD FRAMED PICTURES OF ALL THE GRANDPARENTS —WHAT A SPECIAL TRADITION. I STILL NEED THE SILVER PITCHERS FULL OF HYDRANGEAS FROM THE YARD. THEY'LL BE PERFECT PARADING DOWN THE CENTER OF THE TABLE. WELL, THE MENU IS DONE. NOW, LET ME PUT OUT THE KEEPSAKES FOR EVERYONE IN THAT BASKET IN THE FRONT HALL...MAYBE I SHOULD REPEAT SOME OF THE TOILE IN THERE..." A SOUTHERN MAMA'S PROUD DAY...THE MOST CHERISHED OF OCCASIONS...THE DAY HER BABY IS CHRISTENED...OR IN SOME FAITHS, THE LITTLE ONES ARE "PRESENTED" OR "DEDICATED"...ALWAYS A BLESSED DAY FOR FRIENDS AND FAMILY. HONOR THEM WITH A TIME-TESTED SUMMER BRUNCH.

LAYERED MUSHROOM PASTRY

1	POUND MUSHROOMS, SLICED
¼	CUP CHOPPED ONION
3	TABLESPOONS BUTTER
1	TABLESPOON SHERRY
1	TEASPOON SALT
8	OUNCES CREAM CHEESE, SOFTENED, CHOPPED
1	CUP DRY BREAD CRUMBS
1	CUP SOUR CREAM
⅓	CUP CHOPPED FRESH PARSLEY
¼	CUP FRESH LEMON JUICE
2	LARGE CLOVES OF GARLIC, MINCED
½	TEASPOON PEPPER
20	FROZEN PHYLLO SHEETS
1	CUP BUTTER, ALMOST MELTED

Sauté the mushrooms and onion in 3 tablespoons butter in a skillet over medium heat. Stir in the sherry and salt. Cook for 5 minutes, stirring occasionally; drain. Add the cream cheese. Cook until mixed, stirring constantly. Stir in the bread crumbs, sour cream, parsley, lemon juice, garlic and pepper.

Thaw the pastry using package directions. Place 1 sheet of the pastry on the work surface, covering the remaining sheets with plastic wrap and a moist tea towel. Brush the pastry with some of the melted butter. Repeat the process to form a stack of 10 sheets.

Spoon half the mushroom mixture in a strip along the long edge, leaving a 3-inch border at each end. Roll to enclose the filling, tucking in the ends. Place seam side down on a greased baking sheet with sides. Brush with butter. Repeat the process with the remaining butter, pastry and mushroom mixture for a second roll.

Bake at 375 degrees for 25 to 30 minutes or until light brown. Cool for 5 minutes before slicing.

To serve sixteen

KEEPSAKES

Select a linen hemstitched or embroidered handkerchief or doily for each guest at the christening. Enclose the thought "When you see this keepsake, always think of me, and say a little prayer for what will come to be."

Make inexpensive color copy prints of treasured photographs to place in miniature picture frames and arrange about the buffet table. Remember your family, present and past generations, by incorporating them into the day's celebration.

A new tree or a perennial plant is a special way to commemorate the new addition to the family.

SALMON PATE

SHOWERS OF GIFTS

To be showered with gifts is certainly appropriate for the first-time mother. She will need the "biggies"—a stroller, highchair, and portable playpen—but what about the shower for baby number two? There is always monogrammed or silver anything, but maybe it's time to think of something new.

Treat the mother to something just for her: a basket of goodies to pamper her body and soul; a morning at a spa; or a manicure and pedicure.

Make a tape recording of Gram and Gramps: telling a favorite story; making wishes for the newborn; making a humorous conjecture about how tall, whose nose, perhaps the presidency . . .

Begin a holiday ornament collection for friends and family to add to each year by selecting a design that reminds them of that child's year—the new bicycle, a baseball theme, or a graduation cap. This treasured collection will make a one-of-a-kind wedding gift when that now-grown child marries.

Select an oversized picnic basket and fill it with diapering necessities to use as a second changing area.

2	ENVELOPES UNFLAVORED GELATIN
½	CUP COLD WATER
1	(16-OUNCE) CAN RED SALMON, DRAINED
1	CUP MAYONNAISE
2	TABLESPOONS VINEGAR
2	TABLESPOONS CATSUP
⅛	TEASPOON RED PEPPER
⅛	TEASPOON BLACK PEPPER
15	PIMENTO-STUFFED OLIVES, SLICED
2	HARD-COOKED EGGS, CHOPPED
2	TABLESPOONS SWEET PICKLE RELISH
1	CUP WHIPPING CREAM, WHIPPED
	ORNAMENTAL CABBAGE
	LEMON SLICES (OPTIONAL)
	CHOPPED FRESH PARSLEY (OPTIONAL)
	ASSORTED PARTY CRACKERS

Sprinkle the gelatin over the cold water in a saucepan. Let stand for 1 minute. Cook over low heat until the gelatin dissolves, stirring constantly. Remove from heat.

Remove the skin and bones from the salmon. Flake the salmon in a bowl. Stir in the mayonnaise, vinegar, catsup, red pepper and black pepper. Add the gelatin mixture, olives, eggs and pickle relish and stir well. Fold in the whipped cream.

Spoon into a greased 5½-cup mold. Chill, covered, for up to 2 days or until set. Invert onto a platter lined with ornamental cabbage. Garnish with lemon slices and parsley. Serve with assorted party crackers.

Makes 5½ cups

SPINACH AND CHEESE SQUARES

6   TABLESPOONS WHOLE WHEAT FLOUR
2   EGGS
1   (10-OUNCE) PACKAGE FROZEN CHOPPED SPINACH,
    THAWED, DRAINED
2   CUPS LOW-FAT COTTAGE CHEESE
6   OUNCES CHEDDAR CHEESE, SHREDDED
¼   TO ½ TEASPOON FRESHLY GROUND BLACK PEPPER
⅛   TEASPOON CAYENNE
⅛   TEASPOON NUTMEG (OPTIONAL)
3   TABLESPOONS WHEAT GERM

Beat the whole wheat flour and eggs in a bowl until smooth. Squeeze the moisture from the spinach. Add the spinach, cottage cheese, Cheddar cheese, black pepper, cayenne and nutmeg to the flour mixture and mix well. Spoon into a greased 9x13-inch baking pan. Sprinkle the prepared layers with the wheat germ.

Bake at 350 degrees for 45 minutes. Let stand for 10 minutes. Cut into 1½-inch squares.

To serve twelve

TWENTY-FOUR-HOUR FRUIT SALAD

1   (20-OUNCE) CAN JUICE-PACK PINEAPPLE CHUNKS
1   (8-OUNCE) CAN JUICE-PACK CRUSHED PINEAPPLE
1   (10-OUNCE) PACKAGE MINIATURE MARSHMALLOWS
    (OPTIONAL)
1   POUND RED GRAPES, CUT INTO HALVES
½   CUP SUGAR
1   EGG, LIGHTLY BEATEN
⅛   TEASPOON SALT, OR TO TASTE
1   CUP CHOPPED PECANS
1   CUP (OR MORE) WHIPPING CREAM, WHIPPED

Drain the pineapple chunks and crushed pineapple, reserving 2 tablespoons of the juice. Combine the pineapple with the marshmallows and grapes in a bowl and mix gently.

Mix the reserved juice, sugar, egg and salt in a saucepan. Cook over low heat until thickened, stirring frequently. Let stand until cool. Add to the fruit mixture and mix gently. Stir in the pecans. Chill, covered, in the refrigerator. Fold in the whipped cream. Chill, covered, for 24 hours.

To serve eight

For MARINATED BLUE CRAB CLAWS, *whisk the juice of 2 large lemons, ½ cup extra-virgin olive oil, ½ teaspoon Tabasco sauce and salt and pepper to taste in a bowl. Add 3 bay leaves and the desired amount of blue crab claws. Marinate, covered, in the refrigerator for 2 hours, stirring occasionally; drain. Discard the bay leaves. Serve chilled.*

CHICKEN AND PECAN PASTRY PIE

STUFFED NEW POTATOES

Combine 24 new potatoes and salt to taste with enough water to cover in a saucepan. Boil for 15 to 20 minutes or until tender but still firm and drain. Cut the potatoes into halves. Scoop out the pulp carefully with a melon baller, leaving shells and reserving the pulp. Mix the reserved pulp, 6 cloves of mashed roasted garlic, 2 tablespoons chopped fresh flat-leaf parsley and salt and pepper to taste in a bowl. Add just enough buttermilk to make of a piping consistency. Spoon into a pastry bag fitted with a large star tip and pipe into the potato shells.

1	CUP SHREDDED SHARP CHEDDAR CHEESE
1	CUP FLOUR
¾	CUP CHOPPED PECANS
½	TEASPOON SALT
¼	TEASPOON PAPRIKA
⅓	CUP VEGETABLE OIL
1	CUP SOUR CREAM
½	CUP CHICKEN BROTH
¼	CUP MAYONNAISE
3	EGGS, BEATEN
2	CUPS CHOPPED COOKED CHICKEN
½	CUP SHREDDED SHARP CHEDDAR CHEESE
¼	CUP MINCED ONION
¼	TEASPOON DILLWEED
3	TO 5 DROPS OF TABASCO SAUCE
¼	CUP PECAN HALVES

Mix 1 cup cheese, flour, ¾ cup pecans, salt and paprika in a bowl. Stir in the oil. Press over the bottom and up the side of a 9-inch quiche dish. Prick the bottom with a fork. Bake at 350 degrees for 10 minutes.

Combine the sour cream, broth, mayonnaise and eggs in a bowl and mix well. Stir in the chicken, ½ cup cheese, onion, dillweed and Tabasco sauce. Spoon into the prepared dish. Arrange ¼ cup pecan halves in a decorative pattern over the top. Bake at 325 degrees for 45 to 50 minutes or until light brown.

To serve six

HEAVENLY CHEESE GRITS

4   CUPS BOILING WATER
1   CUP QUICK-COOKING GRITS
1½ TEASPOONS SALT
6   TABLESPOONS BUTTER
1   CUP SHREDDED SHARP CHEDDAR CHEESE
1   TABLESPOON SHERRY
1½ TEASPOONS WORCESTERSHIRE SAUCE
1½ TEASPOONS HOT PEPPER SAUCE
1   EGG, BEATEN
¼   CUP SHREDDED SHARP CHEDDAR CHEESE

Combine the boiling water, grits and salt in a saucepan and mix well. Cook over low heat until most of the water is absorbed. Remove from heat. Stir in butter, 1 cup cheese, sherry, Worcestershire sauce and hot pepper sauce. Fold in the egg. Spoon into a greased baking dish. Sprinkle with ¼ cup cheese.

Bake at 300 degrees for 1 hour or until bubbly. May be prepared 1 day in advance and stored, unbaked, in the refrigerator. Bring to room temperature before baking.

To serve eight

BANANA BLUEBERRY BREAD

2   CUPS SELF-RISING FLOUR
¾   CUP SUGAR
½   CUP BUTTER, SOFTENED
2   EGGS, LIGHTLY BEATEN
3   BANANAS, MASHED
½   CUP (OR MORE) FRESH BLUEBERRIES
½   CUP CHOPPED NUTS (OPTIONAL)

Combine the flour, sugar, butter and eggs in a bowl and mix well. Fold in the bananas, blueberries and nuts. Spoon into an ungreased loaf pan. Bake at 375 degrees for 45 to 60 minutes or until the loaf tests done. Serve with honey butter.

Makes one loaf

FRIED GRITS *are about as close to southern comfort food as you can get. Spoon leftover grits (because, of course, you have made extra) into a square baking pan. Chill for 8 to 10 hours. Cut into squares and sprinkle with salt and pepper. Dust with flour—this is optional, but it reduces the spattering—and fry in a small amount of vegetable oil or bacon grease until brown on both sides. Drain and serve for breakfast or supper.*

LEMON CLOUD DESSERT

CELEBRATION FRUIT DIPS

To make TAFFY DIP, *blend 8 ounces softened cream cheese, 1 cup packed brown sugar and 1 teaspoon vanilla. Or, for* WHITE DIP, *add one 13-ounce jar marshmallow creme and 1 teaspoon vanilla to 8 ounces softened cream cheese. Serve both dips with whole fresh strawberries.*

For DON'T ASK DIP, *process one 16-ounce can cream of coconut, 8 ounces cubed Velveeta, 8 ounces whipped topping and 4 drops of red food coloring in a blender until creamy. Guests will not believe the ingredients, so it's better if we say, "don't ask."*

1   ANGEL FOOD CAKE
1   (14-OUNCE) CAN SWEETENED CONDENSED MILK
    JUICE OF 5 LEMONS
1   CUP WHIPPING CREAM, WHIPPED

Trim the brown edges from the cake with a serrated knife. Tear into bite-size pieces.

Mix the condensed milk and lemon juice in a bowl. Fold in the whipped cream and cake and mix gently. Spoon into a trifle dish. Chill, covered, for 24 hours.

For a finishing touch, refer to To GARNISH, To GARNISH on page 171.

To serve twelve

SUNDAE ICE CREAM TORTE

CRUST

1	CUP CHOCOLATE GRAHAM CRACKER CRUMBS
⅓	CUP MELTED BUTTER
3	TABLESPOONS SUGAR

CHOCOLATE FILLING

½	CUP CHOCOLATE CHIPS
½	GALLON CHOCOLATE ICE CREAM, SOFTENED
⅓	CUP CARAMEL SAUCE
1	CUP CHOPPED MACADAMIA NUTS
½	GALLON VANILLA ICE CREAM, SOFTENED
1	CUP PREPARED RASPBERRY PURÉE
1	PINT FRESH RASPBERRIES

To prepare the crust, mix the crumbs, butter and sugar in a bowl. Press over the bottom of a 9-inch springform pan. Bake at 350 degrees for 8 minutes. Let stand until cool.

To prepare the filling, fold the chocolate chips into the chocolate ice cream in a bowl. Spread in the prepared pan. Freeze for 1 hour. Spread with the caramel sauce. Freeze for 30 minutes.

Fold the macadamia nuts into the vanilla ice cream in a bowl. Spread over the caramel layer. Freeze for 6 hours.

Remove the side of the pan. Spread the raspberry purée over the top, allowing the purée to flow down the side. Garnish with the raspberries.

To serve twelve

ON OCCASION...

lift ordinary brunch drinks to extraordinary levels.

For TOMATO SPRITZER, *mix 24 ounces vegetable juice cocktail, 2 teaspoons lime juice and ½ teaspoon finely chopped fresh mint leaves. Chill. Add 1 to 2 liters of chilled club soda just before serving. Pour over crushed ice. Garnish each serving with a lime twist or celery spear.*

For PINEAPPLE AND MINT LEMONADE, *bring 1 cup sugar and ⅔ cup water to a boil. Boil for 1 minute. Remove from heat. Stir in 46 ounces pineapple juice, 1 cup lemon juice and ⅓ cup chopped fresh mint. Let stand for 15 minutes. Strain into a pitcher, discarding the mint. Pour over ice cubes in tall glasses.*

★★★★ A FOUR-STAR DAY ★★★★

★★★A FOUR-STAR DAY★★★

MENU

BLACK-EYED PEA DIP WITH
BENNE WAFERS

BY CAPTAIN'S ORDERS

MINI BLTs

CABBAGE SLAW SHRED

LAYERED TOMATO AND
MOZZARELLA SALAD

SPINACH SALAD WITH
STRAWBERRIES

CORN BREAD SALAD

KANSAS CITY BRISKET

NOT MAMA'S CHICKEN

STRAWBERRY BROWNIE TORTE

RED, WHITE AND
BLUEBERRY CRUNCH

SIMPLE CHOCOLATE CHIP COOKIES

UNCLE SAM'S HATS

FOUR-STAR LEMONADE

Everyone's invited, including Uncle Sam,
Break out the sparklers, play Kick the Can,
Sing Yankee Doodle, shout hip-hoo-ray!
Red, White, and Blue, A FOUR-STAR DAY!!!

THE SUN IS SHINING BRIGHTLY. FRIENDS AND FAMILY HAVE JOINED FOR AN ALL-AMERICAN CELEBRATION. DINNER ON THE LAWN...HANDMADE DRUMS AND HORNS...EVERY DRESSED-UP BICYCLE GEARS UP FOR AN ANNUAL PARADE. OLD GLORY BILLOWS IN THE EASY BREEZE. TIME TO GATHER FOR MORE BACKYARD GAMES. THE MOON IS PEEKING JUST ABOVE THE TREES. LIGHTNING BUGS HAVE BEGUN TO DISPLAY THEIR MAGIC WHILE THE CHILDREN PLAY FLASHLIGHT TAG. AT THE START OF PATRIOTIC TUNES, EVERYONE HUDDLES TOGETHER. THE "OOHS" AND "AAHS" BEGIN AS FIREWORKS BOOM AND SPARKLE THE ENTIRE SKY...WHAT A DAY THIS HAS BEEN!

BLACK-EYED PEA DIP

1   LARGE VIDALIA ONION, CHOPPED
2   TABLESPOONS BUTTER
1   (16-OUNCE) CAN BLACK-EYED PEAS, DRAINED, RINSED
1   (16-OUNCE) CAN BLACK BEANS, DRAINED, RINSED
1   (14-OUNCE) CAN ARTICHOKES, DRAINED, CHOPPED
½   CUP SOUR CREAM
½   CUP MAYONNAISE
1   ENVELOPE RANCH SALAD DRESSING MIX
2   CUPS SHREDDED MOZZARELLA CHEESE

Sauté the onion in the butter in a skillet until tender. Mix the peas, beans, artichokes, sour cream, mayonnaise and dressing mix in a bowl. Stir in the sautéed onions. Spoon into a round 11-inch baking dish. Bake at 350 degrees for 20 minutes. Sprinkle with the cheese. Bake for 10 minutes longer or until bubbly. Serve with Benne Wafers.

To serve twelve

BENNE WAFERS

1   PACKAGE PIE CRUST MIX
1   CUP BENNE SEEDS (SESAME SEEDS), TOASTED
    COARSELY GROUND SALT

Prepare the pie crust mix using package directions. Stir in the benne seeds. Roll the dough ⅛ inch thick on a lightly floured surface. Cut into small rounds. Arrange on a baking sheet. Bake at 400 degrees until golden brown. Sprinkle with salt. Remove to a wire rack to cool.

Makes three dozen wafers

THE MOO-MOO, WOOF-WOOF ADVENTURE

. . . or An Animal Treasure Hunt

Any number of people may play, but a crowd of 15 or more is the most fun! Choose teams that will allow 4 to 6 children and adults on each team, with an adult as "captain." Ask each captain to choose an animal, but do not tell why.

Scatter several hundred pieces of wrapped penny candy in a large yard or field. Give each captain a paper bag, with the instruction that the object of the game is to collect the most candy. Team members may locate the candy, but only the captain may pick it up. Team members indicate a find by using their chosen animal sound only.

Captains may "steal" another "animal's" candy, so players must be careful of the volume of their woofs and moos. Watch the "animal" come out in everyone. Wild Kingdom has never seen such!

Be sure to have a video camera ready.

MINI BLTs

12 TO 13 SLICES PARTY WHITE BREAD
1 POUND BACON
2 CUPS SOUR CREAM
2 TABLESPOONS MAYONNAISE
½ TEASPOON PEPPER
¼ TEASPOON GARLIC SALT
¼ TEASPOON SALT
CHERRY TOMATOES, SLICED, DRAINED

Cut circles from each slice of bread with a 2-inch round cutter. Arrange the bread rounds on an ungreased baking sheet. Toast at 375 degrees until brown on both sides, turning once. Let stand until cool. Store in a sealable plastic bag.

Fry the bacon in a skillet until crisp. Drain and crumble. Mix the bacon, sour cream, mayonnaise, pepper, garlic salt and salt in a bowl. Spread on the toasted rounds. Top each round with 1 or 2 tomato slices 30 minutes before serving. May top each round with shredded lettuce or serve the rounds on a platter of shredded lettuce.

Makes four dozen rounds

CABBAGE SLAW SHRED

½ CUP SLIVERED ALMONDS
8 TEASPOONS SESAME SEEDS
1 (10-OUNCE) PACKAGE FINELY SHREDDED ANGEL HAIR SLAW MIX
¾ CUP VEGETABLE OR CANOLA OIL
½ CUP SEASONED RICE VINEGAR
¼ CUP SUGAR
1 TEASPOON SALT
1 TEASPOON PEPPER
1 PACKAGE RICE NOODLES

Spread the almonds and sesame seeds on a baking sheet. Toast at 400 degrees for 5 minutes. Let stand until cool. Mix with the slaw mix in a bowl. Chill, covered, in the refrigerator.

Combine the oil, rice vinegar, sugar, salt and pepper in a jar with a tightfitting lid. Shake to mix. Chill in the refrigerator.

Toss the chilled slaw mixture and chilled dressing just before serving. Add the rice noodles and mix gently. Serve immediately. This is a perfect recipe to double to serve a larger crowd.

To serve six

If life gives you lemons, make FOUR-STAR LEMONADE. *To prepare 1 gallon of simple syrup for lemonade, shake 5 pounds of sugar in a gallon jug of hot water until the mixture is clear and dissolved. To make a gallon of lemonade, mix 2 cups lemon juice and 4 cups of the simple syrup in a gallon container. Roll the lemons on a counter or microwave them for 20 seconds to most easily extract the juice. Fill the container with water and crushed ice and stir. Then saunter to the back porch and lay claim to a rocker.*

LAYERED TOMATO AND MOZZARELLA SALAD

DIJON VINAIGRETTE

½ CUP OLIVE OIL

¼ CUP RED WINE VINEGAR

1 TABLESPOON DIJON MUSTARD

1 TABLESPOON MINCED FRESH PARSLEY

1 TEASPOON SUGAR

1 TEASPOON SALT

½ TEASPOON FRESHLY GROUND PEPPER

SALAD

LARGE RIPE TOMATOES, CUT INTO ¼-INCH SLICES

FRESH MOZZARELLA CHEESE, CUT INTO ¼-INCH SLICES

CHOPPED FRESH BASIL

CHOPPED FRESH PARSLEY

To prepare the vinaigrette, whisk the olive oil, wine vinegar, Dijon mustard, parsley, sugar, salt and pepper in a bowl until mixed.

To prepare the salad, layer the tomatoes and cheese alternately on a large serving platter, overlapping the slices on each layer. Sprinkle with basil and parsley. Drizzle with the vinaigrette.

To serve eight

SPINACH SALAD WITH STRAWBERRIES

POPPY SEED DRESSING

½ CUP SUGAR

¼ CUP CIDER VINEGAR

¼ CUP WHITE WINE VINEGAR

¼ CUP SALAD OIL

¼ CUP OLIVE OIL

2 TABLESPOONS SESAME SEEDS

1 TABLESPOON POPPY SEEDS

1½ TEASPOONS MINCED ONION

¼ TEASPOON PAPRIKA

SALAD

16 OUNCES SPINACH AND RED LEAF LETTUCE

1 PINT FRESH STRAWBERRIES, SLICED

¼ CUP SLICED ALMONDS, TOASTED IN BUTTER

To prepare the dressing, mix the sugar, cider vinegar, wine vinegar, salad oil, olive oil, sesame seeds, poppy seeds, onion and paprika in a jar with a tightfitting lid. Cover the jar and shake to mix. Chill until serving time.

To prepare the salad, mix the spinach and red leaf lettuce mixture with the strawberries in a salad bowl. Add the almonds and mix gently. Add the dressing, tossing to coat. May add one 11-ounce can of drained mandarin oranges to the salad if desired.

To serve eight

For a treat BY CAPTAIN'S ORDERS, *wrap ½ slices of bacon around Captain's Wafers and bake them at 300 degrees for 45 minutes or until they are crisp and brown.*

KANSAS CITY BRISKET

FRUIT KABOBS

Thread chunks of fruits onto bamboo skewers, alternating colors and shapes. Apples, bananas, pineapple, melons, pears, kiwifruit, and strawberries are good choices for kabobs. To serve them, cut a watermelon into halves, use a melon baller to cut the better parts, and scoop out the rest. Use a round or star-shape cutter to score the edge. Cut into scallops or points with a sharp knife. Trim the bottom if necessary to help it sit evenly, and arrange the kabobs inside.

1   (5-POUND) BEEF BRISKET
3   TABLESPOONS (ABOUT) ONION SALT
3   TABLESPOONS (ABOUT) CELERY SALT
3   TABLESPOONS (ABOUT) GARLIC POWDER
¼   CUP LIQUID SMOKE
3   TABLESPOONS WORCESTERSHIRE SAUCE
1   CUP BARBECUE SAUCE
¼   CUP RED WINE

Cut a sheet of heavy-duty foil large enough to wrap the brisket generously. Place the brisket in the center of the foil. Sprinkle all sides generously with the onion salt, celery salt and garlic powder until heavily coated. Drizzle with the liquid smoke. Wrap very tightly to seal.

Place the brisket in a roasting pan. Marinate in the refrigerator for 8 to 10 hours. Loosen the foil and discard the marinade. Drizzle with the Worcestershire sauce and rewrap tightly.

Bake at 275 degrees for 5 hours. Fold back the foil edges, exposing the top surface of the brisket and discard the juices. Pour a mixture of the barbecue sauce and red wine over the brisket. Bake for 1 hour longer. Remove the brisket to a cutting board. Slice with an electric knife. Serve hot or at room temperature.

Add shallots during the last hour of baking if desired. Vary the marinade and thus the flavor with this marinade recipe: 2 tablespoons liquid smoke, beef broth to taste, 2 cloves of minced garlic, onion salt and celery salt.

To serve ten to twelve

NOT MAMA'S CHICKEN

2	POUNDS BONELESS SKINLESS CHICKEN BREAST HALVES
½	CUP FLOUR
½	TEASPOON SALT
⅛	TEASPOON PEPPER
2	EGGS, BEATEN
	VEGETABLE OIL FOR FRYING
⅓	CUP SOY SAUCE
⅓	CUP HONEY
1	TABLESPOON DRY SHERRY
1	TEASPOON MINCED GINGERROOT
1	CLOVE OF GARLIC, MINCED OR CRUSHED
2	TABLESPOONS SESAME SEEDS (OPTIONAL)

Cut the chicken into 2-inch pieces or into 1-inch pieces if serving as an appetizer. Mix the flour, salt and pepper in a bowl. Dip the chicken in the eggs and coat with the flour mixture.

Add oil to a skillet to measure ½ inch. Heat over medium-high heat until hot. Add the chicken to the skillet ½ at a time. Fry for 6 to 8 minutes or until golden brown on all sides, turning frequently; drain.

Heat the soy sauce, honey, sherry, gingerroot and garlic in a saucepan until hot. Dip the chicken in the soy sauce mixture. Place on a rack over a baking pan. Sprinkle with the sesame seeds.

Bake at 250 degrees for 10 minutes; brush with the remaining soy sauce mixture. Bake for 10 minutes longer. Serve immediately.

To serve four

ON OCCASION...

include the corn bread in a
CORN BREAD SALAD.

Crumble 8 corn muffins into a salad bowl. Mix 1 drained 8-ounce can green peas, 1 drained 11-ounce can Mexicorn, 2 chopped hard-cooked eggs, ½ to 1 chopped green bell pepper, ½ to 1 chopped onion, ½ to 1 cup mayonnaise and salt and pepper to taste in a bowl. Spoon over the crumbled muffins and toss lightly.

STRAWBERRY BROWNIE TORTE

1   (22-OUNCE) PACKAGE BROWNIE MIX
1   (14-OUNCE) CAN SWEETENED CONDENSED MILK
½   CUP COLD WATER
1   (6-OUNCE) PACKAGE VANILLA INSTANT PUDDING MIX
6   OUNCES WHIPPED TOPPING
1   QUART STRAWBERRIES, SLICED

Prepare the brownie mix using package directions. Spoon into 2 greased round 9-inch baking pans. Bake at 350 degrees for 20 minutes. Let stand until cool.

Combine the condensed milk and cold water in a bowl and mix well. Whisk in the pudding mix. Chill for 5 minutes. Fold in the whipped topping.

Layer the brownie layers, pudding mixture and strawberries ½ at a time on a chilled round serving platter, ending with the strawberries. Chill until serving time.

Slice the brownie layers horizontally into halves for 4 layers if desired. Your company will be so impressed and you will never tell how easy the torte was to prepare.

To serve twelve

RED, WHITE AND BLUEBERRY CRUNCH

3   PINTS MIXED BERRIES
1   TABLESPOON LEMON JUICE
¼   CUP MELTED BUTTER
1   CUP SUGAR
1   CUP FLOUR
1   TEASPOON BAKING POWDER
    SALT TO TASTE
1   CUP MILK

Toss the berries with the lemon juice in a bowl. Pour the butter into a 9x9-inch baking pan, tilting the pan to coat the bottom. Add the berries.

Combine the sugar, flour, baking powder and salt in a bowl and mix well. Stir in the milk. Pour over the berries. Bake at 350 degrees for 35 minutes or until golden brown.

To serve eight

❧

If you ever wondered about the difference between a tart, a torte, and a trifle, here's the answer. A tart is a small pie for an individual serving; it does not have a top crust. It can have a sweet filling such as fruit, jam, or custard, or a savory filling such as meat or cheese. A torte is a rich cake made with beaten egg whites, nuts, fruit, and very little flour. It can have several thin filled layers. A trifle is a rich dessert made of layers of sponge cake soaked in wine or liqueur and served with whipped cream, custard, or fruit.

SIMPLE CHOCOLATE CHIP COOKIES

2 CUPS PACKED BROWN SUGAR
1 CUP BUTTER, SOFTENED
2 EGGS
4 CUPS BAKING MIX
2 CUPS MILK CHOCOLATE CHIPS

Beat the brown sugar and butter in a bowl until blended. Add the eggs, stirring until blended. Mix in the baking mix and chocolate chips. Drop by teaspoonfuls onto an ungreased cookie sheet. Bake at 350 degrees for 10 minutes or until light brown.

Makes three dozen cookies

UNCLE SAM'S HATS

1 QUART RASPBERRY JUICE
1 PINT FROZEN VANILLA YOGURT
2 CUPS COLD WATER
¾ CUP FRESH OR FROZEN BLUEBERRIES

Arrange 10 plastic or paper cups on a tray or baking sheet. Pour enough raspberry juice in each cup to measure 1 inch. Freeze until partially set. Place 1 popsicle stick in the center of each cup. Freeze until set.

Blend 4 large scoops of frozen vanilla yogurt with 1 cup of the cold water in a bowl. Pour enough of the yogurt mixture in each cup to measure 1 inch. Freeze until set.

Process the remaining cup of cold water with 1 large scoop of frozen vanilla yogurt and the blueberries in a blender until smooth. Spoon over the prepared layers. Freeze for 8 to 10 hours.

Slide the popsicles out of the cups to serve.

To serve ten

ICE CREAM SANDWICHES

That hot summer day will probably cause someone to think of an ice cream sandwich. Start with any cookies you might have—Simple Chocolate Chip Cookies, butter cookies, graham crackers, vanilla wafers, or chewy oatmeal cookies. Let your favorite ice cream soften on the counter for 15 to 20 minutes; if it starts to drip down the counter, you have waited too long! Place a small scoop of ice cream on the flat side of a cookie, top with another cookie, and gently press. Roll the ice cream edges in sprinkles, chips, or chopped nuts. Wrap each sandwich in plastic wrap gathered at the top and tied with curling ribbon. Freeze for 1 hour or longer. Theoretically these will keep in the freezer for about a week, but they never last that long!

JUST A NIP IN THE AIR

AND THOSE FIRST

TOUCHES OF AUTUMN...

REMINDERS TO EMBRACE

THE MANY THINGS IN

OUR LIVES THAT WE HAVE

TO BE THANKFUL FOR...

DAYS TO ENJOY AS

A GIFT FROM NATURE...

MENUS

HUNTER'S BREAKFAST

MOUNTAIN RETREAT

1031 PUMPKIN ROAD

HAYRIDES AND HOEDOWNS

A VERY LOVELY EVENING

A NIP IN THE AIR

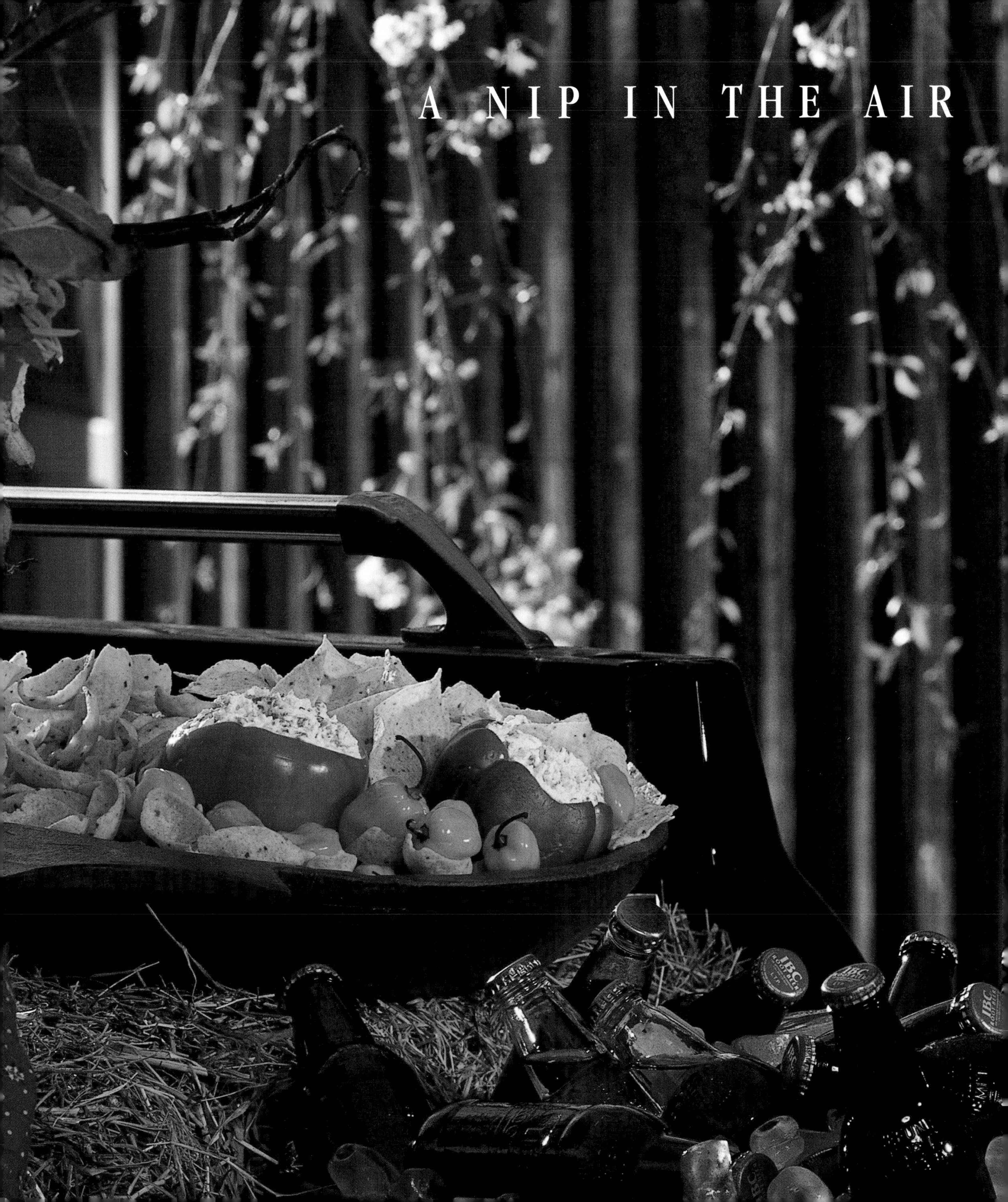

HUNTER'S BREAKFAST

It was cold out there. The sun, coming up between the trees, glints just over the top of the fence line. Time to head back in. The frost begins to melt a bit, but the ground is still crisp under his step. He sees his breath in the chilled air, glad for an extra layer of clothing. Some still find it worth rising early... "Come on, Shep. Bet you're wanting breakfast too..." The fog lifts and he is able to see the house across the field. He sees the kitchen with all the lights on. Looks like folks are starting to stir. And breakfast is almost ready—plates filled with roasted potatoes, peppers and onions, maybe an omelet, sizzled strips of bacon..."Let's get back, ol' boy." A favorite beginning to a crisp fall day. Breakfast is often the simplest of meals made from the most basic of ingredients—grains, fruits, dairy products, eggs, and perhaps meat. Vital for energy, breakfast begins our "every day." Its real intrigue might be that it is the one meal that always speaks of "home."

Hunter's Choice Omelet

2 EGGS
   SALT AND WHITE PEPPER TO TASTE
1 TABLESPOON BUTTER
¼ CUP CRUMBLED COOKED PORK SAUSAGE
¼ CUP SAUTÉED MUSHROOMS
¼ CUP SOUR CREAM

Whisk the eggs, salt and white pepper in a bowl until blended. Heat the butter in a 9- or 10-inch omelet pan over medium heat until melted. Add the eggs, tilting the pan to coat the bottom.

Cook until the edge begins to set. Lift the edge with an ovenproof rubber spatula, allowing the uncooked egg to flow under. Remove from heat when the bottom is thickened but not set. Spread with a mixture of the sausage, mushrooms and sour cream and fold over. Serve immediately.

To serve one

A Well-Seasoned Skillet

Every household needs a cast-iron skillet, seasoned to perfection. This timeless standby conducts heat evenly, allows for cooking at lower temperatures, and keeps food warmer longer. If you aren't lucky enough to have inherited this kitchen treasure, purchase a new one. To season the skillet, wipe it with a thin coat of vegetable shortening (do not use butter or margarine), using a cloth or paper towel and covering the entire surface. Place the skillet in a 300- to 350-degree oven for 45 to 60 minutes. Remove it from the oven and wipe dry with a paper towel. Use only mild detergents to clean the skillet and never use a scouring pad. Wipe it with vegetable shortening after each use and cleaning before storing. Some cooks dry the skillet on the stovetop and allow it to cool before storing. A well-seasoned skillet will turn black with use and develop a thin crust that will seal the surface of the iron and prevent sticking and rust.

RUSTIC ROASTED POTATOES

½ CUP VEGETABLE OIL
6 LARGE RUSSET POTATOES, CUT INTO 1½-INCH PIECES
1 LARGE WHITE ONION, CUT INTO 1-INCH PIECES
2 CLOVES OF GARLIC, SLICED
1 TEASPOON THYME
   SALT AND FRESHLY GROUND PEPPER

Heat the oil in a baking pan at 425 degrees for 15 minutes.

Combine the potatoes, onion, garlic, thyme, salt and pepper in a bowl and mix well. Add the potatoes to the hot oil carefully, stirring to coat. Bake for 1 hour, stirring occasionally.

Broil for 4 to 5 minutes or until the potatoes are crisp.

To serve ten

APPLE TIME PANCAKE

3 LARGE GRANNY SMITH APPLES, PEELED, THINLY SLICED
6 TABLESPOONS SUGAR
1 TEASPOON GROUND CINNAMON
2 TABLESPOONS UNSALTED BUTTER
3 EGGS
½ CUP FLOUR
½ CUP MILK
1 TABLESPOON SOUR CREAM
1 TEASPOON GRATED LEMON ZEST
¼ TEASPOON SALT

Sauté the apples, sugar and cinnamon in the butter in an ovenproof skillet for 3 to 5 minutes. Remove from heat. Spread the apple mixture evenly over the bottom of the skillet.

Beat the eggs in a mixer bowl until frothy. Add the flour, milk, sour cream, lemon zest and salt. Beat until a smooth batter forms. Pour over the apple mixture. Bake at 400 degrees for 25 minutes or until puffed and golden brown. Cut into wedges. Serve immediately.

To serve two to four

❧

Any hunter will be glad to start the day with PEPPERED RANCH BACON. *Sprinkle 1 pound of thick-sliced bacon with coarsely ground black peppercorns, pressing the pepper into the bacon with the back of a spoon. Fry the bacon in a cast-iron skillet over medium heat until crisp and drain.*

SURE SHOT BISCUITS AND SAUSAGE GRAVY

BISCUITS
2 CUPS WHITE LILY SELF-RISING FLOUR
1 CUP WHIPPING CREAM

SAUSAGE GRAVY
1 POUND BULK SAUSAGE, SLICED
2 TABLESPOONS FLOUR
1 CUP (OR MORE) MILK
SALT AND PEPPER TO TASTE

To prepare the biscuits, mix the flour with the whipping cream in a bowl. Drop into 8 mounds onto an ungreased baking sheet. Bake at 400 degrees for 12 minutes.

To prepare the gravy, cook the sausage in a skillet until brown, stirring until crumbly. Remove the sausage with a slotted spoon to paper towels to drain, reserving 2 to 3 tablespoons of the pan drippings.

Add the flour to the reserved pan drippings and mix well. Cook over medium heat until blended, stirring constantly. Whisk in ½ cup of the milk.

Cook over medium-high heat until smooth, whisking constantly. Stir in the remaining ½ cup milk. Cook until of the desired consistency, adding additional milk ½ cup at a time as needed and stirring constantly. Add the sausage and season with salt and pepper. Spoon over hot biscuits.

To serve eight

BISCUIT TRIMMINGS

APPLE BUTTER

Cut 4 pounds of peeled tart apples into quarters. Cook in 1 cup water and 1 cup apple cider until tender, stirring occasionally; drain. Press through a food mill. Mix the apple pulp, the grated peel and juice of 2 lemons, 2 teaspoons cinnamon, 1 teaspoon ground cloves and ½ teaspoon allspice in a saucepan.

Simmer over low heat for 3 to 4 hours or until thickened and dark brown in color, stirring occasionally. Store, covered, in the refrigerator for 1 to 2 weeks or ladle into hot sterilized jars, leaving a ½-inch headspace; seal with 2-piece lids for longer storage.

PEAR HONEY

Peel 10 pears and combine with ½ cup Fruit-Fresh, 1 tablespoon salt and water to cover in a bowl. Let stand for several minutes. Remove the pears 1 at a time and process. Measure 8 to 10 cups ground pears and combine with 8 cups sugar, one 8-ounce can crushed pineapple and ¼ cup lemon juice in a large saucepan; mix well.

Cook over medium-high heat for 30 minutes or until the pears are tender and the mixture is thickened, stirring constantly. Ladle into hot sterilized pint jars, leaving a ½-inch headspace; seal with 2-piece lids. Process in a hot water bath for 10 to 15 minutes.

SAUSAGE PINWHEELS

1   (8-COUNT) CAN CRESCENT ROLLS
8   OUNCES CRUMBLED BULK SAUSAGE, COOKED, DRAINED

Unroll crescent roll dough; press perforations to seal. Sprinkle with the sausage. Roll as for a jelly roll; seal ends. Cut into 1-inch slices.

Arrange the slices on a baking sheet. Bake at 375 degrees for 8 to 10 minutes or until golden brown.

Substitute a mixture of cinnamon and sugar, chopped walnuts and raisins for the sausage for a sweet treat.

Makes one and one-half dozen pinwheels

BANANA BARS

¾   CUP MARGARINE, SOFTENED
½   CUP PACKED BROWN SUGAR
1   EGG
4   CUPS QUICK-COOKING OATS
1½ CUPS MASHED RIPE BANANAS
½   TEASPOON SALT
½   TEASPOON CINNAMON
½   CUP CHOPPED PECANS
½   CUP RAISINS
¼   CUP CHOPPED DRIED APRICOTS

Beat the margarine and brown sugar in a mixer bowl until light and fluffy, scraping the bowl occasionally. Add the egg. Beat until blended. Stir in the oats, bananas, salt and cinnamon. Add the pecans, raisins and apricots and mix well.

Spoon the batter into a greased 9x13-inch baking pan. Bake at 350 degrees for 45 minutes. Cool in pan on a wire rack. Cut into 2-inch bars.

May freeze for future use. Great for hunting and fishing trips, after-school snacks or lunch boxes.

Makes one dozen bars

TAKALONGAPAK

8   OUNCES SPICY BULK SAUSAGE
1   MEDIUM GREEN BELL PEPPER, CHOPPED
1   MEDIUM ONION, CHOPPED
8   EGGS, BEATEN
1   (4-OUNCE) JAR CHOPPED PIMENTOS, DRAINED
½   TEASPOON SALT
¼   TEASPOON FRESHLY GROUND PEPPER
8   FLOUR TORTILLAS
8   OUNCES SHREDDED COLBY-JACK CHEESE

Brown the sausage in a skillet, stirring until crumbly; drain. Add the green pepper and onion. Cook until the vegetables are tender, stirring frequently. Stir in the eggs, pimentos, salt and pepper. Cook just until the eggs are set, stirring gently. Spoon the egg mixture over the tortillas and sprinkle with the cheese. Fold in the ends of each tortilla and roll to enclose the filling. Wrap each tortilla in foil.

Arrange foil-wrapped tortillas in a single layer in a 9x13-inch baking dish. Chill for 8 to 10 hours. Bake at 325 degrees for 20 to 25 minutes or just until heated through.

Grab and go. On a chilly morning, these tortillas make excellent hand warmers too!

To serve eight

ON OCCASION...

greet your returning hunter with a BANANA AND CRANBERRY COMPOTE. *Slice 4 bananas lengthwise into halves. Arrange cut side up in a greased baking dish and brush with 2 tablespoons melted butter. Spoon a mixture of 1 cup whole cranberry sauce, ¼ cup packed brown sugar, 3 tablespoons dry sherry and ⅛ teaspoon salt over the bananas. Bake at 350 degrees for 15 to 20 minutes, basting at least once. Sprinkle with 2 tablespoons roasted slivered almonds just before serving.*

MOUNTAIN RETREAT

MOUNTAIN RETREAT

Menu

Country Pâté

Herbed Sausage Bread

Avocado and Grapefruit Salad
with Tart French Dressing

Baked Quail with Mushrooms

Pan-Fried Mountain Trout

Sautéed Sugar Snap Peas

Rowland's Bleu Cheese Grits

Mountain Apple Pie

Butterscotch Pie

Hot Buttered Rum

Having traversed each curve along the graveled drive, the low wooden porch is a welcome sight. Stacked heavy timbers make for a cozy cabin that rests in the sheltered hillside. Mountain laurel, pine, hickory, and oak exhibit nature's grand touch to the rich landscape. The meandering stream runs full with native trout. Just imagine the day's catch—seared, coated with herbs, and shared with the farm table offerings. Firelight glows and softens the fall of evening...votive candles flicker inside cored apples. Kitchen cupboards, after being lovingly plundered, yield up their assortment of flo-blue china and found flatware. Age-old candlesticks nestle on the table among collected pewter platters, plates, and mugs. A wooded hideaway along the Blue Ridge. Time spent browsing at a country fair or bidding in a local antiques auction house. Cast into a chilled creek. Hike amongst the fall foliage. Or take claim of the porch rocker and do nothing at all...Renew your spirit and discover again the simple pleasures.

COUNTRY PATE

1	SMALL ONION, FINELY CHOPPED
1	CLOVE OF GARLIC, CRUSHED
1	TABLESPOON BUTTER, SOFTENED
8	OUNCES CHICKEN LIVERS
¼	CUP BUTTER, SOFTENED
1	TABLESPOON BRANDY
⅛	TEASPOON THYME
	SALT AND PEPPER TO TASTE

Cook the onion and garlic in 1 tablespoon butter in a skillet over low heat until tender, stirring constantly. Add the livers. Sauté for 5 minutes. Remove from heat. Let stand until cool.

Process the liver mixture in a food processor or blender until smooth. Add ¼ cup butter. Process until blended. Add the brandy, thyme, salt and pepper. Process until smooth. Spoon into a 2-cup terrine or mold. Chill until set.

Invert onto a serving platter. Serve with brown bread and butter and/or melba toast. Serve leftovers as a spread on croissants.

Makes 2 cups

HERBED SAUSAGE BREAD

2	LOAVES FROZEN BREAD DOUGH
1½	POUNDS SEASONED BULK SAUSAGE
2	EGGS
1½	TABLESPOONS PARSLEY
½	TEASPOON OREGANO
⅛	TEASPOON SALT
1	POUND MOZZARELLA CHEESE, SHREDDED
8	OUNCES CHEDDAR CHEESE, SHREDDED
1	TO 2 EGG WHITES, LIGHTLY BEATEN

Thaw the bread dough for 8 to 10 hours. Reserve a small amount of the dough for decoration. Pat the remaining portions of each loaf over the bottom and up the sides of 2 ungreased baking sheets with sides.

Brown the sausage in a skillet, stirring until crumbly; drain.

Beat the eggs lightly in a bowl. Stir in the parsley, oregano and salt. Add the mozzarella cheese and Cheddar cheese and mix well. Stir in the sausage. Spread over the dough. Roll as for a jelly roll. Decorate with the reserved dough in a scroll design. Brush with the egg whites. Bake at 350 degrees for 45 minutes or until golden brown.

Makes two loaves

Baked Quail with Mushrooms

Sauteed Sugar Snap Peas

Sauté 1½ pounds sugar snap peas in ¼ cup butter in a skillet over medium-high heat for 3 to 4 minutes. Sprinkle with ½ teaspoon sugar and salt and pepper to taste and toss to mix. Serve immediately.

⅓	CUP FLOUR
½	TEASPOON SALT
½	TEASPOON PEPPER
8	QUAIL
6	TABLESPOONS BUTTER
8	OUNCES FRESH MUSHROOMS, SLICED
2	TABLESPOONS BUTTER
¼	CUP PLUS 1 TABLESPOON FLOUR
2	CUPS CANNED DILUTED CHICKEN BROTH
½	CUP DRY SHERRY
2	CUPS HOT COOKED RICE

Mix ⅓ cup flour, salt and pepper. Coat the quail on all sides with the flour mixture. Sauté the quail in 6 tablespoons butter in a skillet until brown on both sides. Remove the quail with a slotted spoon to a 1½-quart baking dish, reserving the pan drippings.

Sauté the mushrooms in 2 tablespoons butter in a skillet until tender; drain. Stir ¼ cup plus 1 tablespoon flour into the reserved pan drippings. Cook for 1 minute, stirring constantly. Add the broth and sherry gradually, stirring constantly. Cook over medium heat until thickened, stirring constantly. Stir in the mushrooms. Pour over the quail.

Bake, covered, at 350 degrees for 1 hour. Serve over the hot cooked rice.

To serve four

PAN-FRIED MOUNTAIN TROUT

FRESH BASIL SPRIGS

FRESH OREGANO SPRIGS

FLAT-LEAF PARSLEY SPRIGS

6 TO 12 SMALL TO MEDIUM
WHOLE TROUT, CLEANED

LEMONS, CUT INTO HALVES,
THINLY SLICED

FRESH CHIVES

2 CUPS FLOUR

1 TEASPOON SALT

1 TEASPOON PEPPER

1 CUP BUTTER

½ CUP OLIVE OIL

FRESH LEMON JUICE

Tie the basil, oregano and parsley into small bundles. Stuff each trout with several herb bundles and 2 to 3 slices of lemon. Tie each trout around the middle with chives.

Mix the flour, salt and pepper. Coat the trout with the flour mixture. Fry the trout in a mixture of the butter and olive oil in a skillet for 5 minutes per side or until golden brown; drain. Arrange the trout on a serving platter. Drizzle with lemon juice. Serve immediately.

To serve six to eight

ROWLAND'S BLEU CHEESE GRITS

4 CUPS WATER

2 CUPS CHICKEN BROTH

1 TEASPOON SALT

1 TEASPOON PEPPER

2 CUPS GRITS

¼ CUP BUTTER

8 OUNCES BLEU CHEESE

6 OUNCES BABY BLEU SAGA

Combine the water, broth, salt and pepper in a saucepan and mix well. Bring to a boil. Stir in the grits and butter.

Cook using package directions. Remove from heat. Stir in the cheeses. Serve warm with sliced tomatoes.

To serve six to eight

ON OCCASION...

gather with eight to ten friends, for easy times and lively conversation—a dinner group. Alternate homes and meet once a month. The host house establishes the menu, serves the main dish, and selects a category for each guest to bring, including the appetizer, salad, side dish, bread, or dessert. The meal will come together beautifully with little trouble for anyone.

The evening can be formal, casual, or even a theme party on occasion, according to the hosts' preference. And perhaps the next time you host the dinner group, introduce something unique. Take the opportunity to deliver a humorous heartfelt toast in appreciation of the good company. Tuck a tiny trinket under the plate of each guest—a silly roadside find, like a silver state spoon or a jigger glass from a famous vacation spot. Alter the setting by serving in a different location. Turn off the telephones, televisions, and such. Make the lighting a soothing element. Shuffle place cards to keep conversation spirited. Venture something new—you're among friends!

MOUNTAIN APPLE PIE

AVOCADO AND GRAPEFRUIT SALAD WITH TART FRENCH DRESSING

Mix 1½ tablespoons sugar, 1 teaspoon paprika, 1 teaspoon dry mustard, ½ teaspoon salt and ½ teaspoon white pepper. Add ½ cup vegetable oil gradually, whisking constantly. Whisk in 2 tablespoons fresh lemon juice and 1 tablespoon cider vinegar. Chill, covered, until serving time.

Separate the sections of a chilled grapefruit and cut an avocado into wedges. Arrange the sections and wedges alternately on each of 4 lettuce-lined salad plates. Drizzle with the salad dressing.

CRUST

1½	CUPS FLOUR
½	TEASPOON CINNAMON
½	CUP BUTTER
¼	CUP APPLE JUICE

FILLING

1	CUP SOUR CREAM
¾	CUP SUGAR
¼	CUP FLOUR
1	TEASPOON VANILLA EXTRACT
½	TEASPOON SALT
½	TEASPOON CINNAMON
1	EGG, LIGHTLY BEATEN
6	APPLES, PEELED, SLICED

TOPPING

⅔	CUP FLOUR
¼	CUP PACKED BROWN SUGAR
2	TABLESPOONS SUGAR
¼	CUP PECANS
6	TABLESPOONS BUTTER

To prepare the crust, combine the flour and cinnamon in a food processor container. Process until mixed. Add the butter. Process until crumbly. Add the apple juice gradually, processing constantly until the mixture forms a ball. Chill in the refrigerator. Roll the dough into a 12-inch circle on a lightly floured surface. Fit into a 9-inch pie plate; flute the edge.

To prepare the filling, mix the sour cream, sugar, flour, vanilla, salt, cinnamon and egg in a bowl and mix well. Stir in the apples. Spoon into the prepared pie plate.

To prepare the topping, combine the flour, brown sugar, sugar and pecans in a food processor container. Add the butter. Process until crumbly. Sprinkle over the top. Bake at 350 degrees for 60 to 70 minutes or until golden brown.

To serve six

BUTTERSCOTCH PIE

1   (12-OUNCE) CAN EVAPORATED MILK
1   CUP WHOLE MILK
1   CUP PACKED LIGHT BROWN SUGAR
5   TABLESPOONS FLOUR
½   TEASPOON SALT
3   TABLESPOONS BUTTER
1   TEASPOON VANILLA EXTRACT
3   EGG YOLKS
1   BAKED (9-INCH) PIE SHELL
3   EGG WHITES, AT ROOM TEMPERATURE
6   TABLESPOONS SUGAR

Mix the evaporated milk and whole milk in a bowl. Combine the brown sugar, flour and salt in a double boiler and mix well. Stir in the milk mixture, butter and vanilla. Cook over simmering water until thickened, stirring constantly with a wooden spoon. Cook, covered, for 10 minutes, stirring occasionally.

Beat the egg yolks in a bowl until blended. Stir ¼ cup of the hot custard mixture into the egg yolks; stir the egg yolks into the hot mixture. Cook for 2 to 3 minutes, stirring constantly. Remove from heat. Let stand until cool. Spoon into the pie shell.

Beat the egg whites in a mixer bowl until soft peaks form. Add 5 tablespoons of the sugar gradually, beating constantly until stiff peaks form. Spread over the filling, sealing to the edge. Sprinkle with the remaining 1 tablespoon sugar. Bake at 325 degrees just until light brown.

To serve six

HOT BUTTERED RUM

Nothing could be more welcome in a mountain retreat than HOT BUTTERED RUM *by the fire. Beat 1 pound softened butter, 1 pound light brown sugar, 1 pound confectioners' sugar, 2 teaspoons cinnamon and 2 teaspoons nutmeg in a large freezer-proof bowl until light and fluffy. Fold in 1 quart softened vanilla ice cream until blended. Freeze until firm. To serve, thaw slightly. Spoon 3 tablespoons of the frozen mixture into a large mug. Add 1 ounce rum and the desired amount of boiling water and mix well. Top with whipped cream. Refreeze the unused ice cream mixture for future use.*

1031 PUMPKIN ROAD

MENU

Garlic Spinach Dip

Cheese Artichoke Dip

Bits and Bones

Italian Beef Sandwiches

Bread-and-Butter Pickles

Potato Caskets

Spooky Apple Pizzas

Chocolate Peanut Butter
Boo Bites

Chewy Chocolate Toads

Brown Sugar Bars

Bat's Brew

Boo! It's that scary time of year again! So what'll it be? A ghoulish ghost, an action hero, a beautiful bride (...a ballerina costume next year!). Halloween! Trick or Treat! The one time of year when we can all officially act like nine-year-olds. This time, enjoy the mischievousness outside—then the spilled Bat's Brew is no-big-deal. At five o'clock, add costumed children for a neighborhood monster bash! Have a costume parade! The kids will enjoy seeing each other's "duds" for the night, instead of a brief glance with dad's flashlight as they run down the street...Capture each hooligan on film with an "instant" photo. For a wacky version of ring toss, paint points (50, 40, 30...) on several pumpkins. From a starting line, allow each player three tosses with a hula hoop. Highest total wins!...Set up a "pumpkin-painting" table. Let little hands paint eerie faces on take-home pumpkins using tempera paint and basic brushes for creative magic!...And don't forget mounds of creepy stuff...Now that's a screeeeam!!!

GARLIC SPINACH DIP

1 (10-OUNCE) PACKAGE FROZEN
   CHOPPED SPINACH, THAWED
½ MEDIUM ONION, CHOPPED
1 TABLESPOON BUTTER
2 (6-OUNCE) JARS MARINATED
   ARTICHOKE HEARTS, DRAINED,
   CHOPPED
3 LARGE CLOVES OF GARLIC,
   MINCED

1 CUP FRESHLY GRATED
   PARMESAN CHEESE
½ CUP MAYONNAISE
8 OUNCES CREAM CHEESE,
   SOFTENED
2 TABLESPOONS LEMON JUICE
   COARSELY GROUND PEPPER TO TASTE
   BREADSTICKS AND/OR
   ASSORTED PARTY CRACKERS

Squeeze the moisture from the spinach. Place the spinach in a colander and press to remove any remaining moisture. Sauté the onion in the butter in a skillet until tender; drain. Combine the spinach, onion, artichokes and garlic in a bowl and mix well. Add the Parmesan cheese, mayonnaise, cream cheese, lemon juice and pepper, stirring until mixed. Spoon into a greased 7x11-inch baking dish. Bake at 375 degrees for 25 minutes. Serve hot with breadsticks and/or assorted party crackers.

To serve eight

CHEESE ARTICHOKE DIP

1 (16-OUNCE) CAN ARTICHOKE
   HEARTS, DRAINED, CHOPPED
1 (6-OUNCE) JAR MARINATED
   ARTICHOKE HEARTS, DRAINED,
   CHOPPED
1 (4-OUNCE) CAN GREEN
   CHILES, DRAINED

1 TO 2 TABLESPOONS MAYONNAISE
8 OUNCES COLBY CHEESE,
   SHREDDED
8 OUNCES MONTEREY JACK
   CHEESE, SHREDDED
   CORN CHIPS

Combine the artichokes, chiles and mayonnaise in a bowl and mix gently. Spoon into an 8x8-inch baking pan or a 2-quart baking dish. Sprinkle with the Colby cheese and Monterey Jack cheese. Bake at 325 degrees for 20 minutes or until bubbly. Serve hot with corn chips.

To serve eight

ON OCCASION...

take the easy way out! To feed your hungry goblins, stop by the grocery for pre-cut vegetables from the deli department. Serve them with your favorite commercial dipping sauce. Just drop the entire container inside a hollowed-out gourd.

To decorate the porch for Halloween this year, try a grouping of pie pumpkins rather than decorator pumpkins; they are much easier to carve! Turn them on their sides to use the stem for the nose and carve features as your tradition dictates. Cut a circle in the side on which they sit and place them over votive candles.

No time for carving? A quick trip to the farmers' market will provide an abundance of "fun" vegetables to use to decorate your time-honored pumpkin friend. For facial features, try miniature zucchini, patty pan squash, pearl onions, and baby carrots, using wooden picks to attach them. Don't you think it needs hair made from scallions? Even easier are features drawn on with colored markers.

ITALIAN BEEF SANDWICHES

GARLIC SALT TO TASTE
CRAZY GOURMET SALT TO TASTE
FRESHLY CRACKED PEPPERCORNS TO TASTE
CRUSHED OREGANO TO TASTE
1 (5- TO 6-POUND) SIRLOIN TOP ROUND
½ CUP RED WINE
¼ CUP WORCESTERSHIRE SAUCE
FRENCH ROLLS OR GARLIC BREAD

Sprinkle garlic salt, salt, peppercorns and oregano over all sides of the beef. Place in an oven-cooking bag. Pour the wine and Worcestershire sauce over the beef and seal the bag. Place the bag on a baking sheet.

Bake at 250 degrees for 5 to 6 hours or until of the desired degree of doneness. Let stand for 5 to 10 minutes. Slice and arrange on a serving platter. Drizzle with the pan juices. Serve on French rolls or garlic bread with sliced onions and pickles.

To serve twelve

BREAD-AND-BUTTER PICKLES

6 QUARTS MEDIUM PICKLING CUCUMBERS, THINLY SLICED
6 ONIONS, THINLY SLICED
1 CUP SALT
1½ QUARTS VINEGAR
6 CUPS SUGAR
½ CUP MUSTARD SEEDS
1 TABLESPOON CELERY SEEDS
⅓ TO ¼ TEASPOON CAYENNE

Mix the cucumbers, onions and salt in a crock. Let stand for 3 hours; drain.

Combine the vinegar, sugar, mustard seeds, celery seeds and cayenne in a stockpot and mix well. Bring to a boil. Add the cucumber mixture and mix well. Heat just to simmering, stirring occasionally; do not boil.

Pack the cucumbers and onions into hot sterilized jars. Add the hot syrup, leaving a ½-inch headspace; seal with 2-piece lids.

Makes six pints

Invite moms over for coffee two or three weeks before the annual spooky day for a COSTUME SWAP-RENT-BORROW-SELL PARTY. *Set up a portable clothes rack for an organized exchange. You just might find the needed bunny ears, devil's pitchfork, bigger ballet slippers, or majestic sword!*

SPOOKY APPLE PIZZAS

8   OUNCES CREAM CHEESE, SOFTENED
½   CUP PACKED LIGHT BROWN SUGAR
1   TEASPOON VANILLA EXTRACT
1   (16-OUNCE) LOAF CINNAMON RAISIN BREAD
2   RED DELICIOUS APPLES, CORED
2   TABLESPOONS ORANGE JUICE
¼   CUP CHOPPED PEANUTS OR PECANS

Combine the cream cheese, brown sugar and vanilla in a mixer bowl. Beat at medium speed until smooth, scraping the bowl occasionally.

Cut each bread slice with a 3-inch round cutter. Cut each apple horizontally into 1-inch slices. Brush the slices with the orange juice.

Spread 1 tablespoon of the cream cheese mixture on each bread round. Top with an apple slice and sprinkle with the peanuts.

Makes fourteen pizzas

POTATO CASKETS

1   POUND BACON
6   BAKING POTATOES
     SALT AND PEPPER TO TASTE
8   OUNCES COLBY CHEESE, SHREDDED
8   OUNCES MONTEREY JACK CHEESE, SHREDDED

Fry the bacon in a skillet until crisp. Drain, reserving the bacon drippings. Crumble the bacon.

Pierce the potatoes with a fork. Place on a baking sheet. Bake at 350 degrees for 1 hour or until tender. Let stand until cool. Cut the potatoes lengthwise into halves. Scoop out the pulp, leaving ¼-inch shells. Discard the pulp or reserve for another use.

Brush the potato shells with the reserved bacon drippings. Arrange on a baking sheet. Bake at 350 degrees for 5 to 8 minutes or until light brown. Sprinkle with salt and pepper. Top with the cheese and bacon. Bake for 10 to 15 minutes or until the cheese melts.

To serve twelve

❧

BITS AND BONES *will be a hit among all ages at Halloween parties. Mix 3 cups corn-and-rice cereal, 1 cup bear-shaped grahams or graham cereal, 12 ounces unsalted dry-roasted peanuts and 12 ounces chocolate-coated candies. Store in an airtight container until spooking time.*

CHEWY CHOCOLATE TOADS

CHOCOLATE PEANUT BUTTER BOO BITES

Heat 1 cup butter and 1 cup peanut butter in a saucepan until melted, stirring to blend well. Stir in a mixture of 16 ounces confectioners' sugar and 1 cup graham cracker crumbs. Press into a buttered 9x13-inch dish. Spread with 2 cups melted milk chocolate chips. Chill for 1 to 2 hours or until set. Let stand at room temperature for 15 minutes before cutting into 1-inch squares.

½ CUP SWAMP WATER (MILK TINTED GREEN)

¼ CUP DIRT (BAKING COCOA)

2 CUPS CRUSHED BONES (SUGAR)

½ CUP FAT (BUTTER)

2 CUPS DEAD GRASS (ROLLED OATS)

1 CUP BROKEN PETRIFIED WOOD (COARSELY CRUSHED PRETZELS)

½ CUP SQUASHED BUGS (PEANUT BUTTER)

Combine the swamp water and dirt in a saucepan and mix well. Stir in the crushed bones and fat. Bring to a boil. Boil for 2 minutes, stirring constantly. Stir in the dead grass, petrified wood and squashed bugs. Remove from heat. Stir until the mixture begins to thicken. Drop by tablespoonfuls onto a baking sheet lined with waxed paper. Chill until set.

To serve twelve

BROWN SUGAR BARS

CRUST

   2   CUPS FLOUR

   1   CUP BUTTER, SOFTENED

   ¼   CUP PACKED BROWN SUGAR

FILLING

   3   CUPS PACKED BROWN SUGAR

   ¼   CUP FLOUR

   1   TEASPOON SALT

   4   EGGS, LIGHTLY BEATEN

   2   TABLESPOONS VANILLA EXTRACT

   1   CUP FINELY CHOPPED NUTS

   1   CUP SHREDDED COCONUT

FROSTING

   3   CUPS CONFECTIONERS' SUGAR

   ¼   CUP BUTTER, SOFTENED

      ORANGE JUICE TO TASTE

BAT'S BREW

Simmer 2 quarts apple cider, 1 quart cranberry juice, ½ cup packed brown sugar, 1 teaspoon whole allspice, 1 teaspoon whole cloves, 1 cinnamon stick and ½ teaspoon salt for 20 minutes. Select small rubber creatures at the dime store to place in the punch bowl or in serving cups to spook every ghost and goblin!

To prepare the crust, mix the flour, butter and brown sugar in a bowl. Pat over the bottom and up the sides of a jelly roll pan. Bake at 350 degrees for 12 to 15 minutes or until light brown.

To prepare the filling, combine the brown sugar, flour and salt in a bowl and mix well. Stir in the eggs and vanilla. Add the nuts and coconut and mix well. Spread over the baked crust. Bake for 30 minutes longer. Let stand until cool.

To prepare the frosting, beat the confectioners' sugar, butter and desired amount of orange juice in a mixer bowl until of spreading consistency, scraping the bowl occasionally. Spread over the baked layers. Cut into 1x3-inch bars.

Makes five dozen bars

HAYRIDES AND HOEDOWNS

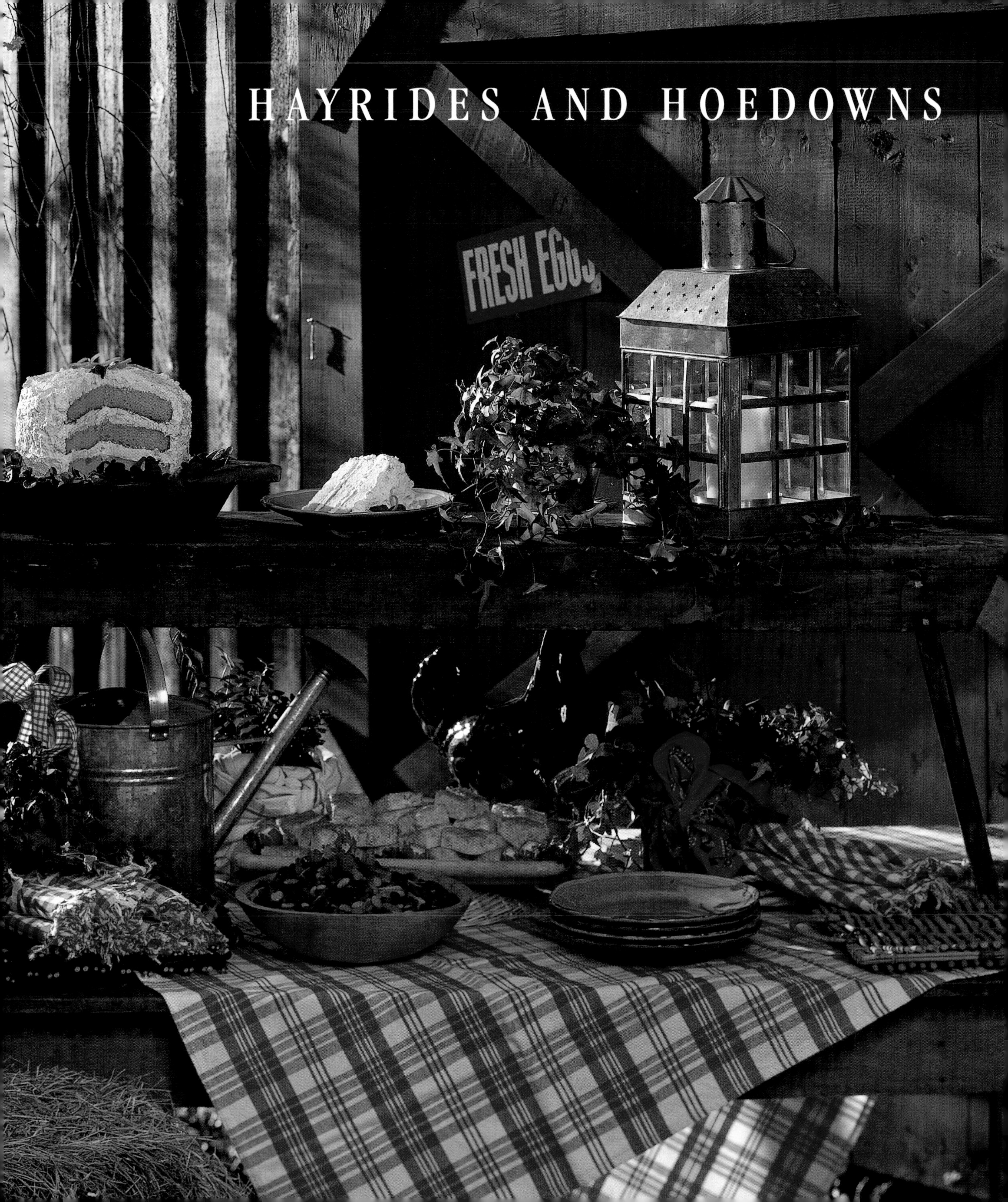

HAYRIDES AND HOEDOWNS

Menu

Green Chile and Bacon Dip

Texas Fudge

Boiled Peanuts

Couscous Salad

Taterlini Salad

Hickory-Smoked Pork Barbecue

Famous Grilled Ribs

Talmadge Farm Barbecued Ribs

Roasted Corn in Husks

Corn Soufflé

Sweet-and-Sour Beans

Hoedown Hoecakes

Pig-Pickin' Cake

Cowboy Spice Cake

Sodie-Floats

Take the basics—red-and-white-checked cloths and old patterned quilts to toss out back… bottles of soda iced down in a big galvanized tub. Then there are handfuls of sunflowers and brown bags of boiled peanuts…Bales of hay tossed into the back of a vintage pickup truck—A grand ole party in the making!!! Pass out red and navy bandannas for the perfect costume and take-home favor. Outline the fence row with heaps o' starry, twinkling lights. Hire a square-dance caller or make a great tape of classic hoedown tunes—start with Roy Rogers and Hank Williams. Join in a hayride or offer pony rides. Maybe cater this time—all the parts or carry out just a few. Host this barn dance for any dinner group, Sunday school class, as a fund-raising event, or…heck, gather up the kinfolk! Grab fiddle and bow—It's time for some hootin' and hollerin'!

Green Chile and Bacon Dip

16 OUNCES CREAM CHEESE, SOFTENED
½ CUP MAYONNAISE
1 TABLESPOON LEMON JUICE
1 (4-OUNCE) CAN CHOPPED GREEN CHILES
½ LARGE ONION, MINCED
½ LARGE GREEN BELL PEPPER, MINCED
10 SLICES CRISP-FRIED BACON, CRUMBLED
1 CLOVE OF GARLIC, CRUSHED
1 GREEN OR RED BELL PEPPER
 CORN CHIPS AND/OR MELBA TOAST

Combine the cream cheese, mayonnaise and lemon juice in a food processor container. Process until smooth.

Combine the cream cheese mixture, chiles, onion, ½ minced green pepper, bacon and garlic in a bowl and mix well. Chill, covered, for 3 to 4 hours.

Cut a slice from the top of the green pepper and discard. Remove the seeds and membranes. Spoon the cream cheese mixture into the green pepper. Serve with corn chips and/or melba toast.

Makes 2 cups

Texas Fudge

2 CUPS SHREDDED MONTEREY JACK CHEESE
2 CUPS SHREDDED COLBY CHEESE
6 EGGS, LIGHTLY BEATEN
1 (4-OUNCE) CAN CHOPPED GREEN CHILES, DRAINED
½ TEASPOON SALT

Combine the Monterey Jack cheese, Colby cheese, eggs, chiles and salt in a bowl and mix well. Spoon into a lightly greased 8x8-inch baking pan. Bake at 350 degrees for 20 to 30 minutes or until the eggs are set.

Serve with your favorite barbecue or Tex-Mex entrées. Adjust the pan size for a thicker or thinner "fudge."

To serve sixteen

No hayride is complete without BOILED PEANUTS. *Rinse 2 pounds raw peanuts in shells until the water runs clear. Combine with 1¼ cups salt and enough water to cover in a saucepan. Boil, covered, for 40 minutes or until the peanuts are tender. Remove from the heat and let stand for 15 minutes; drain. Serve immediately or store, covered, in the refrigerator for up to 1 week. Serve in individual brown bags tied with small cord.*

HICKORY-SMOKED PORK BARBECUE

BRANCHES OF FRESH HERBS (ROSEMARY, SAGE, THYME, ETC.)
1   (10-POUND) PORK SHOULDER WITH BONE
    OLIVE OIL TO TASTE
    SALT AND PEPPER TO TASTE
    HICKORY CHIPS

Arrange 2 sheets of heavy-duty foil in the form of a cross on a work surface. Layer the herbs in the center to form a bed for the pork.

Rub the pork on all sides with olive oil. Sprinkle with salt and pepper. Place the pork over the herbs. Wrap loosely to enclose and seal the edges tightly. Place in a roasting pan. Bake at 250 degrees for 5 hours.

Preheat a smoker. Sprinkle hickory chips soaked in water over the coals. Place the pork on the smoker rack. Open the foil to expose the top and sides of the pork. Smoke for 1 hour. Remove the pork to a platter and shred. Serve with Talmadge Farm Barbecue Sauce on page 159.

To serve eight

FAMOUS GRILLED RIBS

¼   CUP OLIVE OIL
2   TABLESPOONS THYME
2   TABLESPOONS OREGANO
2   TABLESPOONS BASIL
2   TABLESPOONS SAGE
2   TABLESPOONS GARLIC POWDER
2   TABLESPOONS CAYENNE
2   TABLESPOONS RED PEPPER
1   TABLESPOON BLACK PEPPER
1   TABLESPOON SALT
4   SLABS BABY BACK PORK RIBS
    TALMADGE FARM BARBECUE SAUCE (PAGE 159)

Combine the olive oil, thyme, oregano, basil, sage, garlic powder, cayenne, red pepper, black pepper and salt in a bowl, mashing with the back of a spoon to mix. Rub the herb mixture over the ribs. Marinate at room temperature for 1 hour or in the refrigerator for up to 6 hours.

Line a grill rack with heavy-duty foil. Arrange the ribs meaty side up on the foil. Cook with lid down for 1½ hours, checking periodically to make sure the ribs are not burning. Remove the ribs and foil. Baste the ribs with Talmadge Farm Barbecue Sauce. Arrange on the grill meaty side down. Cook for 10 minutes. Serve with extra barbecue sauce.

To serve four

❧

For a rib-tickling treat, apply Everglades Seasoning generously to baby back ribs and place them on the grill.
Baste them every 15 minutes with Mojo Criollo Spanish Marinating Sauce until they
are cooked through. Lip smackin' good!

TALMADGE FARM BARBECUED RIBS

BARBECUE SAUCE

1¼ CUPS CATSUP
1   CUP CIDER OR RED WINE VINEGAR
1   CUP PACKED LIGHT BROWN SUGAR
1   LEMON, SLICED, SEEDED
5   TABLESPOONS WORCESTERSHIRE SAUCE
2   TABLESPOONS DRY MUSTARD
1   TABLESPOON GRATED FRESH GINGERROOT
1   CLOVE (OR MORE) OF GARLIC, MINCED
3   TABLESPOONS UNSALTED BUTTER
    SALT AND FRESHLY CRACKED PEPPER TO TASTE
    LEMON JUICE TO TASTE

RIBS

6   POUNDS RIBS
2   CUPS WATER
1   ONION, SLICED
1   BAY LEAF
½   TEASPOON THYME
    SALT AND PEPPER TO TASTE

ON OCCASION...

serve ROASTED CORN IN HUSKS. *Pull the corn husks back from the ear, leaving them attached at the base of the cob. Discard the silk. Replace the husks and secure by tying at the top with one piece of husk. Soak the corn in enough water to cover for 20 minutes and drain. Arrange the corn on a grill rack positioned 4 to 6 inches from the heat source. Grill for 20 minutes, turning frequently. Serve with assorted* HERBED BUTTERS *on page 244.*

For the barbecue sauce, combine the catsup, vinegar, brown sugar, lemon slices, Worcestershire sauce, dry mustard, gingerroot and garlic in a stainless steel or enamel saucepan and mix well.

Bring to a boil; reduce the heat. Simmer for 15 minutes, stirring occasionally. Stir in the butter. Simmer for 2 minutes, stirring occasionally. Add the salt, pepper and lemon juice and mix well.

Use immediately or allow to stand for 2 to 10 hours to enhance the flavor. Strain and store, covered, in the refrigerator.

For the ribs, place the ribs in a roasting pan. Add the water, onion, bay leaf, thyme, salt and pepper. Bake, covered, at 350 degrees for 40 to 45 minutes. Grill the ribs over hot coals until cooked through, basting frequently with the barbecue sauce.

To serve six

Taterlini Salad

Couscous Salad

Cook 1 package of couscous using the package directions. Whisk together ¼ cup mayonnaise, ¼ cup rice wine vinegar, 1 tablespoon curry powder, 1 teaspoon dry mustard, 1 teaspoon garlic powder and salt and pepper to taste. Mix in the couscous. Fold in 1 drained and chopped 15-ounce can marinated artichokes, 1 chopped red bell pepper, ½ cup chopped pimento-stuffed olives, 4 sliced hearts of palm, 6 sliced green onions and 2 tablespoons capers. Chill, covered, up to 12 hours. To serve as a main course, add 1 pound cooked, peeled, deveined shrimp.

4	MEDIUM RED POTATOES, COOKED, COARSELY CHOPPED
9	OUNCES SMALL CHEESE TORTELLINI, COOKED, DRAINED
1	(8-OUNCE) JAR MARINATED ARTICHOKE HEARTS, DRAINED, CHOPPED
8	OUNCES FRESH MUSHROOMS, SLICED
1	CUP CHERRY TOMATO HALVES
½	CUP CHOPPED RED OR GREEN BELL PEPPER
⅓	CUP CHOPPED GREEN OLIVES
1	TABLESPOON FINELY SLICED FRESH BASIL
1	CLOVE OF GARLIC, MINCED
⅔	CUP ITALIAN SALAD DRESSING
2	TABLESPOONS RED WINE VINEGAR
1	TEASPOON SALT, OR TO TASTE
1	TEASPOON PEPPER, OR TO TASTE
	FRESHLY GRATED PARMESAN CHEESE TO TASTE

Combine the potatoes, tortellini, artichokes, mushrooms, cherry tomatoes, red pepper, olives, basil and garlic in a bowl and mix gently.

Whisk the salad dressing, wine vinegar, salt and pepper in a bowl. Add to the potato mixture, tossing gently to coat. Sprinkle with the cheese. Chill, covered, until serving time.

Tastes even better the second day!

To serve eight

CORN SOUFFLE

1   GREEN BELL PEPPER, CHOPPED
½   CUP CHOPPED ONION
½   CUP MARGARINE
1   (16-OUNCE) CAN WHOLE KERNEL CORN, DRAINED
1   (17-OUNCE) CAN CREAM-STYLE CORN
1   (6-OUNCE) PACKAGE CORN BREAD MIX
3   EGGS, LIGHTLY BEATEN
1   CUP SHREDDED CHEDDAR CHEESE

Sauté the green pepper and onion in the margarine in a skillet until the onion is tender. Remove from heat.

Stir in the whole kernel corn and cream-style corn. Add the corn bread mix and eggs and mix well. Spoon into a greased 9x13-inch baking dish. Sprinkle with the cheese.

Bake at 325 degrees for 45 minutes. Let stand for 5 minutes before serving.

To serve twelve

SWEET-AND-SOUR BEANS

8   SLICES BACON
1   ONION, CHOPPED
¾   CUP PACKED BROWN SUGAR
1   TEASPOON DRY MUSTARD
2   TEASPOONS APPLE CIDER VINEGAR
    SALT AND PEPPER TO TASTE
1   (16-OUNCE) CAN BLACK BEANS
1   (16-OUNCE) JAR OVEN-BAKED BEANS
1   (16-OUNCE) CAN DARK KIDNEY BEANS
1   (8-OUNCE) CAN BABY LIMA BEANS, DRAINED

Fry the bacon in a skillet until crisp. Drain, reserving the pan drippings. Crumble the bacon.

Sauté the onion in the reserved pan drippings until tender. Stir in the brown sugar and dry mustard. Cook until the brown sugar dissolves, stirring constantly.

Add the cider vinegar, salt and pepper and mix well. Stir in the undrained black beans, oven-baked beans, kidney beans and lima beans. Add the bacon and mix well. Spoon into a baking dish.

Bake at 350 degrees for 45 minutes.

To serve eight

Hoedown Hoecakes

1 CUP YELLOW CORNMEAL

1 TABLESPOON SUGAR

½ TEASPOON BAKING POWDER

½ TEASPOON SALT

1½ CUPS MILK

2 EGGS

½ CUP MELTED BUTTER

MAPLE SYRUP OR HONEY (OPTIONAL)

Sift the cornmeal, sugar, baking powder and salt into a bowl and mix well. Add the milk and beat vigorously with a spoon until blended. Add the eggs and beat until the batter is smooth.

Heat a griddle or skillet until hot; brush with some of the melted butter. Ladle ¼ cup of the batter onto the griddle. Cook for 2 to 3 minutes per side or until brown.

Remove to a platter and cover with foil to keep warm. Repeat the process with the remaining batter and melted butter.

Serve with maple syrup or honey.

Makes one dozen hoecakes

Pig-Pickin' Cake

CAKE

1 (2-LAYER) PACKAGE YELLOW CAKE MIX

1 CUP MANDARIN ORANGES WITH JUICE

4 EGGS

½ CUP VEGETABLE OIL

FILLING

1 (20-OUNCE) CAN CRUSHED PINEAPPLE, SLIGHTLY DRAINED

1 (4-OUNCE) PACKAGE VANILLA INSTANT PUDDING MIX

16 OUNCES WHIPPED TOPPING

To prepare the cake, grease and flour three 9-inch cake pans. Beat the cake mix, mandarin orange juice, eggs and oil in a mixer bowl until blended. Fold in the oranges. Spoon into the prepared cake pans. Bake at 350 degrees for 25 minutes or until the layers test done. Cool in pans on wire racks.

To prepare the filling, fold the pineapple and pudding mix into the whipped topping in a bowl.

To assemble, spread the filling between the layers and over the top and side of the cake. Serve cold!

To serve twelve

Cowboy Spice Cake

1 CUP BUTTER, SOFTENED

2 CUPS (SCANT) PACKED DARK BROWN SUGAR

3 EGGS

1 CUP SOUR CREAM

½ CUP FRESH LEMON JUICE

⅓ CUP HONEY

⅓ CUP LIGHT CORN SYRUP

¼ CUP TRIPLE SEC OR ANY ORANGE OR TANGERINE LIQUEUR

1⅔ CUPS ALL-PURPOSE FLOUR

1 CUP WHOLE WHEAT FLOUR

4 TEASPOONS BAKING POWDER

2½ TEASPOONS CRYSTALLIZED GINGER

1 TEASPOON CINNAMON

1 TEASPOON ALLSPICE

1 TEASPOON NUTMEG

1 TEASPOON GROUND CLOVES

1 CUP COARSELY CHOPPED WALNUTS OR BLANCHED SLIVERED ALMONDS

½ CUP DARK RAISINS

Beat the butter and brown sugar in a mixer bowl until creamy, scraping the bowl occasionally. Add the eggs, sour cream, lemon juice, honey, corn syrup and liqueur. Beat until blended, scraping the bowl occasionally.

Mix the all-purpose flour, whole wheat flour, baking powder, ginger, cinnamon, allspice, nutmeg and cloves in a bowl. Add to the creamed mixture and mix well. Stir in the walnuts and raisins. Spoon into a greased and floured 10-inch bundt pan.

Bake at 350 degrees for 1½ hours or until a wooden pick inserted in the center comes out clean. Invert onto a wire rack to cool. Store, wrapped in waxed paper, in a cake tin in a cool, dry environment.

To serve sixteen

Sodie-Floats

The trick to the perfect Sodie-Float is to have all the ingredients ready and cold! cold! cold!

Chill your favorite soda: Tasty choices are root beer, orange soda, lemon-lime soda, and, of course, classic cola. Warm an ice cream scoop in a glass of hot water and use it to place 1 scoop of vanilla ice cream into a frosted mug. Pour the soda of choice over the ice cream and serve it immediately with a straw and a long spoon. Pick out a favorite spot to sit and indulge, because you won't be moving much after. For the ultimate indulgence, teach a child the art.

A VERY LOVELY EVENING

MENU

Regal Shrimp in Phyllo Cups

Bountiful Brie

Romano Spinach Salad

Minted Lamb Chops in
Puff Pastry

Supreme Carrots

Vegetable Terrine with
Mushroom Sauce

Simply Perfect Bread

White and Dark Chocolate
Marbled Mousse Cake

On occasion...we want to entertain more formally. Extend an invitation as perfect as Mrs. Post, develop a time schedule, and organize a shopping list. Then polish, press, and prepare. For this lovely evening, add a few fresh touches...a crystal pitcher of chilled water, a tasty nibble in an heirloom bowl, a cluster of candles. Fill a vase with seasonal blooms, taking less than five minutes—simple is always best. Consider a place card that is a memento...a bundle of chocolate peppermint sticks tied with organdy ribbon, planting bulbs wrapped with netting and raffia. Perhaps, script the guest's name on a square of handmade paper. Lay the card over a folded napkin in the center of each plate. A sumptuous menu, a welcoming table, wonderful company...Honor your guests by sharing in...a very lovely evening.

A Lovely Evening Party Planner

ONE WEEK BEFORE THE PARTY:
- plan the table settings, launder and press the table linens, polish the silver
- select the centerpiece, place cards, and favors
- clean the refrigerator (it's high time anyway!)

THREE DAYS BEFORE:
- check the pantry and make a grocery list
- shop, then rest!

TWO DAYS BEFORE:
- prepare the Vegetable Terrine (do not prepare sauce); chill
- prepare the filling for Regal Shrimp in Phyllo Cups; chill

ONE DAY BEFORE:
- assemble the Minted Lamb Chops in Puff Pastry; chill
- prepare the Romano Salad Dressing; chill
- boil the eggs for the salad; chill
- wash the spinach, dry and wrap in a fresh towel; place in an airtight container; chill
- prepare the Mushroom Sauce for the terrine; chill
- prepare White and Dark Chocolate Marbled Mousse Cake; chill

THE MORNING OF THE PARTY:
- prepare the Bountiful Brie; cover and chill
- prepare the Supreme Carrots up to the tossing stage
- prepare the Simply Perfect Bread; wrap in foil and chill
- prepare salad ingredients; chill

THREE HOURS BEFORE:
- remove the Bountiful Brie from the refrigerator
- enjoy a glass of wine, dress for the party, then don an apron

ONE HOUR BEFORE:
- warm the terrine and sauce, toss the carrots
- assemble the Romano Spinach Salad
- bake the lamb chops, bread, then shrimp
- open all wines and enjoy a very lovely evening

Regal Shrimp in Phyllo Cups

1½	POUNDS SHRIMP, STEAMED, PEELED, CHOPPED
½	CUP MINCED ONION
½	CUP DRAINED WHOLE KERNEL CORN (OPTIONAL)
¼	CUP FINELY CHOPPED CELERY
¼	CUP FINELY CHOPPED RED BELL PEPPER
2	CLOVES OF GARLIC, MINCED
2	TABLESPOONS MINCED DRAINED CAPERS
1	TABLESPOON CHOPPED FRESH CILANTRO
1	TEASPOON CHILI POWDER
	FRESHLY GROUND PEPPER TO TASTE
¾	CUP MAYONNAISE
1	EGG, LIGHTLY BEATEN
1	TABLESPOON DIJON MUSTARD
60	MINIATURE PHYLLO SHELLS

Combine the shrimp, onion, corn, celery, red pepper, garlic, capers, cilantro, chili powder and pepper in a bowl and mix well.

Mix ½ cup of the mayonnaise, egg and Dijon mustard in a bowl. Add to the shrimp mixture, stirring to mix. Add the remaining ¼ cup mayonnaise if needed for additional moisture. Spoon into the phyllo shells. Arrange the shells on a baking sheet.

Bake at 325 degrees for 15 minutes or until heated through.

Makes five dozen

ROMANO SPINACH SALAD

SALAD

2 POUNDS FRESH SPINACH, TRIMMED
10 SLICES CRISP-FRIED BACON, CRUMBLED
2 HARD-COOKED EGGS, CHOPPED
5 GREEN ONIONS, CHOPPED
1 (10-OUNCE) PACKAGE FROZEN GREEN PEAS, THAWED

CREAMY DRESSING

1 CUP SOUR CREAM
1 CUP MAYONNAISE
½ CUP GRATED ROMANO CHEESE
½ TEASPOON LEMON PEPPER
⅛ TEASPOON GARLIC POWDER

To prepare the salad, layer the spinach, bacon, eggs, green onions and peas in the order listed in a large salad bowl.

To prepare the dressing, mix the sour cream, mayonnaise, cheese, lemon pepper and garlic powder in a bowl. Spread over the top of the salad. Chill, covered, for 8 to 10 hours. Toss just before serving.

To serve ten

VEGETABLE TERRINE WITH MUSHROOM SAUCE

½ CUP EACH BUTTER AND FLOUR
1½ CUPS MILK
½ CUP SHREDDED CHEDDAR CHEESE
8 EGGS, LIGHTLY BEATEN
1¼ CUPS CHOPPED BROCCOLI, STEAMED
4 CARROTS, COARSELY CHOPPED, STEAMED
2 CUPS CHOPPED CAULIFLOWER, STEAMED
MUSHROOM SAUCE (BELOW)

Line a 5x9-inch loaf pan with plastic wrap. Heat the butter in a saucepan until melted. Stir in the flour. Add the milk gradually, stirring constantly. Cook over medium heat until thickened, stirring constantly. Remove from heat. Add the cheese, stirring until blended. Let stand for 10 minutes. Stir in the eggs.

Divide the milk mixture into 3 equal portions. Process the broccoli and 1 portion of the milk mixture in a food processor until smooth. Spoon into the prepared pan. Process the carrots with another portion of the milk mixture until smooth. Spoon over the prepared layer. Repeat the process with the cauliflower and remaining portion of the milk mixture. Cover with greased foil.

Place the pan in a larger pan. Add enough boiling water to the larger pan to reach halfway up the sides of the loaf pan. Bake at 350 degrees for 2¼ hours or until set. Let stand for 15 minutes. Invert onto a serving platter. Serve immediately with Mushroom Sauce.

To serve eight

❧

Serve MUSHROOM SAUCE *over a very lovely Vegetable Terrine. Sauté a drained 7-ounce can of sliced mushrooms in ¼ cup butter for 2 minutes. Add 1¼ cups whipping cream and mix well. Simmer for 10 minutes or until slightly thickened, stirring frequently. Serve immediately with the terrine or store, covered, in the refrigerator for 1 day. Reheat before serving.*

MINTED LAMB CHOPS IN PUFF PASTRY

12 (3-OUNCE) RIB LAMB CHOPS, 1 INCH THICK, TRIMMED
    SALT AND PEPPER TO TASTE
2 (17-OUNCE) PACKAGES FROZEN PUFF PASTRY, THAWED
3 TABLESPOONS CHOPPED FRESH MINT
1 EGG YOLK
3 TABLESPOONS WATER

Sprinkle both sides of the lamb chops with salt and pepper. Place on a rack in a broiler pan. Broil 3 to 4 inches from the heat source for 2 minutes; turn. Broil for 2 minutes longer. Freeze the chops for 1 hour.

Unfold 1 sheet of the pastry on a lightly floured surface. Roll into a 12-inch square. Cut into four 6-inch squares; trim the edges. Repeat the process with 2 more pastry sheets, making 12 squares. Unroll the last sheet. Cut out twelve ½- to 1-inch decorative shapes with small cutters. Chill, covered, in the refrigerator.

Place 1 lamb chop in the center of 1 pastry square. Sprinkle with ¾ teaspoon mint. Fold the pastry from the corners over the lamb envelope-style, overlapping slightly in the center. Press edges to seal. Place seam side up 2 inches apart on a baking sheet. Repeat the process with the remaining pastry squares, lamb chops and mint.

Whisk the egg yolk and water in a bowl until blended. Brush over the pastry bundles. Press the decorative pastry shapes gently over the center where the points come together. Brush with the egg yolk mixture. Freeze for 10 minutes. Bake at 425 degrees for 15 to 18 minutes or until pastry is puffed and golden brown.

To serve twelve

ON OCCASION...

tantalize your guests' appetites with a BOUNTIFUL BRIE *crowned with such interesting toppings as brown sugar and toasted sliced almonds; apple slices brushed with lemon juice; dried currants or cranberries; toasted pine nuts; poppy seeds; apricot preserves; chopped fresh basil; or cracked black pepper.*

Start with a whole 5-pound wheel of Brie, then cut away and discard the top of the rind. Trace a circle with a 4-inch bowl in the center of the wheel and fill with 1 topping. Then arrange other toppings in concentric circles to the edge of the wheel. Cut into wedges to serve with crackers or French bread.

SUPREME CARROTS

1½ POUNDS CARROTS, CUT INTO QUARTERS
1½ TABLESPOONS BUTTER
1½ CUPS WATER
1   TABLESPOON SUGAR
½   TEASPOON SALT
⅛   TEASPOON PEPPER
2   TABLESPOONS BUTTER, SOFTENED
1   TABLESPOON PARSLEY FLAKES
1   TABLESPOON CHIVES

Sauté the carrots in 1½ tablespoons butter in a saucepan. Add the water, sugar, salt and pepper. Bring to a boil; reduce heat. Simmer for 30 minutes or until tender; drain.

Toss the carrots with 2 tablespoons butter, parsley flakes and chives just before serving. The flavor is enhanced if made in advance and reheated just before serving.

To serve six

SIMPLY PERFECT BREAD

1   (8- TO 12-OUNCE) LOAF ITALIAN BREAD
¼   CUP ITALIAN SALAD DRESSING
¼   CUP BUTTER, SOFTENED
¼   CUP GRATED PARMESAN CHEESE
3   CLOVES OF GARLIC, MINCED
    FRESHLY CRACKED PEPPER TO TASTE

Cut the loaf diagonally to but not through the bottom into 1-inch slices. Mix the salad dressing, butter, cheese, garlic and pepper in a bowl.

Spread the cut sides of the bread with the dressing mixture. Wrap in foil, leaving the foil partially open at the top.

Bake at 375 degrees for 15 to 20 minutes.

To serve eight

WHITE AND DARK CHOCOLATE MARBLED MOUSSE CAKE

CRUST

1	CUP CHOCOLATE WAFER CRUMBS
3	TABLESPOONS MELTED BUTTER

CHOCOLATE FILLING

14	OUNCES SEMISWEET CHOCOLATE
2	EGGS, LIGHTLY BEATEN
4	EGG YOLKS, LIGHTLY BEATEN
2	CUPS WHIPPING CREAM
4	EGG WHITES

WHITE CHOCOLATE MOUSSE

3	OUNCES WHITE CHOCOLATE
2	EGG YOLKS, LIGHTLY BEATEN
½	CUP WHIPPING CREAM
2	EGG WHITES

To prepare the crust, mix the crumbs and butter in a bowl. Pat over the bottom of a 12-inch springform pan. Chill in the refrigerator.

To prepare the filling, heat the chocolate in a double boiler over hot water until melted, stirring frequently. Stir in the eggs. Add the egg yolks and mix well. Set aside. Beat the whipping cream in a mixer bowl until soft peaks form. Beat the egg whites in a mixer bowl until stiff peaks form. Fold the egg whites and whipped cream alternately into the chocolate mixture. Spoon into the prepared springform pan.

To prepare the mousse, heat the white chocolate in a double boiler over hot water until melted, stirring frequently. Stir in the egg yolks. Set aside. Beat the whipping cream in a mixer bowl until soft peaks form. Beat the egg whites in a mixer bowl until stiff peaks form. Fold the whipped cream and egg whites alternately into the white chocolate mixture. Pour gradually into the center of the chocolate filling and swirl with a knife. Chill, covered, for 3 to 4 hours.

To serve twelve to sixteen

TO GARNISH, TO GARNISH

shaved curls of chocolate; drizzled lines of raspberry sauce; a banding of piped frosting dots; sliced strawberry fans; cocoa or confectioners' sugar sprinkled through a doily; edible flower blossoms

a "fruit flower" of mandarin orange and fresh mint; swirls of lemon, lime, or orange zest; tiny strips of cucumber peel tied in a knot; slices of pimento-stuffed olive, anchovy, or egg; chevrons of smoked salmon

baby shrimp, boiled and peeled; a tomato rose; colorful confetti of finely chopped peppers; sprigs of fresh dill, basil, mint; strips of fresh rosemary, thyme, sage, oregano; tied chive; parsley, parsley, parsley

TRADITIONS GATHERED

FROM MANY HOMES,

ALL CELEBRATING WITH

THE RITUALS THAT

ENRICH OUR LIVES...

TOO QUICKLY EACH

YEAR PASSES, AGAIN NOW

HOLIDAY TIME...

CHERISHED ARE THESE

GLORIOUS DAYS WHEN

HOLLY BERRIES SHINE...

MENUS

A MEAL TO BE THANKFUL FOR

WHEN HOLLY BERRIES SHINE

A CELEBRATION OF LIGHT

MAKING SEASONS BRIGHT

CAN'T WAIT 'TIL MORNING

GOD BLESS US EVERYONE

TRADITIONS GATHERED

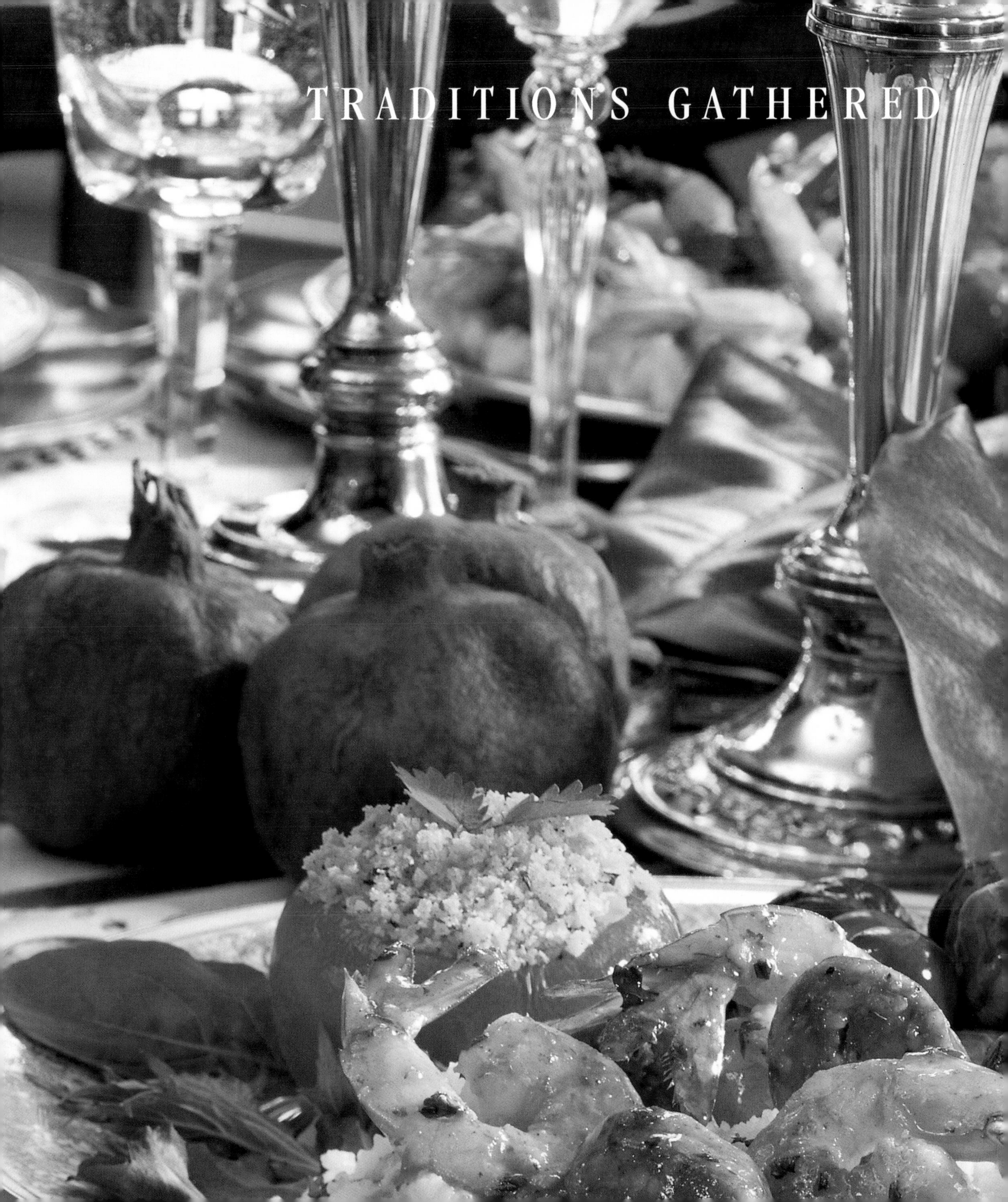

A MEAL TO BE THANKFUL FOR

MENU

SAVORY CHEESE

BLEU CHEESE DIP

GREAT-GRANDMA B'S
CRANBERRY SALAD

CRANBERRY FROZEN SALAD

ROASTED TURKEY

FRIED TURKEY

TRADITIONAL BREAD STUFFING
WITH APPLES AND SAUSAGE

TURNIP GREENS

SWEET POTATO CRUNCH

PEAS WITH PINE NUTS

WHOLE WHEAT ROLLS

WHITE CHOCOLATE PECAN PIE

PUMPKIN CHEESECAKE

MISS AMY'S KAHLÚA

A PAISLEY THROW LANGUIDLY GRACES THE BUFFET, PLAYING HOST TO A COLLECTION OF SHAPELY GOURDS, PUMPKINS, AND FALLEN LEAVES. AMIDST THE ARRANGEMENT RESTS AN URN FILLED WITH CUTTINGS OF EVERGREEN BRANCHES AND THE LAST COLORS OF AUTUMN'S BLOSSOMS. THE ANNUAL GATHERING OF FAMILY AND FRIENDS HAS AGAIN ARRIVED—A HOMECOMING, A SOJOURN, A DAY OF THANKSGIVING. "THANK YOU, LORD, FOR MY MOMMA AND DADDY...AND MY GRANDMA AND GRANDPOPPY AND MY BIG BROTHER AND BABY ELLA...AND THANK YOU FOR MY DOG—MOMMA, HE'S PROB'LY HUNGRY TOO—AND...UMMM...THANK YOU FOR THE TREES...AND MY BIKE—AND-I-REALLY-DID-WANT-TO-RIDE-TO-JACK'S-HOUSE...THANK YOU, GOD, FOR ALL MY FRIENDS...AND FOR MY SCHOOL...AND...UMMM... I PRAY FOR THE SQUIRRELS AND HOPE THEY HAVE ENOUGH NUTS TO EAT. AND THANK YOU FOR ALL OF THE PEOPLE AT THIS TABLE. AMEN." A CHILD'S PRAYER: HOW SIMPLE LIFE WOULD BE IF OUR GREATEST TROUBLES WERE THESE. THANKFULLY, MANY OF US DO LOOK AROUND AND RECOGNIZE THAT WE ARE "THAT BLESSED"...GRATEFUL FOR LIFE'S GIFTS, GREAT AND SMALL...THE GOOD LORD ALMIGHTY GAVE US ALL.

SAVORY CHEESE

8 OUNCES CREAM CHEESE
CHOPPED FRESH DILLWEED
1 (8-COUNT) CAN CRESCENT ROLLS
1 EGG YOLK, LIGHTLY BEATEN
SPRIGS OF DILLWEED (OPTIONAL)
THINLY SLICED SMOKED SALMON
ASSORTED PARTY CRACKERS

Sprinkle the cream cheese block with chopped dillweed. Unroll the crescent roll dough on a lightly floured surface. Press the perforations to form 1 large rectangle. Place the cream cheese in the center of the rectangle.

Wrap the dough package-style around the cream cheese; tuck the ends under. Place seam side down on a baking sheet. Brush with the egg yolk.

Bake using package directions for the rolls. Remove to a serving platter. Garnish with sprigs of dillweed. Surround the log with smoked salmon. Serve with assorted party crackers.

To serve six to eight

GREAT-GRANDMA B'S CRANBERRY SALAD

TOPPING
8 OUNCES CREAM CHEESE, SOFTENED
1 CUP SOUR CREAM
SALAD
1 (20-OUNCE) CAN CRUSHED PINEAPPLE
¾ CUP WATER
1 (16-OUNCE) PACKAGE FROZEN CRANBERRIES
1½ CUPS SUGAR
2 (3-OUNCE) PACKAGES RASPBERRY GELATIN
1 BUNCH SEEDLESS RED GRAPES, CUT INTO HALVES
1 CUP CHOPPED PECANS

To prepare the topping, beat the cream cheese and sour cream in a mixer bowl until creamy. Chill, covered, in the refrigerator.

To prepare the salad, drain the pineapple, reserving ¾ cup of the juice. Combine the reserved juice, water and cranberries in a saucepan. Cook until the cranberries pop, stirring occasionally. Add the sugar and mix well. Simmer until the sugar dissolves, stirring frequently. Stir in the gelatin. Cook until the gelatin dissolves, stirring constantly. Remove from heat. Let stand until cool. Stir in the pineapple, grapes and pecans. Pour into a 2-quart mold sprayed with nonstick cooking spray. Chill until set. Place the mold in hot water for 10 to 20 seconds. Invert onto a serving platter. Top each serving with a dollop of the topping.

To serve eight

The easiest holiday salad of all is CRANBERRY FROZEN SALAD. *Just combine one 16-ounce can whole cranberry sauce, one 20-ounce can drained crushed pineapple and 1 cup sour cream and mix well. Spoon into a shallow round 9-inch dish. Freeze, covered, until firm.*

ROASTED TURKEY

"OVER THE RIVER
AND THROUGH THE
WOODS . . ."

*Take along a special treat for the
youngsters to help while away those
miles to grandmother's house.
Mix cashews, raisins, honey-roasted
peanuts, fish-shaped crackers and
chocolate-covered peanut candies in
the proportions favored by their
appetites. Store the* TRAIL MIX *in sealable
plastic bags until needed.*

1 (15-POUND) TURKEY WITH GIBLETS, THAWED
3 TO 6 CLOVES OF GARLIC
   SALT AND FRESHLY GROUND PEPPER
¾ CUP BUTTER
1 CUP WATER
2½ TABLESPOONS FLOUR

Remove the wing tips from the turkey. Combine the wing tips, giblets, neck and garlic with enough water to cover in a saucepan. Bring to a boil; reduce heat. Simmer for 2 hours. Add 1 cup of water each time the liquid is reduced by half; skim occasionally. Do not add additional water during the last 20 minutes of cooking.

Rinse the turkey and pat dry. Sprinkle the inside cavity and outside surface with salt and pepper. Stuff with Traditional Bread Stuffing with Apples and Sausage on page 175, if desired. Place the turkey breast side up in a 13x18-inch roasting pan. Press pats of butter over the surface. Roast at 500 degrees for 2 hours or until the leg joint moves easily. Remove to a large serving platter, reserving the pan drippings. Let stand for 20 minutes before carving.

Pour the reserved pan drippings into a saucepan. Strain the liquid from the giblets into the saucepan and mix well. Bring to a boil. Whisk in a mixture of 1 cup water and flour. Cook until thickened and smooth, stirring constantly. Season with salt and pepper. Serve with the turkey.

This quick-cooking method will produce a wonderfully moist bird. If any is left over, try Cranberry Mayonnaise on page 46 for a tasty turkey sandwich.

To serve ten to twelve

TRADITIONAL BREAD STUFFING WITH APPLES AND SAUSAGE

20	TO 25 SLICES DRY OR LIGHTLY TOASTED WHITE BREAD
1	POUND BULK SAUSAGE, COOKED, DRAINED, CRUMBLED
¾	CUP COARSELY CHOPPED PEELED APPLE
½	CUP COARSELY CHOPPED ONION
½	CUP COARSELY CHOPPED CELERY
2	TEASPOONS SAGE OR POULTRY SEASONING, OR TO TASTE
	SALT AND PEPPER TO TASTE
2	EGGS, LIGHTLY BEATEN
3	CUPS WATER
½	CUP BUTTER

Tear the bread into ½-inch pieces. Combine the sausage, apple, onion and celery in a bowl. Add the bread and mix well. Mix in the sage, salt and pepper. Add the eggs, kneading until mixed.

Bring the water to a boil in a saucepan. Add the butter, stirring until melted. Pour half the butter mixture over the bread mixture, stirring with a wooden spoon until the mixture is moistened and adheres. Add the remaining butter mixture gradually if needed to achieve an overall moist mixture. Spoon the stuffing into the turkey cavity. Bake at 350 degrees for 4 hours for a 12-pound turkey or roast a 15-pound turkey at 500 degrees for 2 hours. Place the remaining stuffing in a baking dish sprayed with nonstick cooking spray. Bake at 350 degrees for 45 minutes or until golden brown. Do not overbake; stuffing should be moist.

May serve as a side dish substitute for potatoes, pasta or corn on other occasions.

To serve ten to twelve

A NEW TRADITION . . .

Compose an annual Thanksgiving prayer and place a copy at each place setting to be read aloud by all.

Assemble a collection of photographs, both of family attending and those not with you that day . . . thankful for all the times shared.

Select a tablecloth to be signed each year by those in attendance . . . to be used in succeeding years wherever the Thanksgiving meal is served. Designate a family member to embroider the signature for a lasting heirloom.

FRIED TURKEY

TURNIP GREENS

Sauté 6 slices chopped bacon and ¼ cup chopped onion until bacon is crisp and the onion is tender; drain. Tear 4 pounds turnip greens into bite-size pieces. Combine the greens with ½ cup water. Bring to a boil; reduce heat. Simmer for 30 minutes or until tender, adding additional water as needed. Stir in the bacon mixture, ¼ cup apple cider vinegar, 3 tablespoons sugar and ¼ teaspoon salt. Cook for 5 minutes longer.

EQUIPMENT

1	(12-GAUGE) HYPODERMIC SYRINGE WITH A 1½- TO 2-INCH NEEDLE
1	(24- TO 60-QUART) ALUMINUM STOCKPOT WITH DIAL HEAT THERMOMETER
1	(100,000 BTU) LP BURNER

TURKEY

3	BOTTLES HOWARD'S ONION JUICE
2	BOTTLES HOWARD'S GARLIC JUICE
1	BOTTLE HOWARD'S CELERY JUICE
½	CUP BUTTER
1	(10-POUND) TURKEY
	TONY'S CREOLE SEASONING
	CAYENNE OR RED PEPPER
	PEANUT OIL

Combine the onion juice, garlic juice, celery juice and butter in a saucepan. Cook over medium heat until the butter melts, stirring constantly. Draw the hot liquid into the hypodermic syringe and inject it into the turkey at different depths and locations. Discard the needle.

Mix the Creole seasoning and cayenne pepper in equal amounts and place in a shaker. Coat the turkey thickly inside and out with the mixture. Place the turkey in a double layer of sealable plastic bags and seal tightly. Marinate in the refrigerator for 2 to 3 days.

Place the stockpot on the burner and fill ⅔ full with peanut oil. Heat to 300 to 310 degrees on the thermometer. Add the turkey carefully to avoid splash-back while the cavity fills. Fry the turkey for 4 to 5 minutes per pound or until it floats. Test for doneness by cutting into the breast.

Since this is a nontraditional turkey, why not go all the way and serve a North/South Compromise Dressing with it? Instead of dressing made the southern way with corn bread, substitute toasted crumbled white bread for half the corn bread and use canned chicken broth and bouillon for the liquid.

To serve ten

Sweet Potato Crunch

2 (30-ounce) cans mashed sweet potatoes,
    drained
1¼ cups sugar
1 cup milk
½ cup melted butter
4 eggs, lightly beaten
1 teaspoon salt
1 teaspoon cinnamon
1 teaspoon vanilla extract
2 cups chopped pecans
2 cups packed brown sugar
⅔ cup flour
5 tablespoons plus 1 teaspoon melted margarine

Combine the sweet potatoes, sugar, milk, butter, eggs, salt, cinnamon and vanilla in a bowl and mix well. Spoon into a greased baking dish.

Mix the pecans, brown sugar and flour in a bowl. Stir in the margarine. Sprinkle over the prepared layer. Bake at 350 degrees for 35 minutes.

To serve eight

Peas with Pine Nuts

2 green onions
½ cup chicken stock
½ teaspoon sugar
2 (10-ounce) packages frozen peas
½ cup plus 2 tablespoons pine nuts or almonds
3 tablespoons butter
1 tablespoon minced fresh rosemary, or
    1 teaspoon dried rosemary
    Salt and pepper to taste

Chop the green onion bulbs and 2 inches of the tops into ½-inch pieces. Combine the green onions, stock and sugar in a saucepan. Simmer for 3 minutes, stirring occasionally. Add the peas. Simmer until tender; drain. May be prepared to this point 1 day in advance and stored, covered, in the refrigerator.

Sauté the pine nuts in the butter in a skillet for 2 to 3 minutes or until golden brown. Stir in the rosemary. Cook for 1 minute longer. Add the pea mixture and mix well. Cook just until heated through, stirring occasionally. Season with salt and pepper.

To serve eight

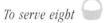

For Bleu Cheese Dip, *combine 8 ounces softened cream cheese, 4 ounces crumbled bleu cheese, ¼ cup milk or cream and ½ teaspoon garlic. Fold in 7 slices crumbled crisp-fried bacon. Spoon into a baking dish. Bake at 350 degrees for 30 minutes. Serve with sliced chilled Granny Smith apples.*

WHOLE WHEAT ROLLS

1 ENVELOPE DRY YEAST
2 TABLESPOONS SUGAR
½ CUP WARM (105 TO 115 DEGREES) WATER
1 CUP BUTTERMILK
¼ CUP VEGETABLE OIL
3 TABLESPOONS HONEY
1 EGG, LIGHTLY BEATEN
1¾ CUPS WHOLE WHEAT FLOUR
1 TEASPOON SALT
⅛ TEASPOON BAKING POWDER
2¼ TO 2¾ CUPS BREAD FLOUR

Dissolve the yeast and sugar in the warm water in a large mixer bowl and mix well. Let stand for 5 minutes. Stir in the buttermilk, oil, honey and egg. Add the whole wheat flour, salt and baking powder. Beat for 3 minutes or until smooth. Mix in just enough bread flour to make a soft dough.

Knead the dough on a lightly floured surface for 8 minutes or until smooth and elastic. Place the dough in a greased bowl, turning to coat the surface. Let rise, covered, in a warm place for 1½ hours or until doubled in size. Punch the dough down.

Shape the dough into 1-inch balls. Place 3 balls in each muffin cup sprayed with nonstick cooking spray. Let rise for 1 hour. Bake at 400 degrees for 12 to 15 minutes or until light brown.

Makes one and one-half to two dozen rolls

WHITE CHOCOLATE PECAN PIE

1 (14-OUNCE) CAN SWEETENED CONDENSED MILK
⅓ CUP WHITE CRÈME DE CACAO
2 EGGS, BEATEN
4 OUNCES WHITE CHOCOLATE, MELTED
2 CUPS CHOPPED PECANS, TOASTED
⅓ CUP MELTED BUTTER
3 TABLESPOONS MILK
2 TEASPOONS VANILLA EXTRACT
½ TEASPOON SALT
1 UNBAKED (10-INCH) DEEP-DISH PIE SHELL
  WHITE CHOCOLATE CURLS

Mix the condensed milk, crème de cacao and eggs in a bowl. Stir in the white chocolate, pecans, butter, milk, vanilla and salt. Spoon into the pie shell.

Bake at 425 degrees for 12 minutes. Reduce the oven temperature to 350 degrees. Bake for 30 to 35 minutes longer.

Top with white chocolate curls. May arrange pecan halves around the outer edge of the pie before baking for a decorative touch.

To serve six

There are several ways to arrange "A WARM PLACE" for bread to rise. Ideally, the temperature should be between 70 and 85 degrees and the bowl should always be covered loosely with plastic wrap or a kitchen towel to avoid drafts. The bowl can be placed adjacent to a heat source or on a rack over a pan of warm water. An oven preheated for less than 1 minute will also work. Some cooks find that the top of a surface next to a clothes dryer that is running will do the trick.

PUMPKIN CHEESECAKE

CRUST

¾ CUP GRAHAM CRACKER CRUMBS

½ CUP FINELY CHOPPED PECANS

¼ CUP PACKED DARK BROWN
   SUGAR

¼ CUP SUGAR

¼ CUP MELTED BUTTER, COOLED

FILLING

1 CUP CANNED PUMPKIN

6 TABLESPOONS SUGAR

3 EGGS, AT ROOM TEMPERATURE

1½ TEASPOONS CINNAMON

½ TEASPOON NUTMEG

½ TEASPOON GINGER

½ TEASPOON SALT

24 OUNCES CREAM CHEESE,
   SOFTENED

6 TABLESPOONS SUGAR

2 TABLESPOONS WHIPPING CREAM

1 TABLESPOON CORNSTARCH

1 TEASPOON VANILLA EXTRACT

TOPPING

¼ CUP CHOPPED PECANS

1 TO 2 TABLESPOONS BUTTER

2 CUPS SOUR CREAM

¼ CUP SUGAR

1 TABLESPOON COGNAC OR
   OTHER BRANDY

1 TABLESPOON MAPLE SYRUP

ON OCCASION...

you might want to serve MISS AMY'S
KAHLÚA. *Bring 4 cups water and
2 cups sugar to a boil and boil for
5 minutes. Remove from heat and stir
in ¾ cup instant coffee, 1 tablespoon
vanilla extract and ⅛ teaspoon salt.
Let stand until cool. Strain through a
cotton or linen tea towel. Add one
750-milliliter bottle of vodka. Pour
into five 12-ounce bottles. Let stand for
2 weeks before serving.*

To prepare the crust, mix the graham cracker crumbs, pecans, brown sugar, sugar and butter in a bowl. Press over the bottom of a 10-inch springform pan. Freeze for 15 minutes.

To prepare the filling, beat the pumpkin, 6 tablespoons sugar, eggs, cinnamon, nutmeg, ginger and salt in a mixer bowl until smooth. Beat the cream cheese, 6 tablespoons sugar, whipping cream, cornstarch and vanilla in a mixer bowl until creamy, scraping the bowl occasionally. Add the pumpkin mixture to the creamed mixture and mix well. Spoon into the prepared pan. Bake at 350 degrees for 40 to 45 minutes. Remove from oven. Increase the oven temperature to 425 degrees.

To prepare the topping, sauté the pecans in the butter in a skillet until crisp; drain. Mix the sour cream, sugar, Cognac and maple syrup in a bowl. Stir in the pecans. Spread over the top of the cheesecake. Bake for 10 minutes longer. Cool on a wire rack for 1 hour. Chill, loosely covered, for 24 hours before serving. Run a knife around the edge of the pan before removing the side.

Garnish each serving with a whipped mixture of 1 cup whipping cream, 2 tablespoons confectioners' sugar and ½ teaspoon cinnamon.

To serve twelve

WHEN HOLLY BERRIES SHINE

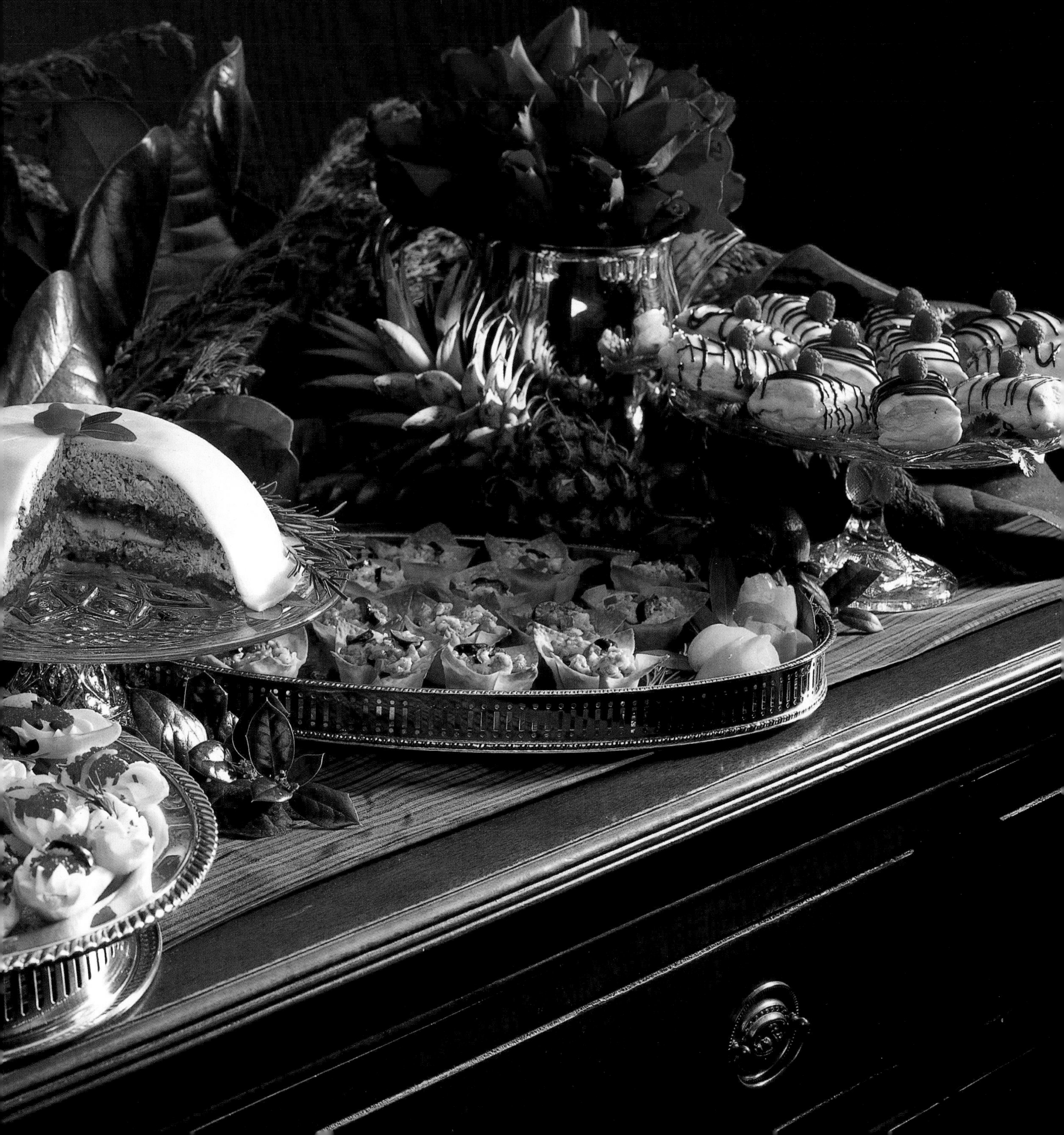

WHEN HOLLY BERRIES SHINE

MENU

Cheese Strata with Basil Tomato Sauce

Stuffed Endive

Pineapple Crown with Red Grapes

Parmesan-Coated Brie

Almost Boursin

Lobster Crostini

Fancy Shrimp Rémoulade

Sausage Stars

Hampton Place Beef Tenderloin

Mushroom Buttons

Lemon Dill Asparagus

Hazelnut Napoleons with Frangelico

Timeless Tassies

Holiday Toffee

Five-Star Coffee Bar

The front door is opened wide for a holiday gathering of friends from near and far. Whether hosting an informal reception or an evening soiree with all the glorious touches, take inspiration from this distinctive December buffet. Your stately sideboard beckons when layered with proud tartan plaid taffeta. The majestic pineapple offers a southern welcome to each and every guest. Rich cedar and shiny magnolia mix with multiple cuttings to form a lush garland, trimming the length of the buffet. An orchestrated series of cake pedestals and shimmering trays at various heights offers selected savories and delectables. Flowering buds band together to form a gentle crown of blossoms, the bouquet resting inside Aunt Eleanor's favorite silver pitcher. Bright red cranberries and fresh citrus fill a vintage crystal vase and support a column of regal iris blooms.

Too quickly each year passes,
again now holiday time,
Cherished are these glorious days
when holly berries shine.

CHEESE STRATA

BASIL TOMATO SAUCE
1 (15-OUNCE) CAN DICED
   TOMATOES
¾ CUP CHOPPED ONION
1 TABLESPOON MINCED FRESH
   GARLIC
2 TABLESPOONS OLIVE OIL
2 BAY LEAVES
½ TEASPOON SUGAR
¼ TEASPOON BASIL
1 (7-OUNCE) JAR OIL-PACK
   SUN-DRIED TOMATOES

STRATA
9 (1-OUNCE) SLICES MOZZARELLA
   CHEESE
8 OUNCES CREAM CHEESE,
   SOFTENED
2 TABLESPOONS BUTTER,
   SOFTENED
½ CUP GRATED PARMESAN
   CHEESE
2 TABLESPOONS PESTO
   SPRIGS OF FRESH BASIL
   (OPTIONAL)

To prepare the sauce, drain the diced tomatoes, reserving ¼ cup of the juice. Sauté the onion and garlic in the olive oil in a skillet over medium heat until the onion is tender. Stir in the diced tomatoes, reserved juice, bay leaves, sugar and basil. Bring to a boil; reduce heat. Simmer for 3 to 5 minutes or until thickened, stirring frequently. Remove from heat. Discard the bay leaves. Stir in the chopped drained sun-dried tomatoes. Chill, covered, for 2 hours or longer.

To prepare the strata, line a 3-cup mold with plastic wrap, allowing an overhang of 6 to 7 inches. Cut 5 slices of the mozzarella cheese diagonally into halves. Arrange the cheese triangles slightly overlapping in the prepared mold so that they resemble the spokes of a wagon wheel. Beat the cream cheese and butter in a mixer bowl at medium speed until creamy, scraping the bowl occasionally. Add the Parmesan cheese and pesto. Beat until smooth. Spread half the cream cheese mixture in the prepared mold. Top with half the sauce.

Cut 2 slices of the mozzarella cheese crosswise into halves. Arrange the cheese rectangles over the prepared layers. Spread with the remaining cream cheese mixture and remaining sauce. Cut the remaining 2 slices of mozzarella cheese into rectangles. Arrange over the top. Fold the plastic wrap over to cover and seal tightly. Place a heavy object on top to compact the layers. Chill for 8 hours or longer. Invert the mold onto a cheese board or serving platter; discard the plastic wrap. Garnish with sprigs of fresh basil. Serve with assorted party crackers or baguette slices.

Makes 3 cups

ON OCCASION...

ensure that your guests mingle by placing several food presentations throughout the living areas. Consider the unexpected . . . serve from a small covered table moved into the center of a room; a tray placed across an ottoman; a fireplace hearth; a bench; the top of a desk . . . places that can be accessed from several sides.

Locate beverage sources separate from the food. There will be spills, so cover the serving counter with plastic or foil, then top it off with a favorite cloth . . . provide several small containers for ice to allow two or more guests to prepare a beverage at one time. Allow 1 pound of ice per guest.

For an open house, furnish seating for about 25 percent of the expected guests. Prepare eight to ten different hors d'oeuvre for the party, allowing two to three per guest.

Encourage guests to linger longer by keeping food and beverages replenished . . . and, like Scarlett, worry about the dishes . . . tomorrow!

PINEAPPLE CROWN WITH RED GRAPES

STUFFED ENDIVE

Separate the spears of 4 to 5 heads of endive. Spoon about 1 teaspoon of filling onto the end of each spear. For fillings, try softened ALMOST BOURSIN, *page 185; sour cream mixed with caviar, smoked salmon, chopped sun-dried tomatoes or chives; or bleu cheese with paper-thin pear or apple slices. Not much time? Use commercially prepared salmon cream cheese and top with caviar.*

16	OUNCES CREAM CHEESE, SOFTENED
1	(8-OUNCE) CAN CRUSHED PINEAPPLE, DRAINED
1	CUP SEEDLESS RED GRAPE HALVES
1	CUP CHOPPED PECANS
¼	CUP CHOPPED GREEN BELL PEPPER
2	TABLESPOONS FINELY CHOPPED ONION
⅛	TEASPOON SEASONED SALT
1	CUP CHOPPED PECANS

Beat the cream cheese in a mixer bowl until smooth. Stir in the pineapple, grapes, 1 cup pecans, green pepper, onion and seasoned salt. Chill, covered, for 1 hour or longer. Shape into a ball. Roll in 1 cup pecans. Chill, covered, in the refrigerator until firm.

Let stand at room temperature to soften slightly before serving. Serve with butter crackers or wheat crackers. May be spooned into your favorite mold, placing 1 cup of the pecans over the bottom of the mold and pressing the cream cheese mixture over the pecans.

Makes 6 cups

Parmesan-Coated Brie

1   EGG, LIGHTLY BEATEN
1   TABLESPOON WATER
½   CUP ITALIAN BREAD CRUMBS
¼   CUP FRESHLY GRATED PARMESAN CHEESE
1   (15-OUNCE) ROUND BRIE CHEESE WITH HERBS
¼   CUP VEGETABLE OIL
    SPRIGS OF FRESH ROSEMARY (OPTIONAL)
    SLICED FRENCH BREAD OR ASSORTED PARTY CRACKERS

Whisk the egg and water in a shallow dish. Mix the bread crumbs and Parmesan cheese in a shallow dish. Dip the Brie in the egg mixture, turning to coat all sides. Coat with the bread crumb mixture. Repeat the process. Chill for 1 hour or longer.

Cook the Brie in the oil in a skillet over medium heat for 2 minutes per side or until golden brown; drain. Arrange on a serving platter.

Garnish with sprigs of rosemary. Serve with sliced French bread or assorted party crackers.

To serve twelve

Almost Boursin

16 OUNCES NEUFCHÂTEL CHEESE, SOFTENED
8   OUNCES WHIPPED BUTTER, SOFTENED
1   CLOVE OF GARLIC, MINCED
½   TEASPOON DRIED BASIL
¼   TEASPOON DRIED OREGANO
¼   TEASPOON DRIED DILLWEED
¼   TEASPOON DRIED MARJORAM
¼   TEASPOON DRIED THYME
½   TEASPOON CRACKED PEPPER

Beat the cream cheese and butter at high speed in a mixer bowl until fluffy. Beat in the garlic, basil, oregano, dillweed, marjoram, thyme and pepper. Chill for 24 hours. Serve with assorted party crackers.

Makes three cups

There are many ways to serve ALMOST BOURSIN. Spread it on tomato halves or spoon into mushroom caps—serve cold, or bake at 350 degrees for 15 minutes or broil until bubbly. Combine 1 cup ALMOST BOURSIN with ½ cup milk and toss with 12 ounces hot pasta. Pipe onto cucumber slices or endive leaves. Spread under the skin of chicken or over skinless chicken. Spoon onto baked potatoes or into mashed potatoes. Use as a sandwich spread in place of mayonnaise.

LOBSTER CROSTINI

½ CUP CHOPPED MUSHROOMS
2 CLOVES OF GARLIC, MINCED
2 TABLESPOONS OLIVE OIL
1 FLORIDA LOBSTER TAIL, COOKED, COARSELY CHOPPED
1 TABLESPOON CHOPPED FRESH ITALIAN PARSLEY
   SALT AND PEPPER TO TASTE
1 BAGUETTE, CUT INTO ½-INCH SLICES
   OLIVE OIL

Sauté the mushrooms and garlic in 2 tablespoons olive oil in a skillet for 3 minutes. Stir in the lobster and parsley. Cook for 1 minute, stirring frequently. Remove from heat. Season with salt and pepper.

Arrange the baguette slices in a single layer on a baking sheet. Brush with olive oil. Bake at 375 degrees for 5 minutes. Broil for 3 minutes or until light brown. Spoon some of the lobster mixture on each slice. Serve immediately.

Makes two dozen crostini

FANCY SHRIMP REMOULADE

1½ CUPS MAYONNAISE
½ CUP CREOLE MUSTARD
½ CUP FINELY CHOPPED GREEN ONIONS
¼ CUP FINELY CHOPPED CELERY
¼ CUP FINELY CHOPPED PARSLEY
2 TABLESPOONS MINCED GARLIC
1 TABLESPOON WORCESTERSHIRE SAUCE
1½ TEASPOONS LEMON JUICE
1 TEASPOON TABASCO SAUCE
   SALT AND FRESHLY CRACKED PEPPER TO TASTE
2 POUNDS PEELED STEAMED SHRIMP WITH TAILS

Combine the mayonnaise, mustard, green onions, celery, parsley, garlic, Worcestershire sauce, lemon juice, Tabasco sauce, salt and pepper in a bowl and mix well. Chill, covered, for 4 hours or up to 10 hours. Adjust seasonings.

Serve with the shrimp. The flavor of the sauce is enhanced if prepared 1 day in advance and stored, covered, in the refrigerator. Allow 3 shrimp per guest when served as an appetizer.

To serve ten to twelve

Everyone likes MUSHROOM BUTTONS. *Mix 1 pound of crumbled crisp-fried bacon or browned sausage, 8 ounces of softened cream cheese and 2 tablespoons minced green onions. Spoon the mixture into fresh mushroom caps. Bake at 375 degrees for 15 to 18 minutes or until the mushrooms are tender but firm.*

SAUSAGE STARS

1   PACKAGE FRESH OR FROZEN WON TON WRAPS,
    CUT INTO QUARTERS
    OLIVE OIL
1   POUND BULK SAUSAGE
1½ CUPS SHREDDED CHEDDAR CHEESE
1½ CUPS SHREDDED MONTEREY JACK CHEESE
1   CUP RANCH SALAD DRESSING
½   CUP FINELY CHOPPED RED BELL PEPPER
1   (2-OUNCE) CAN SLICED BLACK OLIVES, DRAINED

Press the won ton wrap quarters over the bottom and up the sides of miniature muffin cups. Brush with olive oil. Bake at 350 degrees for 5 minutes. Remove to a baking sheet.

Brown the sausage in a skillet, stirring until crumbly; drain. Pat the sausage with a paper towel to remove any remaining fat. Combine the sausage, Cheddar cheese, Monterey Jack cheese, salad dressing, red pepper and black olives in a bowl and mix well. Spoon about 1 heaping teaspoon of the sausage mixture into each shell. Bake for 5 minutes or until bubbly.

Makes forty-eight stars

HAMPTON PLACE BEEF TENDERLOIN

1   (4- TO 5-POUND) BEEF TENDERLOIN, TRIMMED
2   CUPS SOY SAUCE
⅔   CUP DARK SESAME OIL
7   CLOVES OF GARLIC, MINCED
2   TABLESPOONS CHOPPED GINGERROOT
    COARSE SALT AND PEPPER TO TASTE

Place the tenderloin in a nonreactive dish. Whisk the soy sauce, sesame oil, garlic and gingerroot in a bowl. Reserve half the marinade. Pour the remaining marinade over the tenderloin, turning to coat. Marinate, covered with plastic wrap, in the refrigerator for 1 hour; drain. Rub the roast with salt and pepper. Place in a roasting pan.

Sear the tenderloin at 500 degrees for 20 minutes. Reduce the oven temperature to 325 degrees. Bake for 10 minutes. Remove from oven. Let stand for 10 minutes. Return the beef to the oven. Bake for 30 minutes. Remove from oven. Let stand for 10 minutes. Continue the "in and out" process until the desired cooking time is consumed. Bake 17 to 18 minutes per pound for rare and 20 to 22 minutes per pound for medium.

Let stand for 15 minutes before slicing. Heat the reserved marinade in a saucepan and brush over the beef. Cut into thin slices. Serve on yeast rolls with horseradish sauce.

May be prepared 1 day in advance and stored, covered, in the refrigerator.

To serve sixteen to twenty

For LEMON DILL ASPARAGUS, *blanch 1½ pounds of asparagus in 4 quarts boiling salted water for 3 to 6 minutes. Drain and rinse in cold water. Serve with a chilled mixture of 2 cups sour cream, juice and zest of 1 lemon and 1 heaping tablespoon chopped fresh dillweed.*

TIMELESS TASSIES

A TIMELESS TALE . . .

about Mother who used to make
TIMELESS TASSIES *to give to friends*
around the holidays. One year while
Mother was out shopping, the then-
adolescent bottomless-pit son went into
the dining room where the tassies were
laid out—and ate every last one
(calorie count in the five figures)!
Needless to say, Santa brought him
a few coals. The next year, on her
shopping trip, Mother laughed about last
year's fiasco, which was funny—until
she got home. Once again, the tassies
were gone. Lucky for the Bottomless Pit,
he had been away too . . . but the
moaning dogs gave themselves away.
Now at holiday time, Mother sends
magazine subscriptions instead!

PASTRY

3 OUNCES CREAM CHEESE

1 CUP SIFTED FLOUR

½ CUP BUTTER

⅛ TEASPOON SALT

FILLING

¾ CUP PACKED BROWN SUGAR

1 TABLESPOON MELTED BUTTER

1 EGG, LIGHTLY BEATEN

1 TEASPOON VANILLA EXTRACT

⅛ TEASPOON SALT

⅔ CUP CHOPPED PECANS

To prepare the pastry, beat the cream cheese, flour, butter and salt in a mixer bowl until creamy, scraping the bowl occasionally. Chill, covered, for 1 hour or longer. Pat the dough over the bottom and up the sides of miniature muffin cups. To prepare the filling, combine the brown sugar, butter, egg, vanilla and salt in a saucepan. Cook over low heat until blended, stirring constantly; do not boil. To assemble, sprinkle half the pecans over the bottoms of the pastry cups. Spoon about 1 teaspoon of the filling over the pecans. Top with the remaining pecans. Bake at 325 degrees for 25 minutes.

Makes two dozen tassies

HOLIDAY TOFFEE

1 CUP SUGAR

1 CUP BUTTER

3 TABLESPOONS WATER

1 TABLESPOON LIGHT CORN SYRUP

1 (5-OUNCE) PACKAGE SLICED ALMONDS

2 CUPS MILK CHOCOLATE CHIPS

Combine the sugar, butter, water and corn syrup in a skillet. Cook over high heat for 10 minutes or until the mixture begins to thicken, stirring constantly and in 1 direction. Stir in the almonds. Pour onto a greased baking sheet and spread evenly with a spatula or wooden spoon. Sprinkle with the chocolate chips. Let stand until the chocolate begins to melt; spread evenly. Freeze for 1 to 2 hours or until set. Break into bite-size pieces. Store in a box or tin at room temperature.

Makes two pounds

HAZELNUT NAPOLEONS WITH FRANGELICO

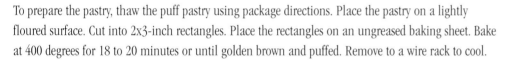

PASTRY

1 (17-OUNCE) PACKAGE FROZEN
    PUFF PASTRY

CUSTARD

2½ CUPS EVAPORATED MILK

1½ CUPS SUGAR

5 TABLESPOONS FLOUR

4 EGG YOLKS, LIGHTLY BEATEN

2 TABLESPOONS BUTTER

½ CUP FRANGELICO OR ANY
    HAZELNUT LIQUEUR

1 TEASPOON VANILLA EXTRACT

ICING

2¼ CUPS SIFTED CONFECTIONERS'
    SUGAR

3 TABLESPOONS MILK

TOPPING

¼ CUP SEMISWEET CHOCOLATE
    CHIPS

To prepare the pastry, thaw the puff pastry using package directions. Place the pastry on a lightly floured surface. Cut into 2x3-inch rectangles. Place the rectangles on an ungreased baking sheet. Bake at 400 degrees for 18 to 20 minutes or until golden brown and puffed. Remove to a wire rack to cool.

To prepare the custard, combine the evaporated milk, sugar, flour, egg yolks and butter in a saucepan. Bring to a boil over medium heat, stirring constantly. Boil for 2 to 3 minutes or until thickened, stirring constantly. Remove from heat. Stir in the liqueur and vanilla. Chill, covered, for 1 hour or longer.

To prepare the icing, mix the confectioners' sugar and milk in a bowl until of spreading consistency. To prepare the topping, heat the chocolate chips in a double boiler over hot water or microwave in a microwave-safe dish until melted.

To assemble, carefully lift off the tops of the pastry. Remove the soft centers to form a well. Spoon the custard into the wells. Replace the tops. Spread the icing on top of each pastry. Let stand until set. Spoon the chocolate into a pastry bag fitted with a small round tip. Pipe the chocolate in a decorative pattern over each pastry. Let stand until set. Store in an airtight container in the refrigerator.

Makes two dozen Napoleons

FIVE-STAR COFFEE BAR

Brew your best blend, then indulge guests with a few of these coffee complements . . .

Flavorful liqueurs . . . Kahlúa, Frangelico, Praline, Grand Marnier, Irish Mint, brandy, amaretto

And . . . heavy cream, fresh whipped cream, granulated raw sugar, sugar cubes, cinnamon sticks, ground nutmeg, white and dark shaved chocolate, rock candy swizzle sticks, Godiva Chocolate truffles.

A CELEBRATION OF LIGHT

O dreidel, dreidel, dreidel
I made it out of clay
And when it's dry and ready
Then dreidel I shall play

THE WEAK CONQUER THE MIGHTY—THAT IS THE VICTORY ACCLAIMED EACH DECEMBER...HANUKKAH, THE FESTIVAL OF LIGHTS! A SMALL BAND OF MACCABEANS DEFEATED THE SYRIAN KING ANTIOCHUS' HUGE ARMY THAT WAS TRYING TO MAKE THE JEWS DISAVOW THEIR RELIGION. WHEN THE TEMPLE WAS CLEAN, THE PEOPLE WISHED TO LIGHT THE MENORAH. THERE WAS ONLY ENOUGH OIL FOR ONE DAY, BUT BY A MIRACLE IT BURNED FOR EIGHT DAYS. TODAY, FAMILIES AND FRIENDS GATHER TO COMMEMORATE THE REDEDICATION OF THE TEMPLE OF JERUSALEM. TOGETHER, THEY LIGHT ONE CANDLE OF THE MENORAH EACH NIGHT FOR EIGHT EVENINGS. CELEBRATE THE FESTIVAL OF LIGHTS!

HERB POTATO CHIPS

5   BAKING POTATOES
    ITALIAN PARSLEY LEAVES
    KOSHER SALT TO TASTE
    FRESHLY GROUND PEPPER TO TASTE

Cut the potatoes into very thin slices. Spray both sides of the slices with olive oil cooking spray. Arrange half the slices in a single layer on a greased baking sheet.

Place 1 parsley leaf on each slice. Top with the remaining slices and press gently. Sprinkle with salt and pepper. Bake at 400 degrees until brown.

Makes four dozen

MARINATED MUSHROOMS

1   (8-OUNCE) BOTTLE RED WINE VINAIGRETTE SALAD DRESSING
1   SMALL ONION, THINLY SLICED
1   TABLESPOON BROWN SUGAR
2   TEASPOONS PARSLEY FLAKES
1   TEASPOON DRY MUSTARD
¼   TEASPOON SALT
36 SMALL FRESH MUSHROOMS, TRIMMED

Combine the salad dressing, onion, brown sugar, parsley flakes, dry mustard and salt in a saucepan and mix well. Bring to a boil. Stir in the mushrooms. Simmer for 5 minutes, stirring occasionally. Cool to room temperature. Chill, covered, for 8 hours or longer, stirring occasionally. Discard some of marinade before serving.

Makes three dozen

MIXED GREENS WITH POPPY SEED DRESSING

Mix ⅔ cup sugar, 1 teaspoon dry mustard and ½ teaspoon salt. Stir in ⅓ cup honey, 3 tablespoons lemon juice, 3 tablespoons white vinegar and 2 teaspoons grated Vidalia onion. Process in a blender at high speed for 1 minute. Add 1 cup salad oil gradually, processing constantly until blended. Fold in 1 tablespoon poppy seeds. Drizzle over a mixture of romaine, iceberg lettuce, red cabbage, chopped carrots, chopped hard-cooked egg and seedless red grapes.

CURRANT-GLAZED CHICKEN

CHICKEN SOUP WITH MATZO BALLS

Make the soup by cooking a 5- or 6-pound chicken with celery, carrots, onion, parsley, fresh or dried dill, salt and pepper. Strain and skim the soup, reserving the meat for dinner and the fat for matzo balls. To make the matzo balls, blend 4 eggs with ¼ cup reserved chicken fat or melted margarine. Add 1 cup matzo meal, 2 teaspoons salt and ¼ cup hot water and mix well. Chill, covered, for 1 hour or longer. Shape the dough into 1-inch balls. Bring 12 cups salted water to a boil and add the matzo balls. Cook, covered, for 20 minutes (don't even peek). Remove to the simmered chicken soup just before serving.

4   BONELESS SKINLESS CHICKEN BREASTS
3   TABLESPOONS BUTTER
½   CUP PREPARED MUSTARD
½   CUP SLIVERED ALMONDS
3   TABLESPOONS BROWN SUGAR
2   TABLESPOONS LEMON JUICE
1   (12-OUNCE) JAR CURRANT JELLY

Sauté the chicken in the butter in a skillet until brown on all sides. Arrange the chicken in a greased baking dish, reserving the pan drippings. Stir the mustard, almonds, brown sugar, lemon juice and jelly into the reserved pan drippings. Cook until the jelly melts, stirring constantly. Pour over the chicken.

Bake, covered with foil, at 350 degrees for 20 minutes. Remove the cover. Bake for 20 minutes longer or until the chicken is cooked through.

To serve four

POTATO VEGETABLE LATKES

2 LARGE POTATOES, PEELED
2 LARGE CARROTS, PEELED
2 MEDIUM ZUCCHINI
1 LARGE ONION
3 EGGS, BEATEN
½ TEASPOON SALT
⅛ TEASPOON PEPPER
¾ CUP MATZO MEAL
   VEGETABLE OIL FOR FRYING

Soak the potatoes in cold water to cover in a bowl; drain. Process the potatoes, carrots, zucchini and onion separately in a food processor until grated; do not purée.

Combine the grated vegetables, eggs, salt and pepper in a bowl and mix well. Stir in the matzo meal. Shape into patties, using 1 to 2 tablespoons of the batter per patty. Fry the latkes in batches in 1 to 2 tablespoons of hot oil in a skillet for 1½ minutes per side, adding additional oil as needed; drain.

To prepare the latkes in advance, fry and drain on paper towels at room temperature for 1 to 2 hours. Reheat on an ungreased baking sheet at 350 degrees for 8 to 10 minutes or freeze for future use and reheat at 350 degrees for 15 minutes.

To serve six

CARROT PANCAKES

6 CARROTS, PEELED, SHREDDED
6 EGGS
¾ CUP MATZO MEAL
½ TEASPOON SALT
   VEGETABLE OIL FOR FRYING
2 GREEN BELL PEPPERS, CHOPPED
2 TABLESPOONS VEGETABLE OIL
2 (8-OUNCE) CANS TOMATO SAUCE
¼ CUP WATER
2 TABLESPOONS SUGAR

Place half the carrots and half the eggs in a food processor container fitted with a steel blade. Process for 30 seconds. Pour into a bowl. Repeat the process with the remaining carrots and eggs and add to the first carrot mixture. Stir in the matzo meal and salt.

Add enough oil for frying to a heavy skillet to measure 1 inch. Heat until hot. Drop the batter by heaping tablespoonfuls into the oil. Fry for 1 minute or until golden brown; turn. Fry for 1 minute or until golden brown. Drain on paper towels. Arrange the pancakes in a 9x13-inch baking dish.

Sauté the green peppers in 2 tablespoons oil in a skillet until tender-crisp. Stir in the tomato sauce, water and sugar. Pour over the pancakes. Bake, covered with foil, at 325 degrees for 15 minutes; remove the cover. Bake for 15 minutes longer.

To serve eight

Serve latkes with CHUNKY APPLESAUCE. *Combine 9 large chopped cooking apples with 1 cup apple cider, ½ cup packed brown sugar, 1 quartered lemon and two 3-inch cinnamon sticks in a large heavy saucepan. Simmer, covered, over low heat until the apples are tender, stirring occasionally and adding water as needed. Cool slightly. Discard the lemon quarters and cinnamon sticks. Chill, covered, until serving time.*

SUFGANIYOT

PACKAGED WITH CARE

Pack cookies and treats in all kinds of containers, which then become part of the gift: a brioche pan, terra-cotta pots, glass vases, French jelly glasses, small buckets, fabric-wrapped boxes. Wrap treats in crisp cellophane, slide them into a container, and tie with a ribbon. When preparing gift breads, rewrap and package them in a new baking pan. Place a handwritten recipe card on top and tie with a fabric ribbon. Print enclosure cards with your family's names, punch a single hole in the corner of each card, and have ready for attaching to a package. It makes for a simple delivery of holiday treats—we'll be waiting!

¼	CUP SUGAR
1	ENVELOPE DRY YEAST
¾	CUP LUKEWARM MILK OR WATER
2½	CUPS FLOUR, SIFTED
1	TEASPOON CINNAMON
2	EGG YOLKS, LIGHTLY BEATEN
⅛	TEASPOON SALT
2	TABLESPOONS BUTTER OR PAREVE MARGARINE, SOFTENED
2	TABLESPOONS APRICOT OR STRAWBERRY PRESERVES
2	EGG WHITES, LIGHTLY BEATEN
	SUGAR OIL FOR DEEP-FRYING
	SUGAR TO TASTE

Mix ¼ cup sugar, yeast and milk in a bowl. Let stand until bubbly. Combine the yeast mixture, flour, cinnamon, egg yolks and salt in a bowl. Knead until the mixture forms a ball. Add the butter. Knead until blended. Let rise, covered with a tea towel, in the refrigerator for 8 to 10 hours.

Roll the dough ⅛ inch thick on a lightly floured surface. Cut into 24 rounds using a juice glass or 2-inch biscuit cutter. Spoon ½ teaspoon of the preserves in the center of half the rounds. Top with the remaining rounds and crimp the edges to seal. Brush with the egg whites. Arrange on a baking sheet. Let rise for 30 minutes.

Add enough sugar oil to a deep skillet to measure 2 inches. Heat to 375 degrees. Drop the doughnuts 5 at a time into the hot oil. Fry until brown on both sides, turning several times; drain. Roll in sugar to taste. Use butter and milk if serving at a milk meal and water and pareve margarine at a meat meal.

The young state of Israel has created many of its own customs. During Hanukkah, these jelly doughnuts, which are fried in oil, are served to symbolize the miracle of the oil that lasted for eight days instead of one.

Makes one dozen doughnuts

HAMANTASCHEN

⅔ CUP UNSALTED BUTTER, SOFTENED

½ CUP SUGAR

1 EGG

3 TABLESPOONS MILK OR WATER

½ TEASPOON VANILLA EXTRACT

2⅓ TO 3 CUPS SIFTED UNBLEACHED FLOUR

APRICOT PRESERVES, PEANUT BUTTER OR CHOCOLATE CHIPS

Combine the butter and sugar in a bowl. Beat with a wooden spoon until creamy. Add the egg. Beat until blended. Stir in the milk and vanilla. Add the flour, stirring until the mixture forms a ball.

Divide the dough into 2 equal portions. Shape each portion into a log 3 inches in diameter. Chill, wrapped in plastic wrap, for 2 to 10 hours.

Remove 1 log at a time from the refrigerator. Cut into ⅛-inch slices. Roll the slices on a lightly floured surface. Place 1 teaspoon of apricot preserves in the center of each round. Pull the outside edges of the rounds to a point and pinch to seal. Place on an ungreased cookie sheet.

Bake at 350 degrees for 20 minutes or until golden brown. Cool on cookie sheet for 2 minutes. Remove to a wire rack to cool completely.

Use your imagination for fillings. Try chopped nuts, chopped apples, poppy seeds or chopped prunes. Traditionally served at Purim, this simple cookie is always enjoyed. The three corners of the cookie represent Abraham, Isaac and Jacob, the founding fathers of Judaism.

Makes three dozen

ON OCCASION...

create little lights for the 8-day celebration. Begin with sheets of beeswax—try using varying shades of blue. With a utility knife and ruler, cut the sheets into 2x4½-inch rectangles. Cut wicking into 5½-inch lengths and knot at one end. Warm the wax with a blow-dryer for 10 to 15 seconds, or just until it is pliable. Place the wicking along the longer edge of the wax, leaving ¾ inch of unknotted wick to hang from one end. Roll the wax carefully around the wick, pressing the seam to seal.

Select inexpensive tin buckets to paint with the traditional colors of Hanukkah and stencil with dreidel, menorah, and star shapes. Fill them with the hand-made candles and you're ready for "special deliveries."

MAKING SEASONS BRIGHT

MAKING SEASONS BRIGHT

MENU

Seafood Parcels with Herb Mayonnaise

Coffeehouse Pecans

Fiery Roasted Pecans

Shrimp and Grits

Brussels Sprouts with Red Grapes

Honey Baked Tomatoes

Gougères

Gabriel's Caramel Cake

Buttermilk Pralines

Homemade Irish Crème Liqueur

Whether you're Old South...or new..., spending time with friends is one of life's best gifts. Engaging conversation and lighthearted laughter are meant to be shared over a splendid meal. A regional favorite, Shrimp and Grits, now boldly makes its way into the dining room. Here, patterned china rests inside golden scalloped-edge chargers. Heirloom linens enhance the polished gleam of the mahogany table. Candlelight reflects in the fine white wine and dances lightly off crystal goblets as Star-of-Bethlehem blossoms reign supreme inside a generations-old compote. Pomegranates and garden greenery mingle with silver candlesticks while Carolina palm fronds fill every window ledge. Clusters of magnolia leaves grace a holiday tree. Not to be outdone, showy leaves encircle potted blooms, artfully tied with organdy ribbons. Bring out your best, however grand or simple, and unite for a special evening. Create enduring memories through the joyous merriment, rich hope, and lasting friendships...that make every season bright.

SEAFOOD PARCELS WITH HERB MAYONNAISE

HERB MAYONNAISE

- 2 EGG YOLKS
- ½ TEASPOON DRY MUSTARD
  SALT AND FRESHLY GROUND
  PEPPER TO TASTE
- ¾ CUP SALAD OIL
- 2 TABLESPOONS WINE VINEGAR
- ½ CUP SNIPPED CHIVES
- ½ CUP SNIPPED WATERCRESS

SEAFOOD PARCELS

- 8 OUNCES SMALL SHRIMP,
  PEELED, DEVEINED
- 1 POUND SCALLOPS

- 2 TABLESPOONS SAKE
  JUICE OF ½ LEMON
  BLACK PEPPERCORNS TO TASTE
- ½ CUP SNIPPED CHIVES
- 2 TABLESPOONS FINELY CHOPPED
  FRESH PARSLEY
- ¼ TEASPOON CAYENNE
  SALT AND FRESHLY GROUND
  BLACK PEPPER TO TASTE
- 8 SHEETS FROZEN PHYLLO
  PASTRY
- ¼ CUP MELTED BUTTER
- 8 CHIVE TOPS, BLANCHED

To prepare the mayonnaise, whisk the egg yolks, dry mustard, salt and pepper in a bowl until thickened. Add 2 tablespoons of the oil 1 drop at a time, whisking constantly. Stir in 1 teaspoon of the wine vinegar. Add the remaining oil in a fine stream, whisking constantly. Stir in the remaining vinegar. Add the chives and watercress and mix well. Chill, covered, in the refrigerator.

To prepare the parcels, reserve 4 of the shrimp. Cook the remaining shrimp and scallops in a mixture of the sake, lemon juice and peppercorns in a large saucepan over low heat just until the seafood begins to change color, stirring frequently; drain. Stir in the chives, parsley, cayenne, salt and black pepper. Thaw the phyllo using package directions. Place 1 sheet of the phyllo on a sheet of waxed paper, leaving the remaining pastry covered with a damp towel to prevent drying out. Brush the phyllo lightly with some of the melted butter. Cut into 4 equal portions and stack. Spoon 2 tablespoons of the seafood mixture on top of the phyllo. Bring up the corners and twist gently to form a parcel. Tie with kitchen twine. Place on a lightly greased baking sheet. Repeat the process with the remaining phyllo, remaining butter and remaining seafood mixture until all the ingredients are used. Bake at 375 degrees for 12 to 15 minutes or until the parcels are golden brown and crisp. May reduce the oven temperature near the end of the baking process to prevent overbrowning. Remove the parcels from the oven and discard the kitchen twine. Tie each with a single strand of chive. Garnish with the reserved shrimp. Serve with the mayonnaise.

To serve four

GEORGIA'S FINEST...

COFFEEHOUSE PECANS
Toast 3 cups Georgia pecan halves in a saucepan over medium heat for 10 to 15 minutes, stirring constantly. Add a mixture of ½ cup sugar, ¼ cup water, 4 teaspoons instant coffee granules, ½ teaspoon cinnamon and ⅛ teaspoon salt. Cook for 3 minutes, stirring constantly. Spread on waxed paper and separate with a fork to cool. Store in an airtight container.

FIERY ROASTED PECANS
Mix 3 tablespoons melted butter, 3 tablespoons Worcestershire sauce, ½ teaspoon salt, ¼ teaspoon garlic powder, ¼ teaspoon cayenne and 6 drops of Tabasco sauce. Stir in 4 cups Georgia pecan halves. Spread in a baking pan. Bake at 300 degrees for 20 minutes, stirring every 5 minutes; drain.

In addition, try CANDIED PECAN CROUTONS on page 32 and BUTTERED PECANS on page 227.

SHRIMP AND GRITS

GIFTS TO GIVE

Candles tied with ribbon—one can never have enough; music— holiday, classical, or a personal favorite compact disc; container of colored sugar—with an invitation to tea; special photograph—slipped inside a frame; copies of Christmas songs—to take caroling with friends; rounds of felt for storing china—one dozen wrapped with a satin cord; unusual silver serving piece—a berry spoon or butter knife— from your local shop of treasures; decorative glass bottle with stopper— filled with HOMEMADE IRISH CRÈME LIQUEUR.

To make HOMEMADE IRISH CRÈME LIQUEUR, *blend 1¼ cups Irish whiskey, 14 ounces sweetened condensed milk, 1 cup whipping cream or light cream, 4 eggs or 1 cup egg substitute, 2 tablespoons chocolate syrup, 2 teaspoons instant coffee, 1 teaspoon vanilla and ½ teaspoon almond extract. Store in an airtight jar in the refrigerator for up to 1 month. Shake well before serving.*

GRITS

12	CUPS CHICKEN BROTH
4½	CUPS COARSE STONE-GROUND GRITS
1	CUP WHIPPING CREAM
	SALT AND WHITE PEPPER TO TASTE

SHRIMP

12	OUNCES SPICY ITALIAN SAUSAGE
1	TABLESPOON OLIVE OIL
2	POUNDS MEDIUM OR LARGE SHRIMP, PEELED, DEVEINED
1½	CUPS CHICKEN BROTH
2	TABLESPOONS FINELY CHOPPED FRESH PARSLEY

To prepare the grits, stir the grits into the boiling broth in a large heavy saucepan over high heat. Reduce the heat and simmer for 5 minutes, stirring constantly. Cook for 20 to 25 minutes longer or until the stock is absorbed and the grits are tender, stirring frequently. Stir in the whipping cream. Cook for 10 minutes longer or until thick and creamy, stirring frequently. Season with salt and white pepper. Cover and keep warm over low heat. Add additional warm chicken broth if the grits become too thick.

To prepare the shrimp, place the sausage on a baking sheet with raised sides. Bake on the top oven rack at 400 degrees for 10 to 15 minutes or until the sausage is firm and the juices run clear. Let stand until cool. Cut into bite-size pieces.

Sauté the sausage in the heated olive oil in a heavy skillet for 2 minutes or until light brown. Add the shrimp. Sauté for no longer than 1 minute or until the shrimp begin to turn pink. Add 1 cup of the broth to deglaze the skillet. Stir in 1 tablespoon of the parsley. Simmer for 1 minute. Add the remaining broth if needed for a thinner consistency.

To assemble, spoon equal portions of the hot grits onto 8 heated plates. Spoon the shrimp mixture over the grits. Sprinkle with the remaining 1 tablespoon parsley. Serve immediately. Allow 6 large shrimp or 8 to 10 medium shrimp per person.

To serve eight

BRUSSELS SPROUTS WITH RED GRAPES

12 BRUSSELS SPROUTS
30 SEEDLESS RED GRAPES
¼ CUP MELTED BUTTER

Trim the bottoms of the brussels sprouts. Make a slash in the shape of a cross in the bottom of each brussels sprout. Place in a steamer basket. Steam over boiling water for 12 to 15 minutes or until tender. Add the grapes. Steam for 1 minute. Spoon into a serving bowl. Drizzle with the butter.

To serve four to six

HONEY BAKED TOMATOES

8 MEDIUM RIPE TOMATOES
4 TEASPOONS HONEY
½ CUP COARSE FRESH BREAD CRUMBS
1 TABLESPOON TARRAGON
2 TEASPOONS SALT
2 TEASPOONS FRESHLY GROUND PEPPER
4 TEASPOONS UNSALTED BUTTER

Cut a slice from the stem end of each tomato and discard; drain. Place the tomatoes cut side up in a buttered baking dish. Drizzle with the honey inside and out, rubbing the honey into the cavities.

Mix the bread crumbs, tarragon, salt and pepper in a bowl. Sprinkle over the tomatoes. Dot with the butter. Bake at 350 degrees for 30 minutes or until the tomato skins begin to wrinkle. Broil for 5 minutes or until the crumbs begin to brown. Serve hot or at room temperature.

To serve eight

DECK THE HALLS . . .

GREENERY CAN BE . . .
boxwood, nandina, lemon leaves, magnolia, pyracantha, mountain laurel, cedar, fir, cypress, smilax, pine, mahonia, ivy, holly, juniper . . . , or any green from your yard . . . tied with a ribbon and placed on the back of dining room chairs for an extra-special touch . . . centered in front of a fireplace and trimmed with fresh pineapple and apples—if it is not cold enough for a fire!

GARLANDS CAN BE . . .
natural and fresh greenery, popcorn, paper chains, penny candy, cranberries, western rope, raffia, wooden beads, drilled pecans, and pine cones; corded roping, paper dolls, jumbo rickrack, cotton jump ropes, ribbon, cut snowflakes, or grapevines.

GOUGERES

1   CUP WATER
5   TABLESPOONS BUTTER
1   TEASPOON SALT
¼   TEASPOON FRESHLY GROUND PEPPER
¼   TEASPOON NUTMEG
1   CUP FLOUR
1   CUP SHREDDED SWISS OR GRUYÈRE CHEESE
5   EGGS, AT ROOM TEMPERATURE
1½   TEASPOONS WATER

Bring 1 cup water, butter, salt, pepper and nutmeg to a boil in a saucepan. Boil until the butter melts, stirring occasionally. Remove from heat. Add the flour. Beat with a wooden spoon until the mixture adheres. Add the cheese. Beat until blended. Add 4 of the eggs 1 at a time, beating until smooth and shiny after each addition.

Drop the dough by small spoonfuls onto a greased baking sheet. Whisk the remaining egg and 1½ teaspoons water in a bowl until blended. Brush the tops with the egg mixture.

Bake in the upper third of the oven at 425 degrees for 20 minutes or until golden brown and doubled in size. Serve immediately.

Makes three dozen

GABRIEL'S CARAMEL ICING

3   CUPS SUGAR
¾   CUP EVAPORATED MILK
¾   CUP MARGARINE
1   TABLESPOON LIGHT CORN SYRUP
1   TEASPOON VANILLA EXTRACT

Spoon ½ cup of the sugar into a stainless steel 2½-quart saucepan or a cast-iron skillet.

Shake the pan to keep the melting sugar evenly spread over the bottom but not on the sides. Stir with a wooden spoon if necessary for even melting; the color will be a little lighter than the skin of an almond and mixture should smoke slightly when ready.

Add the evaporated milk, the remaining 2½ cups sugar, margarine and corn syrup in the order listed and mix well. Cook over medium heat to 238 to 250 degrees on a candy thermometer; mixture will boil vigorously.

Stir in the vanilla. Spread immediately, adding milk if the mixture becomes too stiff to spread. Top your brownies with this decadent caramel icing.

To ice Gabriel's Caramel Cake, page 203

GABRIEL'S CARAMEL CAKE

3   CUPS WHITE LILY FLOUR, SIFTED
2   TEASPOONS BAKING POWDER
¼   TEASPOON SALT
1   CUP 2% MILK
1   TABLESPOON VANILLA EXTRACT
2   CUPS SUGAR
1   CUP MARGARINE
4   JUMBO EGG YOLKS
4   JUMBO EGG WHITES
    GABRIEL'S CARAMEL ICING (PAGE 202)

Let all ingredients stand until room temperature. Sift the flour, baking powder and salt in a bowl. Combine the milk and vanilla in a bowl and mix well.

Beat the sugar and margarine in a mixer bowl until creamy, scraping the bowl occasionally. Beat in the egg yolks 1 at a time. Add the dry ingredients alternately with the milk mixture, beginning and ending with the dry ingredients and mixing well after each addition.

Beat the egg whites in a mixer bowl until soft peaks form. Fold into the batter. Spoon into three 9-inch cake pans sprayed with nonstick cooking spray.

Bake at 350 degrees for 30 minutes or until the layers test done. Cool in pans on wire racks for 10 minutes. Invert onto wire racks to cool completely. Spread Gabriel's Caramel Icing between the layers and over the top and side of the cake.

To serve twelve

ON OCCASION...

treat your family and friends to BUTTERMILK PRALINES. *Toast 2 cups pecans at 300 degrees for 10 to 12 minutes. Combine 3 cups sugar, 1 teaspoon baking soda, ⅛ teaspoon salt, 1 cup buttermilk, ¾ cup light corn syrup and 2 tablespoons butter. Cook over low heat to 234 to 240 degrees on a candy thermometer. Beat until mixture loses its luster and stir in the pecans. Beat until thickened and drop onto waxed paper. When firm, store in an airtight container.*

CAN'T WAIT 'TIL MORNING

MENU

Winter Fruit with
Honey Lime Dressing

Hospitality Ham Steaks

Guest Room Strata

Macadamia Nut French Toast

Walnut Walkaway

Raspberry Coffee Cake

Almond Butter Letters

Fruitcake Cookies

Praline Cookies

Christmas Morning Punch

Cranberry Tea

...PITTER PATTER...PITTER PATTER...CAN YOU HEAR THOSE TINY SLIPPERS TIPTOE ACROSS THE WOODEN FLOOR? IT'S SO EARLY...THE DARK IS JUST BEGINNING TO FADE. YET, A LITTLE FACE SHINES THROUGH THE BANISTER AT THE TOP OF THE STAIRS. SMILING CHEEKS—ROSY, OF COURSE,... BRIGHT EYES—NOT PEEKING. IS IT TIME YET? JUST HAVE TO SLIP ON A ROBE AND HURRY DOWN THE STAIRS. THE MAGIC BEGINS... IT'S CHRISTMAS MORNING! THERE'S MORE THAN A SLEIGHFUL OF TOYS! TINY TREE LIGHTS DANCE OFF PACKAGE WRAPPINGS. SPIRITED BOWS STAND AT ATTENTION, EAGER TO BE SELECTED FOR OPENING. WHAT SPECIAL TREASURE IS HIDDEN JUST INSIDE, WAITING TO FULFILL A HOLIDAY WISH? GROGGY GUESTS AND FUZZY-EYED PARENTS (THE INSTRUCTIONS ALWAYS SAY "EASY TO ASSEMBLE"!) JOIN THRILLED GIRLS AND BOYS. COFFEE IS READY...THE FIRE IS GLOWING AGAIN. EVERYONE CAN DELIGHT ALL MORNING LONG AS A MADE-AHEAD BRUNCH AWAITS— OR...JUST WARMING IN THE OVEN. ENJOY EACH MOMENT OF A DAY SHARED BY OLD AND YOUNG. ONLY ONCE A YEAR...THIS JOY, THIS HOPE, THIS DAY...CHRISTMAS MORNING!

WINTER FRUIT WITH HONEY LIME DRESSING

HONEY LIME DRESSING	SALAD
1 CUP VEGETABLE OIL	1 FRESH PINEAPPLE, CUT INTO
½ CUP DARK RUM	CHUNKS
⅓ CUP FRESH LIME JUICE	SECTIONS OF 6 NAVEL
⅓ CUP HONEY	ORANGES
½ TEASPOON SALT	8 OUNCES SEEDLESS RED
½ TEASPOON DRY MUSTARD	GRAPES, CUT INTO HALVES

To prepare the dressing, combine the oil, rum, lime juice, honey, salt and dry mustard in a jar with a tightfitting lid. Cover the jar and shake to mix. Chill until serving time.

To prepare the salad, combine the pineapple, oranges and grapes in a salad bowl and mix gently. Add the desired amount of dressing, tossing to coat.

To serve twelve

HOSPITALITY HAM STEAKS

1 (6-OUNCE) CAN PINEAPPLE JUICE
4 (4- TO 5-OUNCE) SMOKED OR CURED HAM STEAKS
4 TO 6 FRESH OR CANNED PINEAPPLE RINGS
PEPPER TO TASTE

Pour the pineapple juice over the steaks in a nonreactive dish, turning to coat. Marinate, covered, in the refrigerator for 1 hour, turning occasionally; drain. Place the steaks on a griddle or in a heavy skillet. Cook over medium-high heat for 4 to 5 minutes per side or until light brown. Remove to a platter. Cover to keep warm.

Cook the pineapple on the griddle or in a heavy skillet for 4 minutes per side. Arrange the pineapple rings on top of the steaks. Sprinkle with pepper.

To serve four

FOR A MERRY MORNING...

CRANBERRY TEA
Bring 2 quarts water, 2 cups cranberry juice, 2½ cups unsweetened pineapple juice, 2 cups sugar, one 6-ounce can frozen lemonade concentrate, one 6-ounce can frozen orange juice concentrate, 4 tea bags and 1 tablespoon whole cloves to a boil. Stir in 2 quarts water. Simmer for 20 minutes. Strain the tea and ladle into mugs.

CHRISTMAS MORNING PUNCH
Mix 1 gallon chilled unsweetened apple juice, ½ gallon chilled unsweetened pineapple juice, 4 cups chilled orange juice and 1 cup chilled lemon juice in a punch bowl. Garnish with orange slices. Ladle into punch cups.

GUEST ROOM STRATA

1   (10- TO 12-INCH) LOAF FRENCH BREAD, CUBED
2   CUPS SHREDDED SHARP CHEDDAR CHEESE
1   POUND BACON, CRISP-FRIED, CRUMBLED
1   POUND HOT SAUSAGE, CRUMBLED, COOKED, DRAINED
8   EGGS, LIGHTLY BEATEN
1   QUART MILK
1   TABLESPOON DRY MUSTARD
1   TEASPOON WORCESTERSHIRE SAUCE
1   TEASPOON SALT

Layer half the bread and half the cheese in a buttered 11x14-inch baking dish. Spread with a mixture of the bacon and sausage. Top with the remaining bread and remaining cheese.

Whisk the eggs, milk, dry mustard, Worcestershire sauce and salt in a bowl. Pour over the prepared layers. Chill, covered, for 8 to 10 hours. Bake at 325 degrees for 45 minutes.

To serve twelve

MACADAMIA NUT FRENCH TOAST

1   (16-OUNCE) LOAF FRENCH, ITALIAN OR WHITE BREAD,
    CUT INTO 1-INCH SLICES
⅔   CUP ORANGE JUICE
⅓   CUP MILK
¼   CUP SUGAR
4   EGGS, LIGHTLY BEATEN
½   TEASPOON VANILLA EXTRACT
¼   TEASPOON NUTMEG
⅔   CUP MELTED BUTTER OR MARGARINE
½   CUP CHOPPED MACADAMIA NUTS
    CONFECTIONERS' SUGAR TO TASTE
    NUTMEG TO TASTE
    MAPLE SYRUP

Arrange the bread in a single layer in a lightly greased 9x13-inch dish. Whisk the orange juice, milk, sugar, eggs, vanilla and ¼ teaspoon nutmeg in a bowl until blended. Pour over the bread. Chill, covered, for 8 to 10 hours.

Pour the butter into a 10x15-inch baking pan, tilting the pan to coat the bottom. Arrange the bread slices in a single layer over the butter. Bake at 400 degrees for 10 minutes. Sprinkle with the macadamia nuts. Bake for 10 minutes longer. Sprinkle with confectioners' sugar and/or nutmeg to taste. Serve with warm maple syrup.

To serve four

WALNUT WALKAWAY

8   OUNCES CREAM CHEESE, SOFTENED

½   CUP SUGAR

1   TEASPOON GRATED ORANGE PEEL

1   TEASPOON GRATED LEMON PEEL

½   CUP FINELY CHOPPED WALNUTS OR PECANS

¼   CUP LUKEWARM WATER

1   ENVELOPE DRY YEAST

2   CUPS FLOUR

⅛   TEASPOON SALT

¾   CUP BUTTER, CUT INTO PIECES

1   EGG, AT ROOM TEMPERATURE, LIGHTLY BEATEN

    CONFECTIONERS' SUGAR TO TASTE

ON OCCASION...

make a child's tree.

Use all the handmade decorations, starting with the "preschool past," to mark the passage of time and showcase the personal history of your special child.

Beat the cream cheese in a mixer bowl until light and fluffy. Add the sugar, orange peel and lemon peel. Beat until mixed. Stir in the walnuts.

Microwave the lukewarm water in a microwave-safe cup for 35 seconds. Stir in the yeast. Combine the flour and salt in a bowl. Cut in the butter until crumbly. Add the yeast mixture and egg, stirring until blended. Divide the dough into 2 equal portions. Chill for 5 minutes. Roll one portion into a thin 12x18-inch rectangle on a lightly floured surface. Spread half the cream cheese mixture over the rectangle. Roll as for a jelly roll. Place open edge down on a baking sheet. Fold the ends under. Make a lengthwise slash in the top. Repeat the process with the remaining dough and cream cheese mixture.

Bake at 375 degrees for 22 minutes or until light brown. Cool on the baking sheet for several minutes. Remove to a wire rack to cool completely. Sift confectioners' sugar over the top. Store in an airtight container as this yeast recipe becomes stale quickly.

To serve eight

RASPBERRY COFFEE CAKE

2¼   CUPS FLOUR
¾   CUP SUGAR
¾   CUP BUTTER OR MARGARINE, SOFTENED
¾   CUP SOUR CREAM
1   TEASPOON ALMOND EXTRACT
½   TEASPOON BAKING SODA
½   TEASPOON BAKING POWDER
1   EGG, LIGHTLY BEATEN
8   OUNCES CREAM CHEESE, SOFTENED
¼   CUP SUGAR
2   EGGS
⅓   CUP SEEDLESS RASPBERRY PRESERVES
½   CUP SLICED ALMONDS

Mix the flour and ¾ cup sugar in a bowl. Cut in the butter until crumbly.
Reserve 1 cup of the crumb mixture. Combine the remaining crumb
mixture, sour cream, flavoring, baking soda, baking powder and 1 egg
in a bowl and mix well. Pat into a 10-inch springform pan.

Combine the cream cheese, ¼ cup sugar and 2 eggs in a mixer bowl. Beat
until creamy, scraping the bowl occasionally. Spoon into the prepared pan.
Spread with the preserves. Mix the reserved crumb mixture and almonds in
a bowl. Sprinkle over the top. Bake at 350 degrees for 45 to 50 minutes.
Cool in the pan on a wire rack for 15 minutes before serving.

To serve eight

ALMOND BUTTER LETTERS

3   CUPS SIFTED FLOUR
1½   CUPS BUTTER, SOFTENED
¾   CUP WATER
1   EGG
1   EGG YOLK
1   CUP SUGAR
1   CUP ALMOND PASTE, FINELY CRUMBLED
½   TO 1 TEASPOON ALMOND EXTRACT
1   EGG WHITE, LIGHTLY BEATEN

Combine the flour, butter and water in a bowl, stirring until of a dough
consistency. Chill, covered, for 8 to 10 hours. Whisk the egg and egg yolk
in a bowl until blended. Stir in the sugar, almond paste and flavoring.
Chill, covered, for 8 to 10 hours.

Divide the pastry into 6 equal portions. Roll each portion into a 3x17-inch
rectangle on a lightly floured surface. Spread ⅙ of the filling down the
center of each rectangle. Fold the long side of each rectangle over the
filling to enclose; seal the edges and ends. Brush with the egg white. Place
on a baking sheet. Bake at 350 degrees for 30 to 35 minutes or until
golden brown. May substitute a date-and-nut filling for the almond filling.

To serve six

FRUITCAKE COOKIES

1	TEASPOON BAKING SODA
1	TABLESPOON WATER
3¼	CUPS FLOUR
1	TEASPOON CINNAMON
½	TEASPOON EACH SALT, NUTMEG AND CLOVES
2	CUPS SUGAR
½	CUP SHORTENING
½	CUP BUTTER, SOFTENED
3	EGGS
1½	TEASPOONS VANILLA EXTRACT
1	TEASPOON LEMON EXTRACT
¼	CUP MILK
1	POUND WALNUTS OR PECANS, CHOPPED
8	OUNCES EACH DATES AND RAISINS, CHOPPED
4	OUNCES EACH CANDIED CHERRIES, CANDIED PINEAPPLE AND CITRON, CHOPPED

Dissolve the baking soda in the water in a small bowl. Sift the flour, cinnamon, salt, nutmeg and cloves into a bowl and mix well.

Beat the sugar, shortening and butter in a mixer bowl until creamy. Add the eggs and flavorings. Beat until fluffy, scraping the bowl occasionally. Add the flour mixture and milk alternately, beating well after each addition. Beat in the baking soda mixture. Stir in the nuts and fruit.

Drop by teaspoonfuls onto a greased cookie sheet. Bake at 350 degrees for 15 minutes or until light brown. Cool on the cookie sheet for 2 minutes. Remove to a wire rack to cool completely.

Makes twelve dozen cookies

PRALINE COOKIES

COOKIES

1⅔	CUPS FLOUR
1½	TEASPOONS BAKING POWDER
½	TEASPOON SALT
½	CUP BUTTER OR MARGARINE, SOFTENED
1½	CUPS PACKED BROWN SUGAR
1	EGG
1	TEASPOON VANILLA EXTRACT
1	CUP PECAN PIECES

ICING

1½	CUPS WHIPPING CREAM
1	CUP PACKED BROWN SUGAR
1	CUP CONFECTIONERS' SUGAR

To prepare the cookies, mix the flour, baking powder and salt in a bowl. Beat the butter in a mixer bowl until creamy. Add the brown sugar. Beat until blended. Add the egg and vanilla and mix well. Add the dry ingredients gradually, beating well after each addition. Drop by rounded tablespoonfuls onto an ungreased cookie sheet. Bake at 350 degrees for 10 minutes. Place 4 to 5 pecan pieces on top of each cookie. Cool on a wire rack for 5 to 10 minutes.

To prepare the icing, combine the cream and brown sugar in a saucepan. Bring to a boil, stirring constantly. Boil for 2 minutes, stirring constantly. Remove from heat. Add the confectioners' sugar and beat until smooth. Drizzle over the cookies.

Makes two dozen cookies

RIBBONS *are . . . paper, cord, curling, satin, grosgrain, dotted, floral, plaid, rickrack, raffia, wired, metallic, string, cotton, lace, woven, patterned or plain, vine or bough, fresh or found, simple or fancy . . . the little smile on a package.*

GOD BLESS US EVERYONE

Menu

Crab Meat Butter Spread

Portobello Cream Soup

Always Ambrosia

Cornish Game Hens with
Blackberry Honey

Sweet Tomato Pudding

Haricots Verts with
Holiday Julienne

Mrs. Cratchit's Dinner Rolls

Olde World Almond Torte

What the Dickens?
Bread Pudding

Winter Wassail

Christmas Past, Christmas Present, Christmas Future...the spirit of the season binds each year together, and generations of ritual mark the gift of this glorious day. No time for bah humbug! If by chance Scrooge should cast a curious glance our way, he would surely mend his ways and beg to enter the warm celebration about to begin. Silently checking her list, Mother is in charge. Cherished flatware, holiday china, the damask tablecloth worn by time. Napkins tied with plaid ribbon, holding a new bauble for next year's noble fir. Goblets wait patiently to be filled by Brother, knowing his annual duty. Fruits, nuts, berries, and evergreens all arranged by Sister, her trademark of this treasured family day. The youngest is kept busy creating "original" place cards, while Grandmother puts the finishing touches on dessert...If only the candlesticks could talk... All are seated, in the same places as last year...and the next. Father leads our family in prayer, for God has truly blessed us...everyone!

PORTOBELLO CREAM SOUP

¼   CUP BUTTER
¼   CUP FLOUR
2   CUPS CHICKEN BROTH
½   TEASPOON SALT
¼   TEASPOON PEPPER
1   TO 2 BAY LEAVES
⅔   CUP FINELY CHOPPED CELERY
¼   CUP FINELY CHOPPED ONION
3   TABLESPOONS VEGETABLE OIL
4   TO 5 CUPS SLICED FRESH PORTOBELLO MUSHROOMS
⅔   CUP HALF-AND-HALF

Heat the butter in a saucepan until melted. Add the flour, stirring until blended. Add the broth gradually, stirring constantly. Stir in the salt, pepper and bay leaves. Simmer for 15 minutes, stirring occasionally.

Sauté the celery and onion in the oil in a skillet until tender. Stir in the mushrooms. Cook until the mushrooms are tender, stirring occasionally. Stir into the broth mixture. Bring to a boil; reduce heat. Simmer for 15 minutes, stirring occasionally.

Add the half-and-half gradually and mix well after each addition. Cook just until heated through, stirring occasionally. Discard the bay leaves. Ladle into soup bowls.

To serve four

CRAB MEAT BUTTER SPREAD

Heat 16 ounces softened cream cheese and ½ cup softened butter in a double boiler until blended, stirring frequently. Season with cayenne to taste. Stir in 1 pound crab meat. Spoon into a chafing dish. Serve warm with toast points, thin wheat crackers or melba toast rounds.

ALWAYS AMBROSIA

SECTIONS OF 10 TO 12 NAVEL ORANGES
SECTIONS OF 2 TO 3 BLOOD ORANGES
1 (14-OUNCE) CAN CRUSHED PINEAPPLE
1 CUP FRESH OR CANNED SHREDDED COCONUT
¼ CUP SUGAR (OPTIONAL)
2 BANANAS, SLICED
1 CUP PECAN HALVES, BROKEN

Remove the membranes from the orange sections. Combine the oranges, undrained pineapple and coconut in a large bowl, tossing to mix. Taste and add the sugar if needed. May be prepared to this point 1 day in advance and stored, covered, in the refrigerator.

Add the bananas and pecans 1 hour before serving. Chill until serving time.

To serve twelve

CORNISH GAME HENS WITH BLACKBERRY HONEY

4 CORNISH GAME HENS
   SALT AND PEPPER TO TASTE
2 CUPS WATER
1 CUP HONEY
½ CUP BLACKBERRY JAM
⅛ TEASPOON CINNAMON

Rinse the hens and pat dry. Sprinkle the hens inside and out with salt and pepper. Place in a baking pan. Pour the water around the hens. Bake at 450 degrees for 10 minutes.

Combine the honey, jam and cinnamon in a microwave-safe dish and mix well. Microwave for 1 minute or until the jam melts and stir.

Brush the hens with the blackberry honey.

Lower the oven temperature to 350 degrees. Bake for 40 minutes longer or until the hens are cooked through, basting with the blackberry honey every 15 minutes.

To serve four

For a festive holiday touch, swag ribbon along the handrail of the stairs as garland. Attach it at the newel post, draping it loosely between intervals. Place greenery clusters topped with a bow at the intervals. Try organdy or satin ribbon for a formal look or crisp red plaid for traditional appeal.

SWEET TOMATO PUDDING

2   TABLESPOONS CORNSTARCH
2   TABLESPOONS WHITE VINEGAR
½   CUP CHOPPED ONION
½   CUP CHOPPED CELERY
½   CUP CHOPPED GREEN BELL PEPPER
2   TABLESPOONS BUTTER OR MARGARINE
1   (16-OUNCE) CAN TOMATOES
½   CUP SUGAR
1   TEASPOON BASIL
    SALT AND PEPPER TO TASTE
½   CUP BREAD CRUMBS
1   TABLESPOON MELTED BUTTER

Dissolve the cornstarch in the vinegar in a bowl. Sauté the onion, celery and green pepper in 2 tablespoons butter in a skillet. Add the undrained tomatoes, sugar, basil, salt and pepper. Bring to a boil. Stir in the cornstarch mixture.

Spoon the tomato mixture into a greased 9x9-inch baking pan. Sprinkle with a mixture of the bread crumbs and 1 tablespoon butter. Bake at 400 degrees for 30 to 40 minutes or until brown and bubbly.

To serve four to six

HARICOTS VERTS WITH HOLIDAY JULIENNE

2   POUNDS HARICOTS VERTS, STEMS REMOVED
    SALT TO TASTE
1   RED BELL PEPPER, JULIENNED
1   YELLOW BELL PEPPER, JULIENNED
2   TABLESPOONS OLIVE OIL
¼   CUP BUTTER
3   CLOVES OF GARLIC, MINCED
½   CUP WHITE WINE
    PEPPER TO TASTE

Blanch the haricots in boiling salted water in a saucepan for 2 minutes; drain. Rinse with cold water.

Sauté the red pepper and yellow pepper in the olive oil in a saucepan for 3 minutes or until tender-crisp. Remove the bell peppers to a bowl with a slotted spoon, reserving the pan drippings.

Heat the butter with the reserved pan drippings until melted. Add the garlic. Cook over medium heat for 5 minutes; do not brown. Stir in the white wine. Cook until the liquid is reduced by half, stirring occasionally. Add the haricots and pepper, tossing to coat. Add to the bell peppers and toss lightly. Serve immediately.

Enjoy the luxury of these tiny French green beans.

To serve eight

. . . There is a reason choirs practice, church bells ring, decorations are hung. The comfort of time-worn traditions lets us venture back to another sweet time, makes us remember just how much has been so very good, and opens our eyes again to "believing" . . .

MRS. CRATCHIT'S DINNER ROLLS

5½ CUPS BREAD FLOUR, SIFTED
2 ENVELOPES DRY YEAST
2 CUPS MILK
⅓ CUP SHORTENING
¼ CUP SUGAR
½ TEASPOON SALT
2 EGGS, BEATEN
BUTTER

Mix 2½ cups of the bread flour and yeast in a bowl. Combine the milk, shortening, sugar and salt in a saucepan. Heat just until blended, stirring occasionally; do not boil. Cool for 10 to 15 minutes. Stir into the flour mixture. Add the remaining bread flour and eggs and mix well. Shape into a ball. Place in a greased bowl, turning to coat the surface. Let rise, covered with a tea towel, for 1½ to 2 hours.

Punch the dough down. Knead slightly with floured hands on a lightly floured surface. Shape the dough into 3- to 4-inch squares; do not press the dough down. Place a pat of butter in the center of each square and fold to enclose the butter. Place folded seam down on a greased baking sheet with sides. Let rise, covered with a kitchen towel, for 1½ to 2 hours. Bake at 425 degrees for 12 to 15 minutes.

Makes five to six dozen rolls

OLDE WORLD ALMOND TORTE

TORTE
1 CUP WHOLE ALMONDS
2½ OUNCES SEMISWEET CHOCOLATE
6 EGG YOLKS
1 CUP SUGAR
6 EGG WHITES
CHOCOLATE FILLING
¾ CUP PLUS 1 TABLESPOON BUTTER OR MARGARINE
¾ CUP CONFECTIONERS' SUGAR
1 TEASPOON VANILLA EXTRACT
2½ OUNCES SEMISWEET CHOCOLATE, MELTED
1 EGG
6 OUNCES SLICED ALMONDS, TOASTED

To prepare the torte, chop the almonds and chocolate separately in a food processor. Combine the egg yolks and sugar in a mixer bowl. Beat at high speed for 3 minutes or until pale yellow. Beat the egg whites in a mixer bowl until stiff peaks form. Fold the egg whites, almonds and chocolate into the egg yolk mixture. Spoon into a greased and floured 10-inch springform pan. Bake at 350 degrees for 45 minutes. Cool in the pan on a wire rack.

To prepare the filling, beat the butter, confectioners' sugar, vanilla, chocolate and egg in a mixer bowl until fluffy and of a spreading consistency, scraping the bowl occasionally.

To assemble, slice the torte horizontally into halves with dental floss. Spread the filling between the layers and over the top and side of the torte. Sprinkle the surface with the almonds.

To avoid raw eggs that may carry salmonella we suggest using an equivalent amount of commercial egg substitute.

To serve eight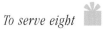

WHAT THE DICKENS? BREAD PUDDING

ON OCCASION...

BREAD PUDDING

1½ CUPS SUGAR

3 EGGS, LIGHTLY BEATEN

2 TABLESPOONS LIGHT BROWN SUGAR

½ TEASPOON NUTMEG

2¾ CUPS WHIPPING CREAM

¼ CUP MELTED BUTTER

4 CUPS FRENCH BREAD CUBES

¾ CUP RAISINS

VANILLA SAUCE

1¼ CUPS WHIPPING CREAM

½ CUP SUGAR

3 TABLESPOONS LIGHT BROWN SUGAR

2 TABLESPOONS BUTTER

1 TABLESPOON FLOUR

1 EGG

⅛ TEASPOON NUTMEG

1 TABLESPOON VANILLA EXTRACT

welcome and warm the gathering with WINTER WASSAIL. *Place 16 whole cloves and 1 teaspoon whole allspice in a tea ball. Combine 6 cups apple cider or juice, 2 cups cranberry juice, ¼ cup sugar, six 1-inch cinnamon sticks and 1 teaspoon bitters in a large saucepan. Add the tea ball, bring to a boil and reduce the heat. Simmer until serving time. Ladle into mugs.*

To prepare the pudding, mix the sugar, eggs, brown sugar and nutmeg in a bowl. Stir in the whipping cream and butter. Fold in the bread cubes and raisins. Spoon into a lightly greased 2-quart soufflé dish or deep baking dish. Bake at 375 degrees for 30 minutes; cover loosely with foil. Cook for 20 to 25 minutes longer. Let stand for 10 minutes before serving.

To prepare the sauce, whisk the whipping cream, sugar, brown sugar, butter, flour, egg and nutmeg in a saucepan. Cook for 10 to 12 minutes or until thickened, whisking constantly. Remove from heat. Stir in the vanilla. Serve warm or at room temperature with the bread pudding.

To serve six to eight

SILVERY SHADOWED DAYS

TO REFLECT UPON OUR LIVES...

HOME FIRES TO KEEP

WINTER'S CHILL AT BAY...

❧

MENUS

NEW FALLEN SNOW

LET'S GEAUX CREOLE

TAKE ME OUT TO THE
BOWL GAME

BLACK TIE OPTIONAL

NEW FALLEN SNOW

"...WITH THIS COLD AIR MASS MOVING THROUGH THE SOUTHERN REGION. SNOWFALL—YES, FOLKS, I SAID SNOWFALL—IS TO BEGIN DURING THE LATE AFTERNOON AND IS EXPECTED TO CONTINUE THROUGHOUT THE NIGHT. WE SHOULD WAKE UP TOMORROW TO REPORTS OF DENSE ACCUMULATIONS..." NEW FALLEN SNOW. FOR A SOUTHERNER, THIS IS A SELDOM-EXPERIENCED OCCURRENCE. MOST CAN COUNT THE OFFICIAL SNOW DAYS ON ONE HAND. MAKES A MESS OF THE WHOLE DAY—ROADS CLOSE, SCHOOL BUSES STAY PUT, OFFICES NEVER OPEN. CARS CAN'T BUDGE FROM THE DRIVEWAYS. AND WE'RE TUCKED INSIDE, JUST WAITING... WAITING THAT IS, FOR SWEET MRS. CUMMINGS'S TELEPHONE CALL AND THE TRADITIONAL INVITATION FOR SOUP AT HER ROUND OAK TABLE. THE FIRST FLURRIES BEGIN AND SHE HEADS FOR THE PANTRY TO CREATE HER VERY BEST POT OF SOUP. YOUNG AND OLD MAKE THEIR WAY OVER— CAREFULLY, OF COURSE, CONTENT TO SPEND THE DAY SHARING WITH THE NEIGHBORS—EXCHANGING RECIPES, GARDENING THEORIES, AND TIPS FOR HOME REPAIRS. CONVERSATION AND CORN BREAD. BETTER BUTTON UP YOUR OVERCOAT. LET IT SNOW! LET IT SNOW! LET IT SNOW!

WINTER CHEESE SOUP

½   CUP MARGARINE
1   CUP MINCED CARROTS
1   CUP MINCED YELLOW ONION
1   CUP MINCED CELERY
½   CUP FLOUR
3   CUPS CHICKEN BROTH
3   CUPS HALF-AND-HALF
2   POUNDS VELVEETA CHEESE, CUBED
1   TABLESPOON FINELY CHOPPED FRESH PARSLEY
    CHOPPED TOMATOES
    MINCED JALAPEÑOS

Heat the margarine in a stockpot until melted. Add the carrots, onion and celery. Sauté until the vegetables are tender but not brown. Add the flour, stirring until mixed. Cook until the mixture turns a light brown, stirring constantly. Add the chicken broth gradually and mix well after each addition. Cook over medium heat until thickened, whisking constantly.

Add the half-and-half and mix well. Stir in the cheese. Cook just until the cheese melts and the soup is heated through, stirring frequently; do not boil. Add the parsley just before serving. Ladle into soup bowls. Top each serving with chopped tomatoes and minced jalapeños.

To serve twelve

ON OCCASION...

you will need a SOUTHERN SNOW SURVIVAL KIT . . .

Matches, candles, flashlight with batteries that work, jacket, long johns, cast-iron skillet, gas in the grill, salt shaker for the steps. Ingredients for S'mores, bottled water, milk and a loaf of bread (you're just supposed to have it!), hot chocolate, Jack Daniel's, board games, playing cards. Pinecones, peanut butter and birdseed for our feathered friends. Camera with film—snap a shot of neighbors' houses blanketed in snow for a springtime surprise in their mailboxes.

DOS EQUIS BEEF STEW

6 MEDIUM ONIONS, CUT INTO ¼-INCH SLICES
½ CUP BUTTER
1 (3½-POUND) CHUCK ROAST, CUBED
2 BOTTLES DOS EQUIS BEER
4 CLOVES OF GARLIC
2 TABLESPOONS BALSAMIC VINEGAR
2 BAY LEAVES
1½ TEASPOONS SALT
½ TEASPOON FRESHLY GROUND PEPPER
¼ TEASPOON THYME
EGG NOODLES, COOKED

Cut the onion slices into halves. Heat 4 tablespoons of the butter in a roasting pan over medium-low heat until melted. Add the onions. Cook for 20 minutes, stirring frequently. Brown the beef in 2 batches in the remaining 4 tablespoons butter in a skillet over medium-high heat. Remove to a platter with a slotted spoon, reserving the pan drippings.

Deglaze the skillet with 1 of the bottles of beer. Add the remaining beer, beef, onions, garlic, balsamic vinegar, bay leaves, salt, pepper and thyme and mix well. Bake, covered, at 400 degrees for 1½ hours. Discard the bay leaves. Serve over hot buttered egg noodles.

To serve six

NOT-SO-BASIC CHILI

12 OUNCES LEAN GROUND LAMB OR GROUND TURKEY
1 YELLOW BELL PEPPER, CHOPPED
1 SPANISH ONION, CHOPPED
4 CLOVES OF GARLIC, CRUSHED
1 BANANA PEPPER, SEEDED, CHOPPED
1 JALAPEÑO, SEEDED, CHOPPED
2 (16-OUNCE) CANS GREAT NORTHERN BEANS
1 (14-OUNCE) CAN CHICKEN BROTH
1 TEASPOON CUMIN
1 TEASPOON DRIED CILANTRO
1 TEASPOON CORIANDER
½ TEASPOON PEPPER
½ CUP LIGHT CREAM (OPTIONAL)
CHOPPED GREEN ONIONS
CHOPPED FRESH CILANTRO

Brown the lamb in a 4-quart saucepan; drain. Stir in the yellow pepper, Spanish onion, garlic, banana pepper and jalapeño. Add the undrained beans and broth and mix well. Stir in the cumin, dried cilantro, coriander and pepper.

Bring to a boil; reduce heat. Simmer for 10 minutes, stirring occasionally. Add the cream and mix well. Cook just until heated through. Ladle into soup bowls. Sprinkle each serving with chopped green onions and chopped fresh cilantro.

To serve eight

For flavor-packed STOCKS . . . *keep a sealable freezer bag in your freezer, continually adding leftover raw vegetable trimmings, garlic and onion skins, celery scraps, etc. When the time arises, add these vegetables to enhance your favorite stock.*

FORT MORGAN SEAFOOD GUMBO

⅔ CUP VEGETABLE OIL
⅔ CUP FLOUR
2 CUPS CHOPPED ONION
1 CUP CHOPPED CELERY
½ CUP CHOPPED GREEN BELL PEPPER (OPTIONAL)
4 CLOVES OF GARLIC, MINCED
¼ CUP CHOPPED PARSLEY
¼ CUP CHOPPED GREEN ONIONS
1½ QUARTS SEAFOOD STOCK OR HOT WATER
1 BAY LEAF
1 TEASPOON THYME
2 TEASPOONS SALT
1 TEASPOON CAYENNE
  BLACK PEPPER TO TASTE
1 (16-OUNCE) CAN CHOPPED TOMATOES, DRAINED
1 OR 2 (10-OUNCE) PACKAGES FROZEN CHOPPED OKRA
8 SMALL CRABS, COOKED, CLEANED
1 POUND UNCOOKED SHRIMP, CLEANED, DEVEINED
1 PINT OYSTERS

FIRST YOU MAKE A ROUX

A roux is the thickening agent for many Gulf Coast dishes, including gumbos, stews, and étouffés. The quickest and easiest way to make a roux is in the microwave. Whisk equal amounts of vegetable oil and flour in an 8-cup glass measure. Microwave on High for 6 minutes. Stir well. Microwave for 30 seconds longer or until the color of a copper penny; stir the mixture. Microwave for 30 seconds longer if necessary, watching carefully to avoid burning. If it burns, discard the whole thing and begin again. You'll be wasting a week's wages on seafood if you put it into a burned roux! The completed roux, with vegetables, can be frozen for later use.

Prepare the roux according to the directions using ⅔ cup oil and ⅔ cup flour. Add the onion, celery and bell pepper to the very hot roux and mix well. Microwave on High for 3 minutes. Stir in the garlic, parsley and green onions. Microwave on High for 2 minutes. Pour off any oil that has risen to the top. Add enough hot water to measure 4 cups.

Place the roux mixture in a 5-quart stockpot. Add the seafood stock, bay leaf, thyme, salt, cayenne and black pepper. Cook over medium heat for 5 minutes. Add the tomatoes and okra. Simmer over low heat for 30 minutes, stirring occasionally.

Add the crab meat, shrimp and oysters with liquor. Cook until the oysters curl and the shrimp are pink; do not overcook. Discard the bay leaf. Serve over steamed rice.

To serve twelve

NAVY BEAN AND COLLARD GREEN SOUP

½   CUP DRIED NAVY BEANS
1   QUART WATER
1   QUART CHICKEN STOCK
2   HAM HOCKS
1   MEDIUM ONION, CHOPPED
1   GREEN BELL PEPPER, CHOPPED
2   BAY LEAVES
    SALT AND PEPPER TO TASTE
1   (16-OUNCE) PACKAGE FROZEN COLLARD GREENS
2   LARGE POTATOES, PEELED, CHOPPED
8   OUNCES CHORIZO OR KIELBASA SAUSAGE, SLICED

Sort and rinse the navy beans. Combine with enough water to cover in a saucepan. Bring to a boil. Boil for 2 minutes. Remove from heat. Let stand, covered, for 1 hour; drain. May soak the navy beans in enough water to cover for 8 to 10 hours.

Combine 1 quart water, stock and ham hocks in a stockpot. Simmer for 20 minutes; skim. Add the navy beans, onion, green pepper, bay leaves, salt and pepper and mix well. Simmer for 1 hour or until the navy beans are tender, stirring occasionally. Stir in the collard greens, potatoes and sausage.

Simmer until the collard greens and potatoes are tender, stirring occasionally. Discard the bay leaves. Ladle into soup bowls.

To serve ten

CRISPY CORNMEAL WAFFLES

1   CUP FLOUR
1   CUP STONE-GROUND YELLOW CORNMEAL
2   TEASPOONS BAKING POWDER
½   TEASPOON BAKING SODA
¼   TEASPOON SALT
2   CUPS BUTTERMILK
1   TABLESPOON MAPLE SYRUP (OPTIONAL)
2   EGGS, LIGHTLY BEATEN
¼   CUP MELTED UNSALTED BUTTER

Mix the flour, cornmeal, baking powder, baking soda and salt in a bowl. Add a mixture of the buttermilk, maple syrup and eggs, whisking just until moistened. Stir in the butter.

Pour about ½ cup of the batter onto a hot waffle iron coated with butter or sprayed with nonstick cooking spray. Bake until brown and crisp. Repeat the process with the remaining batter. Keep the waffles warm in a 200-degree oven until serving time.

Great with your soup of choice!

Makes six waffles

∾

To prepare BROCCOLI CORN BREAD *mix one 9-ounce package corn muffin mix, ½ cup melted butter, ¾ cup sour cream, 1 chopped small onion, 4 eggs and one 10-ounce package of thawed frozen chopped broccoli. Bake at 375 degrees for 30 minutes or until golden brown.*

CABIN FEVER APPLE CAKE

CAKE

2	CUPS SUGAR
1½	CUPS VEGETABLE OIL
3	EGGS
2	TABLESPOONS VANILLA EXTRACT
3	CUPS SIFTED FLOUR
1	TABLESPOON CINNAMON
1	TEASPOON SALT
3	CUPS SLICED PEELED APPLES
¾	CUP CHOPPED PECANS OR WALNUTS

BROWN SUGAR TOPPING

1	CUP PACKED BROWN SUGAR
6	TABLESPOONS BUTTER
¼	CUP EVAPORATED MILK
¼	CUP CHOPPED PECANS OR WALNUTS

To prepare the cake, mix the sugar, oil, eggs and vanilla in a bowl. Add a mixture of the flour, cinnamon and salt and mix well. Stir in the apples and the pecans. Spoon into a greased glass 9x13-inch cake dish. Bake at 325 degrees for 45 minutes. May substitute 1½ cans well drained sliced apples for the fresh apples. Pat dry before combining.

To prepare the topping, combine the brown sugar, butter and evaporated milk in a saucepan. Bring to a boil, stirring frequently. Pour over the hot cake. Sprinkle with the pecans. Let stand for 1 hour before serving.

To serve fifteen

PFEFFERNEUSSE

3¼	CUPS FLOUR
2	TEASPOONS BAKING SODA
1½	CUPS SUGAR
1	CUP BUTTER, SOFTENED
1	EGG
1	TEASPOON CINNAMON
1	TEASPOON GROUND CLOVES
1	TEASPOON GINGER
½	TEASPOON ANISE OIL OR EXTRACT
2	TABLESPOONS CORN SYRUP

Mix the flour and baking soda in a bowl. Combine the sugar and butter in a mixer bowl. Beat at high speed until light and fluffy, scraping the bowl occasionally. Add the egg, cinnamon, cloves and ginger, beating until blended. Mix in the anise. Beat in the corn syrup. Add the flour mixture 1 cup at a time, beating at low speed until blended. Chill, covered, for 1 to 10 hours.

Divide the dough into 8 equal portions. Return all but 1 portion of the dough to the refrigerator. Roll the remaining portion into a log ¼ inch in diameter on a lightly floured surface. Cut the log into ¼-inch slices. Arrange the slices on a cookie sheet. Bake at 375 degrees for 4 to 5 minutes or until light brown. Remove to a wire rack to cool. Repeat the process with the remaining dough.

Makes 4 dozen cookies

LET'S GEAUX CREOLE

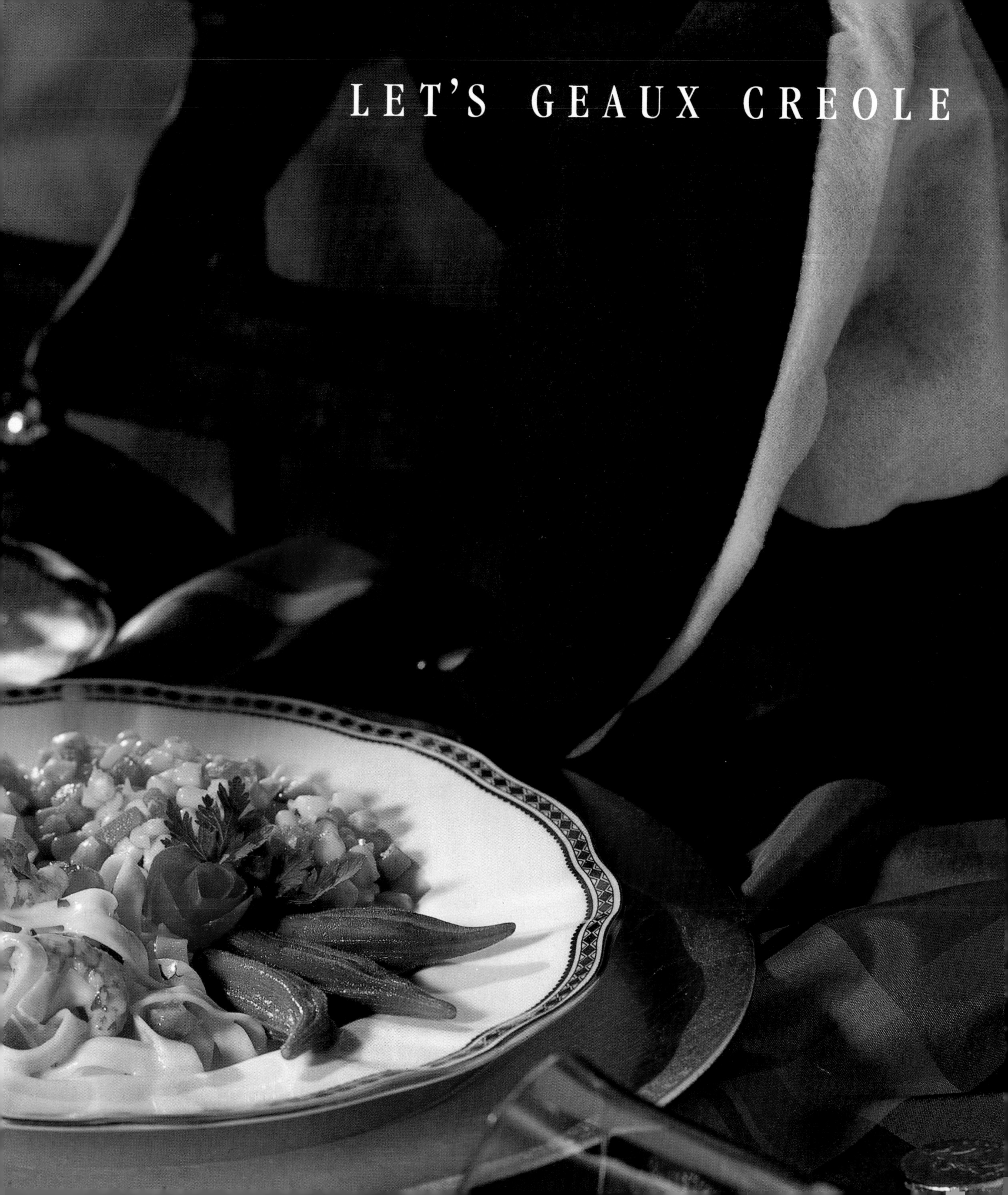

LET'S GEAUX CREOLE

MENU

ARTICHOKE CROUSTADES

BUTTERED PECANS

DELTA SALAD WITH
SWEET-AND-SOUR DRESSING

CRAWFISH FETTUCCINI

OKRA CREOLE

CORN MAQUE CHOUX

CHEESY CORN BREAD

FRENCH BANANA CAKE

CHERRIES JUBILEE

PEEK INSIDE THE CREAKY WROUGHT IRON GATE 'CAUSE THERE'S A WHOLE LOTTA SHAKIN' GOIN' ON! A JUBILEE OF GOLDEN COINS "REIGNS" DOWN LIKE CONFETTI UPON THIS FESTIVE CELEBRATION. IN THE WEEKS BEFORE SHROVE TUESDAY, THOSE IN AND AROUND THE BIG EASY JOIN IN THE REVELRY OF PRE-LENTEN MAGIC—PARADES AND BALLS FOR EVERY "SECRET SOCIETY." AND THE GAIETY CONTINUES FROM THE CREOLE COAST TO OTHER POINTS EAST. EVEN IF YOU'RE LANDLOCKED, CLAIM FAT TUESDAY OR ANY OTHER MYSTICAL NIGHT AS YOUR OWN. JOIN THESE SOUTHERN STANDARDS—CRAWFISH, OKRA, AND CLASSIC CORN MAQUE CHOUX—TO CREATE A CARNIVAL OF FLAVORS. DECADENT DESSERTS AWAIT THE PALATE. OR DISCOVER THE "REAL CHARM" INSIDE A PREORDERED KING'S CAKE. JAZZY PURPLE, GOLD, AND GREEN SILKS DANCE ACROSS THE TABLE. PARCELS OF DOUBLOONS WRAPPED IN CELLOPHANE AND METALLIC RIBBON ENTICE PARTY-GOERS TO THE BANQUET ABOUT TO BEGIN. GOLD TASSELS WRAP EACH FABRIC NAPKIN AS SEQUINED MASKS AND PILES OF PENNY BEADS MARCH DOWN THE CENTER OF YOUR TABLE. NO BASIC BLACK TONIGHT. MASQUERADE FOR ALL!

ARTICHOKE CROUSTADES

CROUSTADES
- 18 SLICES SOFT WHITE BREAD, CRUSTS TRIMMED
- 3 TABLESPOONS MELTED UNSALTED BUTTER

ARTICHOKE FILLING
- 1 (6-OUNCE) JAR MARINATED ARTICHOKE HEARTS, DRAINED, FINELY CHOPPED
- 3 TABLESPOONS MAYONNAISE
- 1 TABLESPOON FINELY CHOPPED SCALLION
- ¼ CUP PLUS 1 TABLESPOON FRESHLY GRATED PARMESAN CHEESE
- SALT AND PEPPER TO TASTE
- FINELY CHOPPED SCALLION TOPS

To prepare the croustades, roll the bread slices to flatten. Trim each slice to form a 2½-inch square. Brush both sides of the bread squares lightly with the butter. Fit the squares into muffin cups, pressing the bread against the sides of the cups. Bake at 350 degrees for 12 to 14 minutes or until the edges are light golden brown.

To prepare the filling, combine the artichokes, mayonnaise, scallion, ¼ cup of the cheese, salt and pepper in a bowl and mix well. Spoon into the croustades. Sprinkle with the remaining 1 tablespoon cheese.

Arrange the croustades on a baking sheet. Broil 6 inches from the heat source for 1 minute or until bubbly. Sprinkle with the chopped scallion tops.

To serve twelve

BUTTERED PECANS

Heat ½ cup butter in a 10x15-inch baking pan at 325 degrees for 5 minutes or until melted. Add 4 cups pecan halves, stirring until well coated. Sprinkle with ½ teaspoon salt. Bake for 30 minutes or until toasted, stirring every 10 minutes; drain.

DELTA SALAD WITH SWEET-AND-SOUR DRESSING

1-800-4MARDIGRAS

Masks and beads are absolutely necessary for the proper celebration of Mardi Gras.

To order purple, gold, and green trinkets, call Oriental Trading at 1-800-228-2269.

For a charm-filled King's Cake, call Gambino's at 1-800-426-9854. They will ship overnight.

SWEET-AND-SOUR DRESSING

1	CUP VEGETABLE OIL
1	CUP SUGAR
½	CUP RED WINE VINEGAR
1	TABLESPOON SOY SAUCE
	SALT AND PEPPER TO TASTE

SALAD

1	CUP CHOPPED WALNUTS
1	(3-OUNCE) PACKAGE RAMEN NOODLES, BROKEN
¼	CUP UNSALTED BUTTER
	FLORETS OF 1 BUNCH BROCCOLI, FINELY CHOPPED
1	HEAD ROMAINE LETTUCE, TORN INTO BITE-SIZE PIECES
4	GREEN ONION TOPS, CHOPPED

To prepare the dressing, whisk the oil, sugar, wine vinegar, soy sauce, salt and pepper in a bowl.

To prepare the salad, brown the walnuts and noodles in the butter in a skillet; drain. Combine the walnuts, noodles, broccoli, romaine and green onion tops in a salad bowl and mix well. Add 1 cup of the dressing, tossing to coat.

May omit browning the walnuts and instead add while tossing salad ingredients.

To serve eight

CRAWFISH FETTUCCINI

    3   MEDIUM ONIONS, FINELY CHOPPED
    2   MEDIUM GREEN BELL PEPPERS, CHOPPED
1½   CUPS MARGARINE
¼   CUP FLOUR
    3   POUNDS CRAWFISH TAILS
¼   CUP PARSLEY FLAKES
    1   POUND VELVEETA CHEESE, CUBED
    2   CUPS HALF-AND-HALF
    2   TEASPOONS JALAPEÑO RELISH
    2   CLOVES OF GARLIC, MINCED
        SALT AND BLACK PEPPER TO TASTE
        RED PEPPER TO TASTE
    1   POUND FETTUCCINI, COOKED, DRAINED
        FRESHLY GRATED PARMESAN CHEESE TO TASTE

Cook the onions and green peppers in the margarine in a large saucepan for 15 to 20 minutes or until tender, stirring frequently. Add the flour and mix well. Cook, covered, for 15 minutes, stirring frequently. Stir in the crawfish and parsley. Cook, covered, for 15 minutes, stirring frequently. Add the Velveeta cheese, half-and-half, relish, garlic, salt, black pepper and red pepper and mix well. Cook, covered, over low heat for 30 minutes, stirring occasionally. Add the fettuccini and toss to mix.

Spoon the crawfish mixture into 2 greased 3-quart baking dishes. Sprinkle with Parmesan cheese. Bake at 350 degrees for 20 to 30 minutes or until brown and bubbly.

This recipe will serve a crowd. Reduce the recipe by ⅔ to serve an average family.

To serve eighteen

OKRA CREOLE

    1   POUND FRESH OR THAWED FROZEN OKRA,
        CUT INTO ⅓-INCH SLICES
    2   TABLESPOONS SAFFLOWER OIL
    2   RIBS CELERY, FINELY CHOPPED
    1   SMALL ONION, CHOPPED
    2   MEDIUM TOMATOES, PEELED, SEEDED,
        COARSELY CHOPPED
½   MEDIUM GREEN BELL PEPPER, FINELY CHOPPED
    1   TEASPOON SUGAR
½   TEASPOON SALT
        FRESHLY GROUND PEPPER TO TASTE

Cook the okra in the safflower oil in a skillet over medium-high heat just until tender, stirring occasionally. Stir in the celery, onion, tomatoes, green pepper, sugar, salt and pepper.

Cook for 5 minutes, stirring constantly. May add ⅓ cup water if vegetable mixture appears too dry. Simmer over low heat for 1 hour or until all of the liquid has been absorbed, stirring occasionally. Serve immediately.

To serve eight

CORN MAQUE CHOUX

8 EARS OF CORN, SHUCKED
1 CUP PEELED CHOPPED TOMATOES OR 1 CUP CANNED
  STEWED TOMATOES
½ CUP COARSELY CHOPPED ONION
½ CUP CHOPPED GREEN BELL PEPPER
½ CUP CHOPPED SCALLIONS
¼ CUP CHOPPED FRESH PARSLEY
1 TEASPOON SUGAR
1 TEASPOON BLACK PEPPER
1 TEASPOON SALT
½ TEASPOON THYME
½ TEASPOON BASIL
2 BAY LEAVES
¼ TEASPOON WHITE PEPPER
¼ TEASPOON CAYENNE
¼ TEASPOON TABASCO SAUCE
½ CUP VEGETABLE OIL

Cut the corn kernels in half lengthwise with a sharp knife into a bowl. Scrape the cob with the back of a knife to remove the pulp and milk. Add to the bowl. Stir in the chopped tomatoes, onion, green pepper, scallions, parsley, sugar, black pepper, salt, thyme, basil, bay leaves, white pepper, cayenne and Tabasco sauce.

Heat the oil in a cast-iron skillet over high heat until hot. Add the corn mixture. Simmer, covered, for 45 minutes, stirring occasionally. Discard the bay leaves.

To serve six

CHEESY CORN BREAD

⅔ CUP FLOUR
⅔ CUP CORNMEAL
2 TEASPOONS BAKING POWDER
¾ TEASPOON SALT
1 (12-OUNCE) CAN YELLOW CORN
  MILK
2 LARGE SCALLIONS, COARSELY CHOPPED
1 MEDIUM JALAPEÑO, SEEDED
⅓ CUP VEGETABLE OIL
2 EGGS, AT ROOM TEMPERATURE
2 TABLESPOONS SUGAR
10 OUNCES COLBY CHEESE, SHREDDED

Mix the flour, cornmeal, baking powder and salt in a bowl. Set aside. Drain the corn, reserving the liquid. Combine the reserved liquid with enough milk to measure ½ cup plus 2 tablespoons.

Combine the scallions and jalapeño in a food processor container. Process until minced. Add the corn, oil, eggs, reserved corn liquid mixture and sugar. Process for 30 seconds.

Add the flour mixture. Pulse 3 or 4 times or just until combined. Do not overprocess.

Sprinkle ¼ cup of the cheese over the bottom of an 11-inch pie plate or baking dish. Spoon the corn mixture over the cheese. Bake at 425 degrees for 18 minutes. Sprinkle with the remaining cheese. Bake for 4 minutes longer or until the cheese melts. Let stand for 10 minutes before serving.

To serve six

FRENCH BANANA CAKE

TOPPING

⅓	CUP STICK BUTTER
1	CUP PACKED BROWN SUGAR

CAKE

1½	CUPS FLOUR
½	TEASPOON BAKING POWDER
½	TEASPOON SALT
¾	TEASPOON BAKING SODA
½	CUP BUTTERMILK
1	CUP MASHED BANANAS
1¼	CUPS SUGAR
⅓	CUP BUTTER, SOFTENED
2	EGGS, BEATEN
1	TEASPOON VANILLA EXTRACT

To prepare the topping, slice the butter into thin pats. Arrange the butter pats over the bottom of a buttered bundt pan. Sprinkle the brown sugar over the butter pats.

To prepare the cake, mix the flour, baking powder and salt in a bowl. Dissolve the baking soda in the buttermilk in a bowl and mix well. Stir in the bananas. Beat the sugar and butter in a mixer bowl until creamy, scraping the bowl occasionally. Add the eggs and mix well.

Combine the flour mixture, buttermilk mixture and butter mixture ⅓ at a time in a bowl, mixing well after each addition. Stir in the vanilla. Spoon into the prepared bundt pan.

Bake at 350 degrees for 40 minutes. Invert onto a serving plate, allowing the topping to drizzle over the top and down the side of the cake for 15 to 20 minutes. Remove the pan.

Cut into slices and serve with whipped cream or vanilla ice cream. The flavor is enhanced if prepared 1 day in advance. If buttermilk is not available, mix 1 teaspoon vinegar with ½ cup milk.

To serve twelve

ON OCCASION...

an event is made an "occasion" by serving CHERRIES JUBILEE.

Heat ¾ cup currant jelly in a chafing dish until melted, stirring occasionally. Stir in 1 drained 16-ounce can of pitted Bing cherries. Pour ½ cup kirsch or brandy into the center of the cherries but do not stir. Heat the mixture. Light very carefully with a fireplace match. Spoon the flaming cherries over vanilla ice cream balls and serve immediately.

TAKE ME OUT TO THE BOWL GAME

Menu

Garlic Buttered Popcorn

Cheesy Pita Chips

Parmesan Popcorn

Barbecued Shrimp

Coach's Special

Seventh Street Salad

The Big Sandwich

Muffuletta

Huddles

Peanut Butter Marbled Brownies

Chocolate Punt Cake

Praline Sauce for Ice Cream

Bushwhackers

No southeastern alumnus, whether ACC or SEC, can overlook Game Day. It's an absolute rite of passage, a ritual of utmost import. If you can't get tickets to your all-time rival contest, then "pull a fake" and score with these party-time treats. Instead of opening a bag of corn chips and rippin' the pop top off a can of bean dip, make these recipe classics at your home field! And the "secret play" is not necessarily one that the university coach knows. It is something that has been taught by southern mamas for generations: Read the sports page at least once a week. A hemline might entice a college man, but a southern gentleman marries the girl who understands punt, pass, and kick! When Game Day arrives, invite the whole conference this year. Set up 50-yard-line seats, with several televisions showing all the different bowl games...line up this menu and satisfy the entire crowd of southern football fans!

BARBECUED SHRIMP

2   CUPS BUTTER
¾   (12-OUNCE) CAN BEER
2   CLOVES OF GARLIC, CRUSHED
2   TABLESPOONS GROUND PEPPER
2   TEASPOONS WORCESTERSHIRE SAUCE
2   TEASPOONS SALT
2   POUNDS JUMBO SHRIMP

Bring the butter, beer, garlic, pepper, Worcestershire sauce and salt to a boil in a stockpot. Add the shrimp. Cook for 5 minutes or until the shrimp turn pink.

Serve in bowls with crusty French bread for dipping in the savory sauce.

To serve four to six

COACH'S SPECIAL

1   LARGE ONION, CHOPPED
2   TO 3 TABLESPOONS BUTTER
2   POUNDS PROCESSED AMERICAN CHEESE, DICED
1   (16-OUNCE) CAN DICED TOMATOES WITH GREEN CHILES
1   POUND SPICY BULK SAUSAGE, COOKED, DRAINED

Sauté the onion in the butter in a saucepan until tender. Add the cheese and undrained tomatoes. Cook over medium heat until the cheese melts, stirring constantly. Add the sausage and mix well.

Spoon the cheese mixture into a fondue pot or chafing dish. Serve warm with tortilla chips, wheat crackers and/or bagel chips.

To serve twelve

A BOWL OF TREATS!

A bowl game wouldn't be complete without popcorn and chips.

For PARMESAN POPCORN, *mix ¼ cup grated Parmesan cheese with 1½ tablespoons melted butter. Toss with 4 cups of popped popcorn.*

For CHEESY PITA CHIPS, *cut 6 pita rounds into halves and split the halves. Brush the cut sides with ¾ cup melted butter and sprinkle with 1½ cups grated Parmesan cheese. Arrange in a single layer on a baking sheet and bake at 350 degrees for 12 to 15 minutes.*

For GARLIC BUTTERED POPCORN, *heat 1 split clove of garlic in ¼ cup margarine or butter. When the butter melts, remove the garlic and stir in 1 tablespoon chopped parsley. Toss lightly with 3 cups of popped popcorn.*

SEVENTH STREET SALAD

1 (6-OUNCE) JAR MARINATED ARTICHOKE HEARTS
¼ CUP OLIVE OIL
4 TO 6 TABLESPOONS (ABOUT) WINE VINEGAR
1 TABLESPOON GRATED PARMESAN CHEESE
1½ TEASPOONS ITALIAN SEASONING
¼ TO ½ TEASPOON GARLIC POWDER
½ HEAD LETTUCE, TORN INTO BITE-SIZE PIECES
½ MEDIUM RED ONION, SLICED, CUT INTO HALVES
1 OUNCE PIMENTO, CHOPPED
ROMA TOMATOES, COARSELY CHOPPED
GRATED PARMESAN CHEESE TO TASTE

Drain the artichokes, reserving the marinade. Chop the artichokes. Whisk the reserved marinade, olive oil, wine vinegar, 1 tablespoon Parmesan cheese, Italian seasoning and garlic powder in a bowl.

Toss the artichokes, lettuce, onion, pimento and tomatoes in a salad bowl. Add the dressing, tossing to coat. Cover the top of the salad with Parmesan cheese. Let stand for 10 to 15 minutes. Toss just before serving.

To serve four

THE BIG SANDWICH

⅓ CUP RED WINE VINEGAR
⅓ CUP VEGETABLE OIL
2 TEASPOONS SUGAR
SALT AND PEPPER TO TASTE
1 RED ONION, SLICED, SEPARATED INTO RINGS
1 LOAF HAWAIIAN BREAD
8 OUNCES HARD SALAMI, THINLY SLICED
8 OUNCES TURKEY, THINLY SLICED
10 OUNCES SMOKED PROVOLONE CHEESE OR
SWISS CHEESE, SLICED
RED OR GREEN LEAF LETTUCE
2 TOMATOES, CUT INTO ⅛-INCH SLICES

Whisk the wine vinegar, oil, sugar, salt and pepper in a bowl. Add the onion and mix well. Marinate, covered, in the refrigerator for 2 to 10 hours. Drain, reserving the marinade.

Slice the top from the loaf of bread and reserve. Remove ¼ of the center carefully, leaving a shell. Freeze the center for future use if desired. Layer the salami, turkey, cheese, lettuce, tomatoes and marinated onions in the shell. Drizzle with the reserved marinade if desired. Replace the top. Chill, wrapped in plastic wrap, for 1 hour before serving.

To serve six to eight

MUFFULETTA

OLIVE SPREAD

1½	CUPS DRAINED RIPE OLIVES
1	CUP DRAINED PIMENTO-STUFFED OLIVES
1	CUP COARSELY CHOPPED CELERY
1	CUP DRAINED PICKLED GARDEN VEGETABLES
½	CUP DRAINED COCKTAIL ONIONS
⅓	CUP OLIVE OIL
⅓	CUP RED WINE VINEGAR
¼	CUP DRAINED CAPERS
8	CLOVES OF GARLIC
1	TEASPOON OREGANO
1	TEASPOON BASIL
¼	TEASPOON GROUND PEPPER

SANDWICH

1	LARGE LOAF SESAME SEED ITALIAN BREAD
	SLICED HAM
	SLICED GENOA SALAMI
	SLICED PROVOLONE CHEESE
	SLICED SWISS CHEESE

To prepare the spread, combine the ripe olives, pimento-stuffed olives, celery, pickled vegetables, cocktail onions, olive oil, wine vinegar, capers, garlic, oregano, basil and pepper in a food processor container. Pulse 10 to 15 times or until finely chopped. May prepare up to 2 days in advance and store, covered, in the refrigerator until serving time.

To prepare the sandwich, slice the loaf of bread horizontally into halves. Layer the ham, salami, desired amount of olive spread, provolone cheese and Swiss cheese on the cut side of 1 bread half. Top with the remaining bread half. Bake, wrapped loosely in foil, at 350 degrees for 20 minutes or until heated through. Cut into slices.

May substitute individual sandwich buns for the loaf. Use approximately ¼ cup of the spread for each sandwich. Brush the outside of the loaf or buns with garlic butter before baking if desired.

To serve eight

PRALINE SAUCE

Combine 2½ cups packed dark brown sugar with 1½ cups light corn syrup and ½ cup margarine in the top of a double boiler. Cook for 8 to 10 minutes and remove from heat. Stir in ½ cup evaporated milk and 1½ teaspoons vanilla. Add 2 cups pecan halves and mix well. Serve immediately over vanilla ice cream with gingersnaps. Store leftovers in the refrigerator.

HUDDLES

2 (3-OUNCE) CANS CHINESE NOODLES
½ CUP BRICKLE TOPPING
2 CUPS WHITE CHOCOLATE CHIPS
2 CUPS BUTTERSCOTCH CHIPS

Combine the noodles and brickle topping in a bowl and mix well.

Heat the white chocolate chips and butterscotch chips in a double boiler over hot water until melted, stirring frequently. Pour over the noodle mixture, stirring just until mixed.

Drop by spoonfuls onto waxed paper. Let stand until cool.

Makes three dozen

PEANUT BUTTER MARBLED BROWNIES

6 OUNCES CREAM CHEESE, SOFTENED
½ CUP SMOOTH PEANUT BUTTER
¼ CUP SUGAR
1 EGG
2 TABLESPOONS MILK
2 CUPS SUGAR
1 CUP MELTED BUTTER
2 TEASPOONS VANILLA EXTRACT
3 EGGS, LIGHTLY BEATEN
¾ CUP BAKING COCOA
1¼ CUPS FLOUR
½ TEASPOON BAKING POWDER
½ TEASPOON SALT
1 CUP MILK CHOCOLATE CHIPS

Beat the cream cheese, peanut butter, ¼ cup sugar, 1 egg and milk in a mixer bowl until creamy, scraping the bowl occasionally.

Combine 2 cups sugar, butter and vanilla in a bowl and mix well. Stir in 3 eggs. Add the baking cocoa and mix well. Stir in a mixture of the flour, baking powder and salt. Add the chocolate chips and mix well. Reserve 1 cup of the batter.

Spoon the remaining batter into a greased 9x13-inch baking pan. Spread with the peanut butter mixture. Drop the reserved batter by teaspoonfuls over the prepared layers and swirl with a knife.

Bake at 350 degrees for 30 to 40 minutes or until a wooden pick inserted in the center comes out clean. Cool in the pan on a wire rack. Cut into bars.

Makes three dozen brownies

CHOCOLATE PUNT CAKE

½   TEASPOON BAKING SODA
1   CUP BUTTERMILK
1   CUP BUTTER OR MARGARINE
1½ CUPS SUGAR
4   EGGS
2½ CUPS FLOUR
1   CUP MINIATURE SEMISWEET CHOCOLATE CHIPS
2   (4-OUNCE) BARS GERMAN'S SWEET BAKING CHOCOLATE, MELTED, COOLED
⅓   CUP CHOCOLATE SYRUP
2   TEASPOONS VANILLA EXTRACT
4   OUNCES WHITE CHOCOLATE, CHOPPED
2   TABLESPOONS PLUS 2 TEASPOONS SHORTENING
½   CUP MINIATURE SEMISWEET CHOCOLATE CHIPS

ON OCCASION...

knock 'em cold with BUSHWHACKERS. *Combine 1 part rum with 1 part dark crème de cacao, 1 part Kahlúa, 1 tablespoon Coco Lopez coconut oil and 2 scoops of your favorite ice cream in the blender. Add 2 teaspoons Nestlé Chocolate Quik if desired. Process with crushed ice until smooth and serve in a tall glass.*

Dissolve the baking soda in the buttermilk and mix well. Set aside. Beat the butter in a mixer bowl until creamy, scraping the bowl occasionally. Add the sugar gradually, beating constantly at medium speed until light and fluffy. Add the eggs 1 at a time, beating well after each addition.

Add the buttermilk mixture alternately with the flour, beating well after each addition. Stir in 1 cup chocolate chips, German's sweet chocolate, chocolate syrup and vanilla just until mixed. Spoon into a greased and floured 10-inch bundt pan. Bake at 300 degrees for 1 hour and 25 to 35 minutes or until the cake springs back when lightly touched with the fingertips. Invert onto a serving platter immediately. Let stand until cool.

Combine the white chocolate and 2 tablespoons of the shortening in a double boiler. Bring the water to a boil; reduce heat to low. Simmer until blended, stirring frequently. Remove from heat. Drizzle over the cake.

Heat ½ cup chocolate chips and the remaining 2 teaspoons shortening in a saucepan over low heat until blended, stirring constantly. Let stand until cool. Drizzle over the white chocolate.

To serve twelve

BLACK TIE OPTIONAL

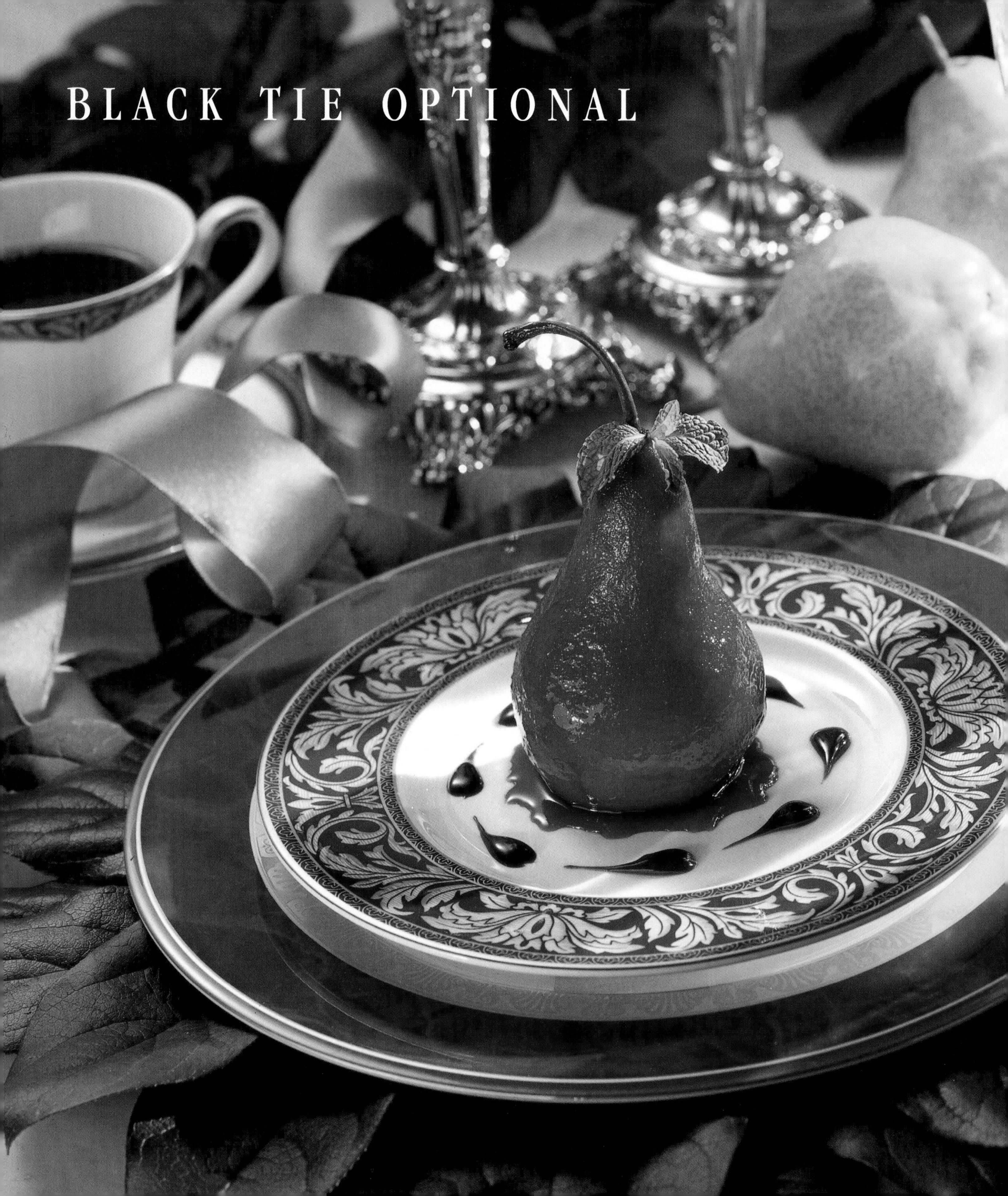

BLACK TIE OPTIONAL

MENU

Coconut Shrimp with
Curry Mustard Sauce

Miss Sally's Crab Bisque

Red Leaf Lettuce Salad with
White Wine Dressing

Four-Peppercorn Pork Roast

Dinner Jackets

Bassano Asparagus

No-Reservation Rolls

Herbed Butters

His Majesty's
Mocha Cream Torte

Cabernet Sauvignon
Poached Pears

Kir Royale

You are cordially invited...to dinner at eight. An evening of elegance, a sparkling celebration, a reason to "dress to the nines"—peau de soie and pumps. An indulgent interlude, a midnight supper, a dinner party...just because! Men in bow ties and ladies in their evening finery anticipate an event to remember. Beribboned bottles of Champagne splits, a preview of the jubilation to follow, serve as place cards and as a fond keepsake of the affair. Crisp hem-stitched linens and radiant crystal set a smart-looking table. Filigree-edged plates are layered over banded chargers. A wreath of lemon leaves creates a verdant surround at each place setting. Luscious double-faced satin ribbons gracefully intertwine brilliant candelabras. Then...a single poached pear—enhanced with the finest of wines—rests in a puddle of sweet chocolate...a divine ending...on occasion.

Coconut Shrimp with Curry Mustard Sauce

Curry Mustard Sauce

- 1 CUP MAYONNAISE
- 2 TABLESPOONS MINCED ONION
- 2 TABLESPOONS PREPARED MUSTARD
- 2 TABLESPOONS SUGAR
- 2 CLOVES OF GARLIC, MINCED
- 2 TEASPOONS MINCED FRESH PARSLEY
- 2 TEASPOONS LEMON JUICE
- 1 TEASPOON CURRY POWDER
- TABASCO SAUCE TO TASTE

Shrimp

- ¼ CUP LEMON JUICE
- ½ TEASPOON SALT
- ½ TEASPOON CURRY POWDER
- ¼ TEASPOON GINGER
- 2 POUNDS SHRIMP, PEELED, DEVEINED, BUTTERFLIED
- 2 CUPS FLOUR
- 2 TEASPOONS BAKING POWDER
- ½ TEASPOON SALT
- 1¾ CUPS MILK
- 1½ CUPS (ABOUT) FLOUR
- 1 (14-OUNCE) PACKAGE FLAKED COCONUT
- VEGETABLE OIL FOR DEEP-FRYING

To prepare the sauce, whisk the mayonnaise, onion, mustard, sugar, garlic, parsley, lemon juice, curry powder and Tabasco sauce in a bowl until mixed. Store, covered, in the refrigerator until serving time.

To prepare the shrimp, combine the lemon juice, ½ teaspoon salt, curry powder and ginger in a bowl and mix well. Add the shrimp, tossing to coat. Marinate, covered, in the refrigerator for 1 hour or longer. Drain, reserving the marinade.

Mix 2 cups flour, baking powder and ½ teaspoon salt in a bowl. Whisk in the milk until blended. Stir in the reserved marinade.

Coat the shrimp in 1½ cups flour. Dip in the batter and roll in the coconut. Fry the shrimp in 375-degree oil in a deep fryer for 2 to 3 minutes or until golden brown on all sides; drain. Serve immediately with the sauce.

To serve ten

Red Leaf Lettuce Salad with White Wine Dressing

Drain and chill the sections of an 11-ounce can of mandarin oranges. Arrange over red leaf lettuce and sprinkle with 4 ounces of crumbled feta cheese and ¾ cup toasted walnuts. Whisk together ½ cup white wine vinegar, 2 teaspoons sugar, ¼ cup salad oil and garlic powder and kosher salt to taste. Drizzle over the salad.

MISS SALLY'S CRAB BISQUE

3 TABLESPOONS BUTTER
5 TABLESPOONS FLOUR
1½ QUARTS HALF-AND-HALF
1 POUND LUMP CRAB MEAT, SHELLS REMOVED
¼ CUP SHERRY
1 TABLESPOON WORCESTERSHIRE SAUCE
½ TEASPOON TABASCO SAUCE
SALT AND WHITE PEPPER TO TASTE

Heat the butter in a saucepan until melted. Whisk in the flour. Cook for 2 to 3 minutes or until blended, stirring constantly; do not brown. Add the half-and-half gradually, mixing constantly. Cook until slightly thickened, stirring constantly.

Stir in the crab meat, sherry, Worcestershire sauce, Tabasco sauce, salt and pepper. Cook just until heated through, stirring frequently. Ladle into soup bowls.

Our Charleston friends search for she-crabs to add the roe to the bottom of the soup bowls. To be "semi-authentic" substitute chopped hard-cooked egg yolks.

To serve eight

BASSANO ASPARAGUS

3 POUNDS ASPARAGUS, TRIMMED
SALT TO TASTE
1 CUP EXTRA-VIRGIN OLIVE OIL
JUICE OF 3 LEMONS
PEPPER TO TASTE
1 TABLESPOON CHOPPED FRESH PARSLEY
6 HARD-COOKED EGGS, FINELY CHOPPED

Cook the asparagus in just enough boiling salted water to cover in a skillet for 3 to 5 minutes or just until tender-crisp; drain.

Whisk the olive oil, lemon juice, salt and pepper in a bowl. Stir in the parsley. Pour over the asparagus, tossing to coat.

Arrange the asparagus on a serving platter. Sprinkle with the eggs. Serve at room temperature.

May be prepared 6 to 8 hours in advance and stored, covered, in the refrigerator. Bring to room temperature before serving.

To serve ten

FOUR-PEPPERCORN PORK ROAST

1	(4½-POUND) BONELESS PORK LOIN, TIED
	SALT TO TASTE
3	TABLESPOONS UNSALTED BUTTER, SOFTENED
2	TABLESPOONS FLOUR
¼	CUP MIXED PEPPERCORNS, CRUSHED
¼	CUP FLOUR
1¾	CUPS CHICKEN BROTH
1	CUP WATER
2	TABLESPOONS RED WINE VINEGAR, OR TO TASTE
	SPRIGS OF FRESH ROSEMARY

Pat the roast with a paper towel. Sprinkle with salt. Mix the butter and 2 tablespoons flour in a bowl until of a paste consistency. Coat the top of the roast with the paste mixture. Sprinkle the peppercorns over the paste mixture and press lightly.

Place the roast on a rack in a roasting pan. Roast on the middle oven rack at 475 degrees for 30 minutes. Reduce the oven temperature to 325 degrees. Roast for 1½ to 1⅔ hours longer or until a meat thermometer registers 160 degrees. Transfer the roast to a cutting board, reserving ¼ cup of the pan drippings. Let stand for 10 minutes.

Whisk ¼ cup flour into the reserved pan drippings in the roasting pan. Cook over medium heat for 3 minutes, stirring constantly. Add the broth and water gradually, whisking constantly. Bring to a boil. Stir in the wine vinegar and salt. Simmer until thickened or of the desired consistency, stirring constantly.

Discard the twine from the roast. Cut the roast into ½-inch slices. Arrange the slices on a serving platter. Garnish with rosemary. Serve with the sauce.

To serve ten

DINNER JACKETS

Cut a slit in the tops of 4 baked Idaho potatoes and carefully remove the pulp, leaving the skins intact. Mash the potato pulp with a fork. Cook 2 minced cloves of garlic in 2 tablespoons unsalted butter over low heat until tender but not brown. Combine the garlic butter and potato pulp with ½ cup sour cream, 2 ounces crumbled mild bleu cheese, 1 tablespoon chopped fresh parsley and 1 tablespoon chopped fresh chives. Add salt and pepper to taste and mix well. Spoon into the potato skins, mounding slightly, and sprinkle with paprika. Bake for 15 minutes, sprinkle with additional chives and serve immediately. This can be prepared in advance and reheated for 30 minutes when ready to serve.

HIS MAJESTY'S MOCHA CREAM TORTE

A FINISHING TOUCH

Prepare HERBED BUTTERS *in quantities
when herbs are fresh to store in the
refrigerator or freezer to always have on
hand. Serve them on breads, chicken,
beef, eggs, fish, or sandwiches. They can
be pressed into a small bowl or shaped
into a log, chilled in plastic wrap for an
hour or longer, and cut into patties.
Or check your local gourmet store for
molds in the shapes of stars, rounds,
and flowers.*

*For the basic recipe, to 8 ounces
of softened unsalted butter, add
1 of the following herbs: 3 tablespoons
minced fresh tarragon, ¼ cup minced
fresh chives, ½ cup minced fresh
basil, ½ cup minced fresh oregano,
½ cup minced fresh marjoram,
½ cup minced fresh dill, 5 cloves
of minced garlic.*

*Herbed Butters are especially good
on* NO-RESERVATION ROLLS. *Just
allow frozen rolls to rise using the
package directions. Brush them
with olive oil, sprinkle with sea salt
and bake. Too easy!*

TORTE
- 6 EGG YOLKS, AT ROOM TEMPERATURE
- ½ CUP CONFECTIONERS' SUGAR
- 3 TABLESPOONS BAKING COCOA
- 6 EGG WHITES, AT ROOM TEMPERATURE
- ⅛ TEASPOON CREAM OF TARTAR
- ½ CUP CONFECTIONERS' SUGAR

FILLING
- 1½ CUPS WHIPPING CREAM
- ½ CUP CONFECTIONERS' SUGAR
- ¼ CUP BAKING COCOA
- 2 TABLESPOONS KAHLÚA

GARNISH
- CHOCOLATE CURLS
- CONFECTIONERS' SUGAR

To prepare the torte, grease a jelly roll pan and line with waxed paper, leaving a 2-inch overhang on each end. Beat the egg yolks in a mixer bowl at high speed for 3 minutes or until thick. Add ½ cup confectioners' sugar and baking cocoa gradually, beating constantly at low speed. Beat the egg whites in a mixer bowl at low speed until foamy. Add the cream of tartar. Beat at high speed until soft peaks form. Add ½ cup confectioners' sugar 1 tablespoon at a time, beating constantly until stiff but not dry peaks form. Fold into the egg yolk mixture. Spread the batter in the prepared pan. Bake at 400 degrees for 12 to 15 minutes or until the top springs back when lightly pressed with the fingertips. Invert onto a towel sprinkled with additional baking cocoa. Discard the waxed paper. Let stand until cool.

To prepare the filling, beat the whipping cream in a mixer bowl at low speed until soft peaks form. Add the confectioners' sugar, baking cocoa and Kahlúa. Beat at medium speed until of spreading consistency.

To assemble the torte, line the edges of a platter with 4 strips of waxed paper. Cut the torte crosswise into 4 equal portions with a serrated knife. Place 1 portion on the platter. Spread with ⅓ of the filling. Repeat with the remaining portions and filling, ending with a torte layer. Trim the edges if necessary to even, discarding the waxed paper. Chill, covered with foil, or freeze, wrapped in foil, if desired. Let the frozen cake stand in the refrigerator overnight before serving.

Spread with a mixture of 1 cup melted chocolate chips, 2 tablespoons melted unsalted butter, 2 tablespoons light corn syrup and 3 tablespoons milk. Garnish with chocolate curls and confectioners' sugar.

To serve twelve

CABERNET SAUVIGNON POACHED PEARS

4 PEARS
LEMON JUICE
1½ CUPS CABERNET SAUVIGNON
1½ CUPS SUGAR
2 TEASPOONS VANILLA EXTRACT, OR 2 VANILLA BEANS
WHIPPING CREAM
SPRIGS OF FRESH MINT OR CINNAMON BASIL

Peel the pears, leaving the stems intact. Remove the cores from the bottom. Place the pears in a bowl. Add a mixture of lemon juice and water to cover.

Bring the wine, sugar and vanilla to a boil in a saucepan. Simmer for 5 minutes, stirring frequently. Add the pears stem side up. Simmer for 15 to 20 minutes or until the wine mixture is of a syrupy consistency and the pears are tender, basting frequently. Remove the pears to a platter. Cook the syrup until reduced, stirring frequently.

Cover the bottom of 4 dessert plates with the syrup. Place a pear in the center of each plate. Drizzle with whipping cream and garnish with sprigs of mint or cinnamon basil.

To serve four

ON OCCASION...

greet guests with sparkling flutes of KIR ROYALE. *Just mix 5 ounces of Champagne with ¼ ounce of crème de cassis and add a twist of lemon. It will make you feel like royalty!*

CONTRIBUTORS

Thank you to our generous supporters—for your ideas, energy, and products, making this cookbook possible.

The Whitlock Inn of historic Marietta
Alexis Edwards, Innkeeper
"the most beautiful Bed & Breakfast
in Georgia"

M. L. Jarvis, Inc. in Vinings Jubilee
Margaret Hathaway
Atlanta, Georgia

C'est Moi
Susan Kolowich
Atlanta, Georgia

El Charro Restaurant
Tucson, Arizona

The Flag Company
Kennesaw, Georgia

Gabriel's Desserts
Johnnie and Ed Gabriel
Marietta, Georgia

Galla's Package Beer and Wine
Bob Galla and Mike Galla
Marietta, Georgia

Leoni Ley-Mitchell Catering
Marietta, Georgia

Merry Times Party Rental, Inc.
Mary and Doug McNeel
Marietta, Georgia

Rowland's Catering, Inc.
Rowland Stanfield
Atlanta, Georgia

Carolyn Schallmo
Polymer Clay Design
Marietta, Georgia

Thank you to our many contributors. Thank you for sharing from your recipe files, your family albums, your dining tables, and your southern kitchens. And it is our sincere hope that no one has been overlooked.

Jennie I. Adams
Laurie Arrington
Wilma Ashcraft
Libby Astrachan
Susan Alexander Aulebach
Joanna Jernigan Austin
Maureen Bangert
Margaret Seawell Barfield
Sandra Barfield
Lori Manning Barger
Kim Barker
Ellen Cook Barnes
Joan Brogden Barnhill
Jean Barr
Lisa Stockwell Barrett
Linda Bartmess
Lang Baumgarten
Trish Bennett
Sue Bentley
Laurie Bivins
Nancy Black
Jean Blazek
Virginia Blomgren
Nancy M. Bodiford
Melissa Bottoms
Sue Boudreaux
Michelle Bowden
Rachel Dare Bowen
Susann Meadows Braden
Virginia Braden
Susan Gann Brasfield
Gayle Brewner
Velma Brewner
Lisa A. Bronson
Sarah Alice Bronson
Julia Harper Brown
Mark Brown
Sharen Brown

Gerri Bryan
Nancy Hubbard Bryan
Priscilla Gatewood Buege
Maggie Bunch
Ann Marie Burley
Diane M. Busch
Reneé Burzin Busdicker
Jennifer Bush
Nancy Butler
Jeff Byrd
Rachel Doan Byrd
Brandi Calhoun
Claudia M. Calhoun
Isabel Cardoso
Ellen Mitchell Carmack
Sharon Carson
Kim Connell Churchill
Marion H. Cianciolo
Lynn Claussen
Kathryn Keeter Coffee
Peter Coleman
Caroline Collar
Katherine Seiler Collar
Catherine Collier
Ginger Collier
Sandra Colson
Anna Conley
Jane Cooley
Stephanie Corley
Mikel Sutton Crowley
Crissi Calhoun Czerniawsky
Lillian Budd Darden
Marcelle B. David
Debbie Denhard
Sandi Hollomon Dennis
Joan DeRose
Brandi Diamond
Renie Cordell Dixon

Gail Dolan
Christine Doran
Suzanne C. Duda
Linda Duffy
Maryann Durnien
Patty Hughs Eagar
Laura S. (Sis) Eastland
Beth Eckford
Ellen Elleman
Mike Elleman
Carroll Farber Elliott
Jean Fleming
Marina Fleming
Carolyn Fontenot
Lee Rainey Fowler
Claire Francis
Matt Francis
Debbie Smith Freeman
Shelia Garnette Frey
The Neighbors of Freyer Drive
Vicki Gardner
Linda C. Garner
Kathy Garrett
Tracy Geisel
Judi Gertz
Carol Giddens
Jenny Glover
J. Marty Godfrey
M. Martina Goscha
Elizabeth (Dolly) Wright
   Gregory
Laurie Gregory
Janet Hall
Laura Wilson Harding
Dorothy Christian Harrison
Virginia Webb Harrison
Mary Rainey Hart
Meg Tysinger Hartin

C O N T R I B U T O R S

Jan S. Hatfield
Joyce Hatfield
Lexis Hay
Jennifer Gardner Helms
Shelley Southerland Hill
Vickey Watts Hogan
Cheryl M. Holland
Sheri Hollomon
Donna Hudson
Blanch Williams Hurt
Najda M. Hutchinson
Beth Hyman
Farin Lovinger Jaeger
Nancy B. Johnstone
Beverly P. Jones
Helen Jones
Jane Jones
Torey Mahrenholz Keene
Mildred Hamrick Keeter
Laura King
Cheryle Kirk
Jennifer Sewell Kloet
Catherine M. Kossler
Estelle Kyler
Charlotte Lamm
Susan Lamothe
Bonnie Lanier
Mary Anne Lanier
Nancy Price Law
Martha Wyatt Lawson
Beryl E. Lillard
Betty Lillard
Livvy Kazer Lipson
Beth Locandro
Lainnie Lowrey
Rhonda Maloy
Jane P. Manning
Judy Manning
Dorothy Jean Martin
Jeff Martin
Joanna Prater Martin
Johanna Amos Martin

Marie Wiselogel Martin
Susan Morgan Martin
Desiree de Toit Mastracchio
Stephanie McAllister
Alison L. McCall
Ruth Tatum McClendon
Cheryl McColl
Beverly Webb McCollum
Kathi McGarry
Caroline McKethan
Gina McKethan
Mary T. McKethan
Ann McMurray
Megan McMurray
Ron Meadows
Diana Wiegand Mears
Lisa Forrest Mensch
Ann Militades
Becky Miller
Cary Freeman Miller
Linda Allen Milligan
Margaret W. Mitchell
Polly Mitchell
Paige Hutto Monteith
Carol Montie
Sally Heubach Morgan
Renae Morse
Shereyl J. Mulkey
Esther Barnes Mulling
Susan Murphey
JoAn Nathan
Stephanie Nelson
Viki Busdicker Nelson
Betty Jean Newman
Charles S. Newman
Michi Rainey Newman
Amanda Robertson Nicholls
Ginny Northcutt
Ann Alvarez Novit
Jan Hardy Osmon
Maggie Overstreet
Andrea Parker

Laura Patterson
Jean Pavalina
Jane Rooks Perrie
Leigh Farrar Pharr
Susan S. Phillips
Andrea Pope
Edna Ree Porter
Judy Prater
Paula Prather
Anita Jo Rainey
J. L. Rainey
Mardelle L. Rainey
Debbie Rampley Randall
Leigh Ann Rapp
Norma Ree
Sarah J. Reed
Tammy New Renno
Vicky Richards
Marni Roake
Brent Robertson
Joyce McClendon Robertson
Katie Braden Robertson
Dorothy Romans
JoAnn Rossi
Lynette Rossi
Marsha Ellzey Roy
Martha Lee Sanders
Anne Scandlyn
Libba Schell
Lisa G. Schneiderman
Heather Longdon Schoeman
Candice C. Scott
Dana Scott
Jan Scott
Gini S. Seely
Nancy Egan Seiler
Liz Serrao
Lorrie Shaw
Ginger Sheilds
Virginia Boling Shields
Caroline Sierra
Kim Silva

Jill Wyatt Smith
Joyce Clarke Smith
Shae H. Smith
Mrs. E. H. Sparkman
Jane Waters Stoddard
Nancy Harder Stowell
Yancey Summers
Valerie Surasky
Alison Crowson Talbert
Leslie Anne Tarabella
Sana Thomas
Sandra Thomas
Jennifer Thompson-Redmond
Joanne M. Thurston
Bonnie Sinclair Tippett
Sandy Stripling Tolar
Jeanne Tonkin
Marianne Trapnell
Dianne Van Voorhees
Diane B. Vaughan
Annie Maud Vick
Joyce Vick
Bonnie Wagoner
Doris Walker
Frankie Henderson Webb
Renee Porter Webster
Julie Bess White
Susie White
Ginger Wiener
Kitty Wilks
Evelyn Cuffel Williams
Mary Frances Williams
Allison B. Wood
Gladys Teem Worley
Jane Gregory Worley
Melissa Robertson Worley
Michelle Wallace Wyant
Ann Whorton Wyatt
Hazel Holcombe Wyatt
Janet Young
Pam Younker
Kris Anne Zenoni

INDEX

SOUTHERN...ON OCCASION

A COMPANION TO INSPIRE GRACIOUS LIVING

Name
_____

Street Address
_____

City _____ State _____ Zip _____

Phone
_____

YOUR ORDER	QUANTITY	TOTAL
Southern . . . On Occasion $24.95 per book		$
Case of 6 *Southern . . . On Occasion* $135.00 per case		$
Georgia On My Menu $15.95 per book More time-tested recipes from JLCM		$
Shipping & Handling ($3.50 for first book; add $1.50 for each additional book)		$
Georgia residents add 5% sales tax		$
TOTAL		$

[   ] Check enclosed. Please make check payable to THE JUNIOR LEAGUE OF COBB-MARIETTA, INC.

[   ] Charge to: [   ] VISA   [   ] MasterCard

Account Number _____ Expiration Date _____

Cardholder Name
_____

Signature
_____

To order by mail, send to: THE JUNIOR LEAGUE OF COBB-MARIETTA, INC.
P.O. Box 727 • Marietta, Georgia 30060 • 770.422.5266 • 770.427.2253 Fax

Proceeds benefit the many projects of The Junior League of Cobb-Marietta, Inc.

Photocopies accepted.

ON OCCASION...

*we celebrate a special day, welcome a
new tradition, rejoice with friends
and family. And on occasion . . .
we simply gather, for splendid food
and spirited conversation.*